Joan Finchley, a professional actress and dramatic teacher, has taught acting at Boston University, New York University, and the Western Australian Academy of Performing Arts.

AUDITION!

A Complete Guide for Actors with an Annotated Selection of Readings

JOAN FINCHLEY

A SPECTRUM BOOK

Prentice-Hall, Inc., Englewood Cliffs, New Jersey 07632

Library of Congress Cataloging in Publication Data

Finchley, Joan.
    Audition! : a complete guide for actors with an
annotated selection of readings.

    "A Spectrum Book."
    Includes index.
    1. Monologues.   2. Acting—Auditions.   I. Title.
PN2080.F56   1984   792'.028   84-9943
ISBN 0-13-052093-4
ISBN 0-13-052085-3 (pbk.)

10 9 8 7 6 5 4 3 2 1

This book is available at a special discount when ordered
in bulk quantities. Contact Prentice-Hall, Inc., General
Publishing Division, Special Sales, Englewood Cliffs, N.J. 07632.

Editorial/production supervision by Chris McMorrow
Cover design by Hal Siegel

ISBN 0-13-052093-4

ISBN 0-13-052085-3 {PBK.}

PRENTICE-HALL INTERNATIONAL, INC., *London*
PRENTICE-HALL OF AUSTRALIA PTY. LIMITED, *Sydney*
PRENTICE-HALL CANADA INC., *Toronto*
PRENTICE-HALL OF INDIA PRIVATE LIMITED, *New Delhi*
PRENTICE-HALL OF JAPAN, INC., *Tokyo*
PRENTICE-HALL OF SOUTHEAST ASIA PTE. LTD., *Singapore*
WHITEHALL BOOKS LIMITED, *Wellington, New Zealand*
EDITORA PRENTICE-HALL DO BRASIL LTDA., *Rio de Janeiro*

FOR NAÏLA AND FOR DALE

CONTENTS

FOREWORD

The Actor's Needs

The need of a young actor to act is stronger than the intelligent layman can understand. The world might think that this ambition is motivated by the desire for money, success, and fame. Even if the actor says this is his aim, it is still only partially true. If there could be a slogan, it would be: "Join the theatre and give back to the world part of the greatness each young actor feels is in him." The actor is fighting for a way of life. The theatre differs from many other professions because it is a way of life.

Acting as an expression includes a rare thing—soul satisfaction—which is not very concrete, yet very important to his growth. If you don't understand that acting has this level of expression, that it is an art form, you are only adding to the confusion which already exists.

The material presented here includes many, many ways in which the actor might present himself to those who need to see him work on his craft.

The unusually varied selections will open many interesting doors, both for the actor and his audience.

Along with other creative powers released in the actor,

Miss Finchley's book will challenge him as he grows to the whole range of dramatic literature.

Everyday reality is not enough for the actor. He must find an art form with which to express this reality—life! When he becomes an actor, he achieves an independence and an ability to grow as long as he lives. Even if you take the platform away from him, he will grow; he has the tools, the training, and the discipline. To grow is his deepest and truest need when he says: "I want to be an actor."

STELLA ADLER

PREFACE

Auditioning is an unnatural act. I can think of few professions in which a prospective employee, applying for a job, must present himself or herself in the manner that actors do. Can you imagine an automobile mechanic walking into a garage and being told he must reassemble an engine in front of, say, 30 other mechanics before getting the job? Or imagine a pastry chef being asked to bake strudel in front of 30 Hungarian restaurant owners! That would be *one crowded kitchen*!

Besides being unnatural, auditioning is an act whose rewards are uncertain. As we in the professional theatre all know, the casting of a show has often already been done over rounds of beer and cups of coffee. If anyone complains, the director can always say, "Sorry, ducks, but I didn't like your audition." In amateur productions, roles are often assigned to the actor or actress who can also help with the lighting when Ralph gets ill.

Unnatural? For certain. Inequitable? Surely that. Solutions? None at the moment. The system is here to stay.

Two positive ways of confronting the situation are (1) to experiment with the audition guidelines set forth in this book, and (2) to discover and develop fresh, first-rate literature with which to audition.

My primary intention in writing this book is to aid in the selection of that literature. The book contains nondramatic audition material (fiction, nonfiction, poetry, and newspaper and magazine articles) for the professional theatre artist and for the student of drama.

Unconventional material can be of extraordinary value to an actor because a casting director or teacher has fewer assumptions and expectations about the piece. The circumstances and biography of a character's life can be created from your own imagination and tailored to your own needs. You are not at the mercy of both the character and the play's reputation.

For example, in *A Streetcar Named Desire*, Blanche DuBois is an elegant, delicate, and sensual lady from the South who later escapes into a psychotic world when things go wrong. Allan Felix in *Play It Again, Sam* is homely, nervous, and shy and has difficulty meeting women.

To illustrate further: Over the course of a casting day, a director is likely to hear 15 versions of Blanche DuBois or Allan Felix. Rather than concentrate on your acting skills, the director is unhappily comparing your performance with the one(s) he or she so fondly recalls: namely Vivien Leigh's or Uta Hagen's. (Of course, as you move farther away from Broadway, associations such as these become less frequent.) With the Allan Felix role, none of the 15 versions the director has just witnessed will ever compare with his own brillant performance of that role in a recent dinner theatre engagement in Paramus, New Jersey.

The same values can apply to directors. By being receptive to nondramatic audition material, your mind is freed from past associations with the selection you are hearing. You are able to concentrate *solely* on the actor's performance. A director once told me she welcomed unconventional material because it helped her gain further insight into the actor "as a person." An actor's choices can often reflect his or her personality.

This book is not an indictment of conventional plays; I fully acknowledge their value as timely works of art. However, parting with certain musty classics, at least for audition purposes, could prove to be a wise choice. Nondramatic selections contain all the essential elements of a good audition piece: rich language, vivid images, and an expansive emotional range.

HOW TO USE THIS BOOK

1

Several selections in this book appear in their entirety. Because of stringent copyright laws, however, I have excerpted many, giving the reader only impressions of their language and content. Where permission to reproduce a piece (in any form) has been denied, I have chosen to describe it instead.

The selections are briefly summarized. These summaries are not intended as literary criticism but, rather, are designed to highlight facts and assumptions about the character and circumstances.

The nature of this book disallows categorizing the selections by age or gender. Instead, I have grouped them by subject matter and style. The first 18 selections are mainly humorous and contemporary character studies: "Popping Up in 60 Minutes," Erma Bombeck, Woody Allen. The next 16 selections are sociological/psychological character studies: *Children in Jail, In Cold Blood*. The seven selections that follow deal mainly in Americana: *Hillbilly Women, Growing Up Southern*.

The final section is devoted entirely to poetry. Rarely is an actor called upon to audition with (nondramatic) poetic material. However, poetry does have a strong place and purpose in training the young actor who is preparing for classical roles. It can be an excellent springboard in mastering the works of Shakespeare, Webster, Congreve, and the like. Poetry provides the imagery, rhythm, meter, figurative language, and musical devices that must be comprehended if an actor wishes to perform classical, dramatic works.

In *Voice and the Actor* Cicely Berry comments on the value of poetry in training the actor's voice:

> . . . the demands it makes are very particular and quite subtle, yet its extravagance encourages you to do extravagant things which are not untrue. This has nothing to do with what kind of acting you want to do; it is not just for the person who wants to do mainly classical acting but for those using all kinds of text. The point is, you find inflections happen which, if they had been calculated, would seem false but which, if they spring from the stimulation of a text, are quite true. Speeches from plays are not always helpful as they cannot be done without

reference to character and interpretation and other issues than voice immediately become important.

Out of the vast repertoire of British and American poetry, selecting which poems to use was no easy task. Many of them were chosen because they illustrate well the aforementioned literary elements—imagery, meter, rhythm, and so on—whereas others seem to embody more dramatic elements: character, action, and different levels of emotion. In the end, I asked my own students which ones were both useful and pleasurable to them.

Before each selection, you will find the title of the source. If it suits your needs, obtain the source (readily available at good libraries and bookstores), which, of course, contains the material in its entirety. To further assist you, I have included the author, publisher, date of publication, specific page(s) where the piece begins and ends, and an indication of whether the specific pages are from the paperback or hardcover edition. Although I have suggested age and gender, no overall rule applies. Much of this material can be performed by a range of ages and by actors of either sex.

Next, you will find an abbreviation of the type of audition circumstance the material is best suited for (see chart below). A scene from *Sophie's Choice* would not be recommended for the Turnpike Dinner Theatre, nor would "Popping Up in 60 Minutes" be apropos for a classical repertory company.

Repertory Theatre	REP
Off-Broadway	OB
Summer Stock	SS
Dinner Theatre	DT
Drama School/	
Acting Class	DS
Agents	A

Finally, after each piece there is a section entitled "Treatment." I offer brief insights into the character, content, or style of the piece and at times suggest a few acting guidelines to help you get started. This section is not meant to be an intensive character study nor a lengthy acting manual. My hope is simply to provide the actor with a base from which to work.

To avoid redundancy, I often refer you to characters from other selections because the emotional levels, content, and style are similar. The same guidelines can be considered for other characters.

This format is slightly altered in the poetry section. All the poems appear in their entirety, and only where the selection is obscure do I note its source. The audition circumstance is left to the actor's own discretion. Realistically, however, the best place for the performance of these poems would probably be the classroom.

Unlike dramatic literature, poetry is not always clearly defined with regard to character, intent, or circumstance, and for the most part is a personal experience. With that considered, I have resisted the temptation to include summaries and/or acting guidelines as I do with the other nondramatic selections in this book. For the insatiable scholar, an oversupply of literary criticism is readily available in every library and/or college bookstore.

The greatest effort on the part of actor, director, or teacher lies in the editing. All of these selections need to be neatly trimmed down to a realistic playing time, usually 3–5 minutes. Editing material for audition purposes is a highly subjective process. What appeals to one actor may seem insignificant and mundane to another. The best method of editing is to ask yourself these questions:

1. What fascinates me about what the character says?
2. What part(s) of the speech do I personally connect with?
3. Which parts of the speech provide the best dramatic possibilities?
4. Which parts best reveal information about the character's intentions and feelings?

The rest is oftentimes excess, and you can easily eliminate it without obstructing the clarity or content of the speech.

4

If you have the luxury of time, you will want to read the entire text of the source as you would any dramatic script. The process of investigating this material can be stimulating and informative and can hopefully lead you down other paths. It serves a twofold purpose: the discovery of first-rate audition material and exposure to a diverse body of literature.

All the material in this book has been "tested" by actors, writers, directors, and teachers. It was through their cumulative opinions that the final selections were made.

FOOD
FOR THOUGHT

2

A good chef would agree that haute cuisine cannot be created without adhering to the advice and instructions given in a first-rate cookbook. Similar rules apply to the audition process. There is a basic recipe that the actor must tend to. Once you have learned the recipe, cook the meal. If the meal turns out well, is tasty and esthetically pleasing, you have done your job. Relax and enjoy your creation. If the meal turns out poorly and your taste buds tell you it is far from a culinary delight, a few options are available to remedy the situation:

Repeat the recipe
Change the recipe
Discard the recipe

Such is the case with the audition guidelines that appear in the following section. It is important to remember that no two actors are alike. What fills the need (and gets the job) for one actor may be unsuitable for you. Always remain flexible. A rigid actor is a dead one.

At the end of this section, I refer you to a few good books on acting and auditioning to further assist your mission. But proceed with caution: you cannot learn about acting from any text. You can be guided, but you cannot be taught.

While writing this book, I met a well-known actress who won an Academy Award for her performance in a recent film. She told me: "I hate books about acting; I've never read one. I got to where I am today by just *doing* it. By throwing myself into the ring—again and again and again and then once more."

For this reason, I have resisted all temptation to turn the following chapter into a didactic treatise. Instead, I have chosen those guidelines which are commonly overlooked by most actors, both professional *and* amateur.

Further Reading

Respect for Acting by Uta Hagen with Haskel Frankel. New York: Macmillan, Inc., 1973.

Audition by Michael Shurtleff.
New York: Walker Publishing Company, 1978.
Presence of the Actor by Joseph Chaiken.
New York: Atheneum Publishers, 1980.

THE RECIPE

3

Keep a File

My undergraduate days were spent at a first-rate theatre training school. One semester, since the school was in close proximity to New York City, I applied for permission to pursue an independent study on audition techniques (anything to get out of Beginning Lighting Design 101).

I was well aware I could not accept an acting job (should I have actually landed one), because my primary commitment was to the training program. But I welcomed the restriction. It freed me from the tension and despair ("Please, God, I need this job!") that seemed to be the plight of so many actors I observed. I knew my day would come soon enough. Instead, I went from "mock audition" to "mock audition" watching, waiting, participating. I kept a note card on each audition I attended and ended up with a file much in the form of a diary, which I still refer to now and then. Sometimes when I look at it, I swallow hard and say, "I can't believe I used to do that." Here are a few entries from it:

> Attended an audition for a musical comedy today. Chose to sing a tune from a musical currently running on Broadway. Knew it was the wrong choice when I heard a loud "ugh" coming from the dark. The auditors were tired of it. My guess is they had heard that song at least fifty times that day.

Moral: Do not choose a song from a current show. Wait until its reputation has a chance to simmer.

> This week I met with a well-known acting teacher, to audition for a place in his acting class. We chatted extensively. I wondered at what point he was going to ask the inevitable question: "What are you going to do for me?" He never did. Instead he simply said, "You're very good, aren't you?" I looked him straight in the eye, and with all the conviction I could muster up replied, "Yes, I am."

Moral: If given the opportunity to converse with an auditor, take full advantage. Demonstrate your sincerity, wit, charm, and intelligence. Remain positive about yourself and your talent. (P.S. I never had to do my audition piece, and was invited to join the class.)

If you are inexperienced at the audition game, I recommend travelling this route. For the well-seasoned actor, I am not encouraging auditioning for the sake of auditioning, but I do wish to convey the importance of simply keeping a record. This system is as valuable as any "How to Audition" class might be and surely more economical.

Being Seen

Regardless of how wonderful a performance you give, it will not matter if it cannot be seen. If you are auditioning in a legitimate theatre equipped with at least a few lighting instruments, take a moment to find the light. That is where your audition should take place, not in the dark. If uncertain as to whether you are in the light, simply ask the auditors. They will be more than happy to tell you.

In many instances, you will find yourself auditioning in well-lit rehearsal studios, hotel rooms, or classrooms. Chances are you will have no control over the situation and will not have to concern yourself with the lighting.

Being Heard

If given the opportunity, find out *beforehand* in what size room your audition will take place. Then, adjust your vocal range accordingly. Many actors misinterpret the term projecting to mean shouting. If you do not know the size of the audition space, be prepared to shift vocal gears at a moment's notice.

The best preparation is to rehearse your scene in different-sized rooms. Ask a friend to sit in the last row and note which sections of your speech are inaudible or incomprehensible. Sharpening this skill involves extensive vocal training. For your assistance I refer you to *Voice and the Actor* by Cicely Berry (Macmillan Publishing Company, Inc., 1973) and *Freeing the Natural Voice* by Kristen Linklater (Drama Book Specialists, 1976). Both, however, will be of more value under the tutelage of a proper vocal coach.

Attire

If attending a general audition, go for the unobtrusive look. Garish outfits can impede an auditor's ability to concentrate on your audition. But if you are being considered for a specific role, dress appropriately. For example, if the role is Masha from *The Three Sisters*, you might best save your designer jeans for another occasion.

Warming Up

The purpose of warming up before an audition is to tune and relax the actor's instrument. Every actor knows what works for him or her. Some vocalize, others meditate, still others run their speech 50 times backwards. If you need to work this way and insist on warming up a few minutes before the actual audition, by all means proceed. The best place to prepare is *at home*. Quiet, private spaces are rarely available at the audition site. For me, the ladies' room never quite fits the bill.

Do what *you* have to do. However, keep in mind that it is unrealistic to think you can achieve a proper vocal, physical and psychological warm-up under adverse conditions. I would aim for one of the above. Many actors I know prefer an activity that has little to do with the audition itself: reading, balancing your checkbook, or writing letters.

Most professional actors will tell you that when acting becomes a full-time career and auditioning a way of life, the need for extensive preparation of this nature will subside. You just go do it!

Get Help

You can rehearse a scene or monologue numerous times. Hopefully you will improve upon it with each run-through, but you can reach a point where monitoring yourself becomes impossible. Find an audience. It does not necessarily have to be an acting teacher. Try the speech on anyone who will listen to you: friends, parents, landlords, exterminators. By rehearsing for a diverse audience, you will gain the confidence so needed when the time comes to perform. This process will will answer an all-important question: "Do I know it?"

I think the ultimate test of confidence is to run into a shoe store, find the nearest clerk, and begin reciting your piece. If he doesn't call the cops—that is, if he *believes* you—then you're a success!

Eye Contact

You have several options available:

1. You can address imaginary characters in empty chairs (place them downstage, please), but it is unnecessary to focus the entire speech on them. The auditors accept the convention; they know the characters are part of your scene. *Refer* to the characters from time to time, but do not remain immobilized in front of them. In real life, no one stares directly into the eyes of a person they are talking to, for the entire time.

2. If auditioning for *one* auditor, some actors like to make direct eye contact. If relieves them of the burden of talking to make-believe people. But be careful. Some auditors are threatened and uncomfortable with direct confrontation. Others may welcome the intimacy of it. So ask. Simply say; "Do you mind if I use you?"

3. If you are auditioning for several auditors and your speech is of the "Friends, Romans, countrymen" genre, address the entire group, and no one auditor will feel uneasy. This technique can heighten the effect of your speech and presence on the stage.

Props

True, props can be your friend. They are an additional tool in the acting process, since they reveal information about your character and can further the action of a scene. However, the very nature of the audition situation is one of anxiety and stress. One less thing to worry about is one less thing that can go wrong. Every actor has his or her story to tell about the lighter that wouldn't light or the alarm clock that refused to go off. For some mysterious reason, the gods are never on our side when we need them. *Minimize your props.*

Dialects

Unless requested to do so, avoid dialects. Actors often mistake the use of dialects for good acting. They get caught up in the rhythmic flow of the dialect and forget the scene's real intentions. If you must use one, rehearse the scene in your own speech, tagging the dialect on last. If you have a sharp ear for language, recordings are the best source for learning dialects.

Further reading

Foreign Dialects: A Manual for Actors, Directors and Writers, by Lewis Herman and Marguerite Shalett Herman. New York: Theatre Arts Books, 1973.

More Stage Dialects by Jerry Blunt. New York: Harper & Row, 1980.

A Pronouncing Dictionary of American English by John S. Kenyon and Thomas A. Knott. Springfield, MA: G. & C. Merriam Company, 1953.

Choice of Material

Choose something you like. If you rehearse your piece a few times and discover it isn't working, drop it. If you do not, the piece can become your nemesis, making the work sheer drudgery.

Choose a piece whose speaker is close to your age and suitable to your physical attributes. If you do not know yourself well enough, seek the advice of someone you trust. Your choice should say something about you, reflecting your personality, intelligence, and imagination.

Just in case you are asked to do something else, do not be caught off guard. Always have extra material *prepared*. I recommend knowing five classical and five contemporary speeches, ready to be performed at a moment's notice. To best demonstrate your versatility and range, these selections should be of a contrasting nature.

Being prepared in this manner shows the auditors you are a serious actor who has done his or her homework and knows what the audition game is all about.

Obtain the Script

If you know what role you are auditioning for, obtain a copy of the script beforehand. Take full advantage of the opportunity by reading it thoroughly and becoming very familiar with your particular scene(s).

Your responsibility does not end there. Familiarity with a text does not mean you can act it. Make some decisions about the scene. What does my character want? What is my relationship to the other characters in the scene? One can *never* know what a director wants, and it is usually a waste of precious time to try to find out. By making specific choices, you have something to go on, something to play.

Listen to yourself and enjoy what you have prepared. I know an actor (employed and successful) who, before each audition, gives this little speech: "If I am on the wrong track and interpreting the script contrary to your vision, please stop me." It saves their time and yours. If you are doing good work, chances are they will not stop you.

Cold Readings

If you ask, most directors will allow you to have a look at the script before your reading. But *you* have to ask. If the reply is negative, don't fret. You will never know what you are capable of doing unless you try. This could be your chance to shine. With spontaneity, humor, and great aplomb, accept the challenge. Travel this unknown territory as if you have been there a thousand times!

Résumés

A few simple rules here, and you are in business. Produce an 8 × 10 black and white photograph with a résumé attached. Both items must represent you accurately: a picture that looks like you and a résumé that is truthful.

While I was teaching at a well-known university one summer, my students were constantly asking, "What if my credits are few and far between?" My reply was simply, "So what?" List them anyway and never apologize. Bow down to no one. Do not confuse subservience with modesty: the former is obsequious, the latter essential.

Waiting Room Etiquette and Survival

An open audition is one that everyone and anyone may attend—and does. Waiting long hours at audition centers, surrounded by other contenders, may be unnecessary for you at the career stage you have arrived at. Presumably you have something called a scheduled appointment. If so, count your blessings and feel free to skip this section.

I handed these questions to a group of actors I interviewed at an open audition call in New York City. The actors I spoke to are named Kenn, Jacki, Janis, and Donna.

What happens when you sign up to audition early in the day and realize you won't be called on for several hours? What do you do with your time?

KENN: I use the time well. I make sure I have a list—made the night before—of constructive activities I can accomplish. I catch up on letter writing, read, make phone calls.

JACKI: I'm the queen of the coffee shops. I patronize one after the other. One more Danish and I'll be ready for Weight Watchers!

JANIS: I go home. Now and then I check in to see how fast things are moving.

What if you don't live near the audition site?

JANIS: I have friends all over this town. If I know I'm going to be near one of them, I'll drop by. At least it's a quiet place to rest. I phone the night before. If they're not going to be home, I manage to get a set of keys. Why, I've got keys to over a dozen apartments in this city.

What makes "hanging around" the audition site so objectionable?

KENN: Are you kidding? It scatters your energy and deflates your morale.

How so?

KENN: Some actors can be disrespectful and unrestrained. You get sucked into their conversations. It's impossible not to eavesdrop.

Usually conversations about the negative aspects of the business—the job they didn't get, the director who was a tyrant, or the show that closed. It's okay to complain, I'm not saying that. But do they have to do it for all the world to hear?

DONNA: It really kills me when they start showing their latest photos and résumés. I don't think the audition waiting room is the place for it. I guess I'm just uptight about competition and don't need to be reminded of what I'm up against. I'm nervous enough thinking about my audition.

KENN: Acting/auditioning is about talking yourself *into it*. By participating in or encouraging negative patter, you defeat that frame of mind.

Isn't there a quiet place you can escape to?

DONNA: If there is, I'm usually the first one to find it!

Beware the Beast

By the tender age of nine, I had relinquished all belief in mythical creatures. Santa Claus, the tooth fairy, the stork and the boogieman would have to find housing elsewhere, for I was on to bigger and better things.

When I entered the acting profession, it was frightening to learn that one of these creatures had resurfaced. Namely, the boogieman. He was back. He returned in the form of a fat, cigar-smoking "gentleman," promising fame, fortune, and the opportunity of a lifetime. There is usually a price for the promises he will make and never keep. Don't pay it! Keep your clothes on and slam the door loudly as you exit.

You may be asking, "How will I know if I am doing business with a shady non-professional?" A few clues: he likes to disguise himself as an agent, producer, casting director, mentor, or acting teacher. He can usually be found holding auditions at his apartment (instead of a bona fide audition center), casting an all-nude version of *Uncle Vanya*, or crediting himself for the successful careers of well-known celebrities ("I gave Julie Harris her first lucky break").

Chances are you will fall prey to such a beast at least once in your career—chalk it up to experience and take heed next time.

Every actor has his or her story to tell. An actress described the following experience:

It had been a slow year with few acting jobs in sight. I was getting bored and restless. In response to an ad in the trade papers, I sent a photo and résumé to a casting director in Caracas, Venezuela. They were looking for a young actress to play the lead role in a feature film. Several months later I received a telegram:

Dear Ms. Smith,

After considering hundreds of actors, we have cast you in our film. We will be contacting you in the very near future to discuss your availability.

A transatlantic telephone call soon followed the telegram. An appointment was made for the next week. I was to meet the producer and director at a hotel in New York City to obtain a script and sign the necessary contracts ($2500 a week!!). I hung the phone up and screamed for ten minutes: "There is a God! I've gotten a job!" My bags were packed.

When I arrived at the hotel I was met by a little man who barely spoke English. (Where were the producers and director?) He wanted me to "read" for him. Since this was the first mention of an audition, it certainly made sense to do so. He pushed a button on a cassette recorder. Wild jungle music came blasting out of the tiny machine. I thought Johnny Weismuller would come swinging by any minute.

My suspicions were already beginning, but I decided not to prejudge the situation. I *desperately* wanted this to be real. I *needed* this to be real. A bit later, the little man narrated from the script and asked me to "act out" the following directions:

As you run frantically through the jungle you stumble and fall to the ground. Upon looking up, a young woman appears, claiming to be a Lesbian Countess. You are immediately seduced by her beauty and kindness. You take The Countess in your arms (jungle music building) and kiss her passionately. Clumsily, you begin to remove your clothing. . .

Need I go on? I walked over to the cassette player and clicked it off. I asked the gentleman one question: "What is the name of this film?" He replied, "Barbara, The Lesbian Countess of Caracas." (A Venezuelan named Barbara??) I knew I had been had. I gathered my things and headed for the door. (He pleaded with me to stay, apologizing profusely.) As I approached the elevator in the lobby I saw a young woman get off. I could tell by her appearance that she was the next victim. I cornered the woman and relayed my experience, strongly advising her not to go in. When I finished my diatribe she looked at me and said, "I'm going in anyway—just in case."

If You Blow It

If you forget your lines or feel you have gotten off to a bad start, ask if you may begin again. The answer will usually be yes. The best advice is not to lose control and end up hating yourself when it is over. With each audition, it gets easier and easier. Really it does.

Occasionally, there is a bright side to our blunders, as illustrated in this good letter I received from a young actress:

Dear Joan,

I was recently reminded of an incident I witnessed a few years back.

I was at The Southeastern Theatre Conference (S.E.T.C.) spring auditions where hundreds of actors, singers, and fire jugglers are herded through a crowded assembly hall with one minute and eight bars of music to prove their worth. I was number 317.

Number 316 was ushered to the stage. He nodded to the accompanist to push the button on the portable cassette player he had brought with him. "We got sunlight on the sand. . ." He went stone blank. The tinny recording played on enthusiastically. A sympathetic producer (really!) sang softly to the frozen, white-faced young man, to try and get him back on the track: "We got mangoes and bananas you can pick right off the tree. . ." The producers at nearby tables joined in: "We got volleyball and ping pong and a lot of dandy games. . ." The young man began to nod vaguely: "What ain't we got?" Everyone, at the top of their lungs—"We ain't got dames!"

The room exploded in thunderous applause and cheers!! The young man, having finally been awakened from his stupor, bowed and exited. Unfortunately for me, the laughing and cheering hadn't subsided when my minute and eight bars began. But I gave it my shot. A couple of hours later, I took a look at the callback board. Do you know that creep 316 got called back by everybody there?

Truly,

Miriam D.

Eavesdropping: Snippets of Conversation Overheard at Audition Calls

"Auditioning has nothing to do with acting. Once you get the job, a new set of rules applies. Your responsibilities are to the work. You no longer have to sell yourself; you've already done that. You've been bought."

"The theatre is a wonderful life if you are fortunate enough to be working in it."

"The theatre is a terrible life. I should have gone to medical school."

"I just keep in mind that auditioning is part of being an actor. This is my job. Some folks punch a clock—I wake up every morning, I audition. I'm just not getting paid, that's all."

"Why am I here? Well . . . when I wake up in the morning, I just can't think of anything I'd rather do with my life."

"I'm doing everything I can do. I sent photos and résumés, I audition for everything and anything, I talk with agents, I talk with directors, I talk to my psychiatrist. It may seem like a waste of time—it is to my parents. But at least when I'm old and gray, I can say I tried, I did everything I could."

"I like to pretend that the two-minute auditions I give three days a week *are* my performances. My audition *is* the show. It opens and closes in two minutes, the same day. But that's okay because I'm grateful there's another two-minute show to do tomorrow. It's when the auditions stop—when there just isn't anything to go to—that's when I'll panic. That's when I'd better stop dreaming."

"Auditioning gives me a chance to memorize some wonderful works of literature. It's a great feeling to know I can recite practically anything from Shakespeare to Sam Shepard at the drop of a hat."

"I met my wife at an audition."

"The way I see it, with unemployment soaring in every other profession, why not be an actor? I would feel really envious if all my non-actor friends were gainfully employed in their chosen fields. But they're not. Be an actor, the time is ripe!

When It's Over

When you have finished the audition, go home. Forget about it. Once you leave, there is nothing more you can do. Fill your life with activities which have little to do with acting and the business of acting. Go to karate class, write your memoirs, cook a great dinner. Promise you will not sit home and wait for the phone to ring!

A little voice in me is saying, "Great advice to give, impossible to take." Try.

THE SELECTIONS

4

Even Cowgirls Get the Blues by Tom Robbins

Paperback edition: Bantam Books, Inc., 1977

Chapter 15

Begins: Page 53: "Please don't think me immodest, but I'm really the best."

Ends: Page 55: "Maybe birds are stupid at that."

Suggested age and gender: Broad age range; male or female

Recommended for: REP, OB, DS, A

Summary

Sissy Hankshaw is a small-town gal from the honky-tonk tobacco fields of southern Virginia. She is outrageous! She is beautiful! She is adventurous! She is handicapped.

Born with an oversized set of thumbs ("They grew while she ate her grits and baloney; they grew while she slurped her Wheaties and milk"), there was little hope for anything else in life but to give herself completely to hitchhiking.

In this scene, Sissy has been given a truth serum by Dr. Goldman, one of several "specialists" she encountered (in hope of a cure), and tells of her hitchhiking triumphs.

Excerpt

Please don't think me immodest, but I'm really the best. When my hands are in shape and my timing is right, I'm the best there is, ever was or ever will be.

When I was younger, before this layoff that has nearly finished me, I hitchhiked one hundred and twenty-seven hours without stopping, without food or sleep, crossed the continent twice in six days, cooled my thumbs in both oceans and caught rides after midnight on unlighted highways, such was my skill, persuasion, rhythm. I set records and immediately cracked them; went farther, faster than any hitchhiker before or since. . . .

There is no road that did not expect me. Fields of daisies bowed and gas pumps gurgled when I passed by. Every moo cow dipped toward me her full udder. . . . I am the spirit and the heart of hitchhiking, I am its cortex and its medulla, I am its foundation and its culmination, I am the jewel in its lotus. And when I am really moving, stopping car after car after car, moving so freely, so clearly, so delicately that even the sex maniac and the cops can only blink and let me pass, then I embody the rhythms of the universe, I feel what it is like to *be* the universe, I am in a state of grace.

You may claim that I've an unfair advantage, but no more so than Nijinsky, whose reputation as history's most incomparable dancer is untainted by the fact that his feet were abnormal, having the bone structure of bird feet. Nature built Nijinsky to dance, me to direct traffic.

Treatment

• The dictionary defines *caricature* as a picture or description in which certain features or qualities are exaggerated or distorted to produce an absurd effect. It is tempting to make Sissy Hankshaw a caricature since the context of this material borders on the absurd. Make her a real person, with real feelings and needs. Taken seriously, the humor which is built into the text will emerge effortlessly. Have fun with this character as she is—vivacious, energetic, and colorful.

• The images in this piece are strong ones—for example, "Fields of daisies bowed and gas pumps gurgled when I passed by." The actor must substitute his or her own personal experiences to make these images spring to life. To find the reality of this character you have to examine your own life experiences and sensations. You may never have hitchhiked, but perhaps you remember skiing down a mountain at top speed, the beautiful snow and fresh air exhilarating your senses much the way Sissy becomes exhilarated when she is hitchhiking on the open road. The stronger the image(s) the more believable it becomes for you and your audience.

Working: People Talk About What They Do All Day and How They Feel About What They Do by Studs Terkel

Paperback edition: Avon Books, 1978

Book 5: "Footwork." Conrad Swibel

Begins: Page 365: "Reading gas meters, it's kind of a strenuous business."

Ends: Page 370: "It's to occupy your day, ya know? To pass the time of day."

Suggested age and gender: Broad age range; male

Recommended for: REP, OB, SS, DT, DS, A

Summary

Conrad Swibel, a gas meter reader from the Midwest, takes great pride in his work and meets each new day with vigor and a fine sense of humor.

Excerpt

Reading gas meters, it's kind of a strenuous business. . . . You have the blue shirt with the gas company on a patch. . . . They give you a badge with your ID picture. That helps you get in. They try to keep us on the same route so people will get used to you. People are suspicious.

I've been bit once already by a German shepherd. And that was something. It was really scary. It was an outside meter the woman had. I read the gas meter and was walking back out and heard a woman yell. I turned around and this German shepherd was comin' at me. The first thing I thought of was that he might go for my throat, like the movies. So I sort of crouched down and gave him my arm instead of my neck. He grabbed a hold of my arm, bit that, turned around. My arm was kinda soft, so I thought I'd give him something harder. So I gave him my hand. A little more bone in that. So he bit my hand.

. . . The big subject of conversation with us is dogs and women. . . . If you see a nice lady sitting there in a two-piece bathing suit—if you work it right and they'll be laying on their stomach in the sun and they'll have their top strap undone—if you go there and you scare 'em good enough, they'll jump up. To scare 'em where they jump up and you would be able to see them better, this takes time and it gives you something to do. . . .

Usually women follow you downstairs to make sure that maybe you're not gonna take nothin'. . .Of course, if she's wearing a nice short skirt, you follow her back up the stairs. (*Laughs*)

Treatment

• This is a simple, straightforward monologue. Conrad Swibel says exactly what he means and *tells* you how he feels about it. The actor needs to assume very little to interpret this character; the subtext is minimal: "I've been bitten once already by a German shepherd and that was something. It was really *scary*. . .[Almost every time you'll go into a house, they jump on you and sniff ya and if you do three hundred homes in a day, it gets *aggravating.*"]

• Find the variety of the speech. Each tale Conrad tells "to pass the time of day" must be different from the next one. By attacking this character in the simplest, most obvious way, its many colors and textures will surface. An intensive, psychological investigation into the character's body and soul is probably unnecessary. Just go with it, and see what happens.

Working: People Talk About What They Do All Day and How They Feel About What They Do by Studs Terkel

Paperback edition: Avon Books, 1975

Book 5: "Footwork." Babe Secoli

Begins: Page 375: "We sell everything here. . .From potato chips and pop—we even have a genuine pearl in a can of oysters."

Ends: Page 380: "I look forward to comin' to work. I enjoy it somethin' terrible."

Suggested age and gender: Broad age range; female

Recommended for: REP, OB, SS, DT, DS, A

Summary

Babe Secoli is a supermarket checker and has known no other work. Babe delights in knowing she's a master at her craft, and would not change her position in life for anything. She embraces each day with competence, wit, arrogance, and zeal.

Excerpt

You sort of memorize the prices. It just comes to you. I know half a gallon of milk is sixty-four cents; a gallon, $1.10. You look at the labels. A small can of peas, Raggedy Ann. Green Giant, that's a few pennies more. I know Green Giant's eighteen and I know Raggedy Ann is fourteen. I know Del Monte is twenty-two. But lately the prices jack up from one day to another. Margarine two days ago was forty-three cents. Today it's forty-nine. Now when I see Imperial comin' through, I know it's forty-nine cents. You just memorize. One the register is a list of some prices, that's for the part-time girls. I never look at it.

I don't have to look at the keys on my register. I'm like the secretary that knows her typewriter. The touch. My hand fits. The number nine is my big middle finger. The thumb is number one, two and three and up. The side of my hand uses the bar for the total and all that.

I use my three fingers—my thumb, my index finger, and my middle finger. The right hand. And my left hand is on the groceries. They put down their groceries. I got my hips pushin' on the button and it rolls around on the counter. When I feel I have enough groceries in front of me, I let go of my hip. I'm just movin'—the hips, the hand, and the register, the hips, the hand, and the register. . .(*As she demonstrates, her hands and hips move in the manner of an Oriental dancer.*) You just keep goin', one, two, one, two. If you've got that rhythm, you're a fast checker. Your feet are flat on the floor and you're turning your head back and forth.

Somebody talks to you. If you take your hand off the item, you're gonna forget what you were ringin'. It's the feel. When I'm pushin' the items through I'm always having my hand on the items. If somebody interrupts to ask me the price, I'll answer while I'm movin'. Like playin' the piano.

Treatment

• To begin work on this character, observe various checkers at supermarkets in your neighborhood. This will give you a clearer picture of a typical day in the life of Babe Secoli. You may want to observe the following:

1. How do the checkers move?
2. How do they handle food?
3. How do they bag their groceries? (They all seem to have different techniques.)
4. Do they sit or stand?

• If given the opportunity, make "small talk" as your groceries are being checked. Learn as much as you can.

• Physicalize this character. The things she *does* are as important as how she feels about doing them. Observing "real life" situations can help in this process. Once you get the externals flowing, the internal needs of the character should surface with ease.

• Babe Secoli is intelligent, poignant, and alert.

American Dreams: Lost and Found by Studs Terkel

Hardcover edition: Pantheon Books, 1980 (also available in paperback: Ballantine Books)

"Onward and Upward": Sharon Fox

Begins: Page 61: "I'm just one of millions."

Ends: Page 63: "If I can leave something behind creative, that
  I've done, maybe I'll be important to somebody."

Suggested age and gender: Broad age range; female

Recommended for: REP, OB, SS, DT, DS

Summary

Sharon Fox is a messenger at the Board of Trade in
Chicago. Her sideline is collecting autographs. Among her most
celebrated are those of Sylvester Stallone, Jack Ford, Yul Bryn-
ner, and Buster Crabbe.

She thinks of herself as a quiet, dull person. Collecting
autographs adds importance and glamour to her life. She is a
delightful personality: warm, endearing, and humorous.

Excerpt

I've grown up with these people, watching them on TV. I never
had many friends, so it was a substitute. I decided to go one
step further and meet these people instead of admiring them
from afar. My mother has an autographed picture of Jean Har-
low. So maybe it's in the genes somewhere. (*Laughs*)

I live at home. I never liked hanging out on street corners
or going to parties. I don't drink or smoke. We're a churchgo-
ing family, Baptist. My parents are all I've got, I'm all they've
got. They never had any hobbies. They have no real outside
interest, outside of me. They want to see me happy, and they're
interested in what I'm doing. Whatever I do reflects them.

They're like living through me. This is one country where you can do anything, and they prove it every day.

Are you familiar with Brenda Starr? I can identify with her. She's glamorous, not what I am. She's got this great love in her life, Basil St. John, which I don't have. She goes on all these exciting capers.

Treatment

• I cannot decide whether to laugh or cry at Sharon Fox. Perhaps that is the beauty of the speech. She claims to be a dull person, yet her experiences ("I met Prince Charles and he kissed me for my birthday") and attitudes ("If I can leave something behind creative, that I've done, maybe I'll be important to somebody") suggest otherwise. Perhaps the challenge of this speech is to work against that claim, concentrating on her humorous, passionate, and ingenuous qualities.

• Each experience she has triggers a different set of emotions and reactions. Make them bigger than they seem. On meeting Prince Charles she is not merely pleased but awestruck. On being sketched into the Brenda Starr comic strip, she is grateful and impressed.

• Sharon Fox is the kind of girl I would put at the top of my guest list and invite to a dull dinner party.

Letters from the Earth by Mark Twain; edited by Bernard DeVoto

Hardcover edition: Harper & Row Publishers, Inc., 1962 (also available in paperback: Harper & Row Publishers, Inc.)

"Letter II"

Begins: Page 8: "I have told you nothing about man that is not true."

Ends: Page 12: "He is a marvel—man is! I would I knew who invented him."

Suggested age and gender: Broad age range; male

Recommended for: OB, DS

Summary

In the guise of Satan, Mark Twain reports (to the archangels Gabriel and Michael) his observations on the "curious inhabitants of the planet Earth." He finds their ways and beliefs preposterous and astounding.

In Letter II, he describes man's invention of heaven: "It has invented a heaven. . . . guess what it is like! In fifteen hundred eternities you couldn't do it. The ablest mind known to you or me in fifty million aeons couldn't do it. Very well, I will tell you about it." He proceeds to do so in the style that has come to be known as vintage Twain: wildly funny, vigorous, and imaginative.

Excerpt

In man's heaven, EVERYBODY SINGS! The man who did not sing on earth sings there; the man who could not sing on earth is able to do it there. This universal singing is not casual, not occasional, not relieved by intervals of quiet; it goes on, all day long, and every day, during a stretch of twelve hours. And EVERYBODY STAYS; whereas in the earth the place would be empty in two hours. The singing is of hymns alone. Nay, it is of ONE hymn alone. The words are always the same, in number they are only about a dozen, there is no rhyme, there is no poetry: "Hosannah, hosannah, hosannah, Lord God of Sabaoth, (sic) 'rah! 'rah! 'rah! siss!-boom! . . .a-a-ah!"

Treatment

• One weekend, I found myself in Chapel Hill, North Carolina, with nothing to do. A friend told me Hal Holbrook was in town with his one-man show, "Mark Twain Tonight," and suggested I see it. The show prompted me to include this material among my selections. I found it to be very playable and wildly funny.

• Treat this piece as an artist would treat a blank canvas. Choose a persona or voice that suits your creative instincts. Twain suggests the guise of Satan as one possibility. But a more playable character might be an ex-priest turned flaming agnostic who in the style of an ambitious politician, must spread his views throughout the world. Try them both on for size.

• It would help to read as much Mark Twain as possible. Perhaps you can piece together material from other works. Hopefully, working in this manner will tempt you to research and compile works of other great writers. This is how one-man (-woman) shows are born. If you are a versatile performer, perhaps this is a direction in which you may want to go. Twain is a good place to start.

Catcher in the Rye by J. D. Salinger (not reproduced here)

Little, Brown & Company, 1945

Chapter 1

Begins: "If you really want to hear about it."

Ends: "If there's one thing I hate, it's the movies. Don't even mention them to me."

Suggested age and gender: Young; male

Recommended for: REP, OB, DS, A

Summary

Holden Caulfield is both the protagonist and the narrator of *Catcher In The Rye*, a chronicle of a sixteen-year-old boy who escapes to New York after flunking out of his third prep school.

In this opening scene, it is implied that Holden has had a nervous breakdown and speaks to us from an institution. ("I'll just tell you about this madman stuff that happened to me around last Xmas before I got pretty run-down and had to come out here and take it easy.") In a cry of mixed pain and pleasure, he unravels the memories of his "lousy childhood."

It is Holden's language that provides the dramatic excitement, the surprises, and the clues to his character. One learns about Holden not necessarily from his actions, but rather, from the way in which he expresses himself.

Treatment

• Read the entire book. If you have already done so, read it again. Try not to approach this piece from a literary point of view. That choice will not help you act it. Besides, you have already done that in high school English. Try to read the book as you would any dramatic script, looking for the answers to the following questions:

1. What is Holden's relationship to his parents, sister, brother, schoolmates, and so on?
2. What are his needs and demands in life?
3. What *would* make Holden happy?
4. What physical choices can be determined about him? How does he walk, run, shave, etc.?
5. What does his choice of language reveal?

• Be careful not to make this speech a one-note rendition of "Blues in the Night." Find the nuances, the different levels. Holden doesn't hate everything. Moments of pleasure and humor peep through his sarcasm and anger. It is almost as though he doesn't want to *get caught* feeling good about anything.

"Baby Gets a Tattoo" by Deanne Stillman
The Village Voice, October 21–27, 1981
This selection appears in its entirety.
Also by Deanne Stillman: *Getting Back at Dad*, Wideview Books,
    1981
Suggested age and gender: Broad age range; male or female
Recommended for: REP, OB, SS, DS

Summary

After much anxiety about getting a tattoo, the character
in this piece heads for Woodstock, New York in pursuit of re-
nowned tattoo artist Spider Webb. Despite overhearing horri-
fying screams (another subject being tattooed) in the waiting room
of Spider's tattoo cottage, the character courageously endures,
and in the end acquires a lovely tattoo in a very secret place.

Excerpt

Don't tell my mom that I have a tattoo because she'll probably kill me. She says you can't be buried in a Jewish cemetery if you have a tattoo, and even if you could, Jews shouldn't
do cheap things like painting their bodies (permanently). Only sailors and marines and stevedores who get drunk and stumble into cheap parlors in places like Hong Kong and the water-
front of Cleveland get tattoos, not Jews. So don't tell my mom,
okay?

The tattoo that I got is really neat. I'm sorry, but I can't
tell you what it looks like or even where it is because it's supposed to be a surprise for the people who get to see it. In other
words, it's not on my right or left arm, or my neck, or my
feet. (Hint: it's not on my thighs, either.)

I got the tattoo the day after some people with a crowbar
pried off the door to my loft and ripped me off. Here's what

they took: two gold necklaces and an amethyst ring and two strings of pearls my grandmother gave me before she died. All the jewelry had street and sentimental value. They also took a gram of cocaine and left me one line. That turned out to be a good thing because it gave me enough energy to call the police. My friend Bob arrived first and surveyed the scene of the crime. (Bob has a tattoo too; it's a small one and you can hardly see it, but his mom noticed it one day, and she got mad.) Bob said, "It's time for a piece of jewelry no one can steal."

I had been thinking about getting a tattoo for a long time, but I never looked at it that way. So Bob and I went to Woodstock to visit our friend Spider Webb, known in tattoo circles as the best tattoo artist in the tri-state area, if not the whole world. I told him what I wanted and where I wanted it and he said to think about it overnight and if I still wanted it the next day, I should come back.

I thought about it all night, which is what I had been doing for months, but it seemed like a good idea to think about it one more time. I thought about all the reasons I shouldn't get a tattoo. First of all, I thought about how mad my mom would get. Would I be rejected by a Jewish cemetery? Then I thought about how I might not like the tattoo next week. Then I worried about how much it would hurt to get the tattoo. Then I thought that certain people would think I was copying Janis Joplin, even though it was about 15 years later. Then I thought some people would think I was getting a tattoo just because of that new Bruce Dern movie called *Tattoo*. And then I thought about how mad my mom would get. Would she tell me to go join a circus?

I didn't care. I wanted to become a member of the world's oldest cult. I wanted to partake of a ritual that knows no national boundaries. I wanted to have a piece of art that I could always wear. I wanted a permanent decoration, something that would look great with everything. I wanted to surprise my friends and confuse my enemies. Also, I was pretty drunk.

I went back to Spider Webb's the next day. His place is not a tattoo parlor, it's a tattoo cottage. He says that if you want the kind of tattoo you get in a tattoo parlor, you should go down the street to the local tattoo parlor, where the guy outlines all his tattoos in black ink. Spider's place is right near the Woodstock town green, next to a place that does ear-piercing. If you really want to make your mom mad, you could stop there after you get your tattoo.

While you're waiting for Spider, you can sit on a couch and read his book, *Pushing Ink*. It says that Jennie Churchill and Barry Goldwater have tattoos, something that may convince you to either stay or leave, depending on your point of view. It also says, "The tattoo will let you know if it wants you, and where."

When I arrived, Spider was finishing up another tattoo. I heard a woman's screams coming from the room where he was working. I knocked on the door and asked if I could take a peek. No one seemed to mind. In fact, the woman seemed excited that someone wanted to witness her screams. Spider was carefully tattooing a long-stemmed rose on the woman's foot. It covered a scar. The tattoo was truly beautiful, a perpetual blossom climbing up from between two toes. Every time Spider applied the needle, the woman shrieked. And this was only her foot! I started to panic.

Spider soon emerged. I asked why the woman screamed so much. "Some people are screamers," he said, and smiled. Then he asked me if I still wanted my tattoo. I said yes. He said he thought that I still did, and last night had drawn a special design based on my description of the tattoo I wanted. It was beautiful—but about three inches too big.

Spider likes to work big because that's the way he thinks. I asked him to scale it down and he asked me again if I really wanted the tattoo. I said yes. He smiled and scaled it down. When the size was right, I went inside his studio and he went to work.

I won't go into all the details because it might scare you. And I don't want to do that because a tattoo is definitely something worth getting if you really want one. I will say that it hurt. I'm not a screamer so I didn't scream. But I think I invented several dozen words consisting of consonants during the two-hour-long session. I will also say that if anyone can make getting a tattoo a pleasure, it's Spider Webb.

That's because Spider Webb is like Groucho Marx on angel dust. A Zen Rodney Dangerfield. Captain Kangaroo with an electric needle. If Spider had his own TV show, the announcer would say, "Kids, Spider Webb is a professional. Check with mom before trying to imitate Spider. . ." Spider Webb looks like the kind of guy who has a secret. And he does. He tells you his secret through the colors that he carefully pushes under your skin. He inserts a needle flowing with red ink. "You know what they say," he says. I'm splayed out in pain. "What?"

"A fool and his money are soon parted." And then Spider Webb laughs, as if sharing a private joke with the ancients. Is this what Egyptian tattoo artists told Cleopatra when she had reached the point of no return?

My tattoo is all healed now, and it's the nicest piece of art that I have. If you know Spider Webb's work, you know it looks like a Spider Webb tattoo. I unveiled it a couple of weeks ago, and my friends wanted to know where I got it and how much it cost. (Spider's prices start at $50.) No one mentioned Janis Joplin or Bruce Dern. A couple of people mentioned the Stones' new album, "Tattoo You."

Well, at least they can't call me chicken. And when I walk down the street, I know there must be a lot of people, maybe as many as the number that live in Pennsylvania, who have tattoos that only their closest friends know about. I know that there are a lot of people who have jewelry that no one can steal. It's a feeling I get. Spider says that sometimes you can just tell when someone has a tattoo.

But don't tell my mom, okay?

Treatment

I share the following notes which were taken while watching an actress audition with this monologue.

1. I enjoyed the actress enjoying herself. This speech has great comic potential. She subtly captured its off-beat humor without pushing for laughs.

2. The story seemed to roll off her tongue as though she had *recently* experienced it. There was a sense of excitement and immediacy to her delivery.

3. The piece was well edited.

4. I travelled with her on a journey which began in fear ("Please don't tell my mom") and insecurity (". . .When I arrived, Spider was finishing up another tattoo. I heard a woman's screams coming from the room where he was working.") and ended with feelings of relief and satisfaction.

Lady Oracle by Margaret Atwood (not reproduced here)

Simon & Schuster, 1976

Chapter 5

Begins: Page 42: "My Mother named me after Joan Crawford."

Ends: Page 51: "Besides, who would think of marrying a moth-
ball?"

Suggested age and gender: Broad age range; female

Recommended for: REP, OB, SS, DT, DS, A

Summary

Among other imperfections, Joan Foster was a grossly
overweight child. She kept a photograph of herself on a dresser,
but when asked about it, claimed it was that of a favorite aunt.
She managed to conceal this secret and many others (she wrote
Gothic romances under a pseudonym) throughout her adult life.

In this piece she describes the many ways her disapprov-
ing mother tried to deal with her daughter's shortcomings. "When
I was eight or nine my Mother would look at me and say mus-
ingly, "To think that I named you after Joan Crawford!" She goes
on to describe how Mother, hoping to make Joan less chubby,
enrolled her in Miss Flegg's dancing school, where she performed
such memorable routines as "Tulip Time," "Anchors Aweigh,"
and "The Butterfly Frolic."

It is this particular memory, and the author's detailed
description of it, that provide a monologue of wit, compassion,
and sentiment.

Treatment

See Treatment from *Working* (Conrad Swibel), *American Dreams: Lost and Found* and *California and Other States
of Grace.*

"Popping Up in 60 Minutes" by **Russell Baker** (not reproduced here)

New York Times Magazine, Sunday Observer Column, March 2, 1980 (also available on microfilm)

Begins: "In my first dream about appearing on *60 Minutes,* Harry Reasoner did the interviewing."

Ends: "If Tom Snyder refuses to take my case, it's curtains."

Suggested age and gender: Broad age range; male or female

Recommended for: REP, OB, SS, DT, DS, A

Summary

In this piece the narrator dreams that the *60 Minutes* crew has asked him to appear on their television show for an interview. They wish to interrogate him about his faulty toaster. In the course of the piece he finds the members of the *60 Minutes* news team in different rooms of his house.

Morley Safer explains that the team is doing an exposé on people who waste energy: "Poets who burn the midnight oil. . .condemned murderers who insist on being electrocuted instead of hanged." He goes on to say they are now interested in the character's toasting habits.

Dan Rather discovers that the toaster has to be warmed up before it will toast the bread. He asks, "Is is not a fact that you prefer to keep this ancient, outmoded toaster which is so dilapidated that the toast has to be pushed down, not just once, but twice?" In a fit of paranoia, the character seizes the toaster, rushes into the bedroom, slams the door, only to hear:

"True or False?" The voice is familiar. "You are a toaster batterer." It is none other than Mike Wallace.

In despair, the character pleads guilty, throwing himself on the mercy of Shana Alexander and James Kilpatrick.

Treatment

See Treatment from *Working* (Conrad Swibel and Babe Secoli). In addition: your reaction to each confrontation and to each interviewer must vary. The speech begins with the most amiable interviewer. You are relaxed and confident. You move on to the next interviewer—paranoia sets in. You are at last confronted with the most vicious of the three interviewers. By this time you are a vision of pathos and frenzy, begging for mercy from anyone who can help you. As the "plot" progresses, the comedy builds.

Getting Even by Woody Allen

Paperback edition: Warner Paperback Library (published by arrangement with Random House, Inc.)

"A Little Louder Please"

Begins: Page 82: "On the night of the performance, the two of us—I in my opera cape and Lars with his pail—."

Ends: Page 84: "I don't like to be bothered once I'm asleep."

Suggested age and gender: Broad age range; male

Recommended for: SS, DT

Summary

This gentleman has been plagued since childhood by his inability to understand the art of pantomime.

In this piece, he and Lars (his window-washer) attend a pantomime entitled, *Going to a Picnic*. His "mimetic shortcomings" are enhanced and his confusion thickens as he struggles to interpret the performance.

Excerpt

The mime now proceeded to spread a picnic blanket, and instantly my old confusion set in. He was either spreading a picnic blanket or milking a small goat. Next, he elaborately removed his shoes, except that I'm not positive they were his shoes because he drank one of them and mailed the other to Pittsburgh. I say "Pittsburgh," but actually it is hard to mime the concept of Pittsburgh, and as I look back on it, I now think what he was miming was not Pittsburgh at all but a man driving a golf cart through a revolving door or possibly two men dismantling a printing press.

Treatment

• See Treatment from *The Grass Is Always Greener Over the Septic Tank* and *Even Cowgirls Get the Blues.*

• In addition: The difficulty of this piece is in creating a believable, three-dimensional character. By doing so you voyage one step beyond the comedy routine and into a character an audience can empathize and identify with.

The Grass Is Always Greener Over the Septic Tank by **Erma Bombeck** (not reproduced here)

Hardcover edition: McGraw-Hill Book Company, 1976 (also available in paperback: Crest/Fawcett)

Chapter 7: "It Comes with the Territory"—Loneliness

Begins: Page 91: "No one talked about it a lot, but everyone knew what it was."

Ends: Page 98: "By the way, could you call and let me know how Lisa makes out on *As The World Turns*."

Suggested age and gender: Middle-aged; female

Recommended for: SS, DT

Summary

While chatting over a cup of coffee with neighbor Helen, our character reveals a case of the housewife blues. Boredom and restlessness abound. The symptoms are evident: "The other day I flushed a Twinkie down the toilet just to please Jack LaLanne." She goes on to confess: "I would have graduated from college this June. That's right. If I had just found my car keys, I could have picked up my B.A. and could be one of those women who only wash on Saturdays and freeze their bread."

As with all the writings of Erma Bombeck, humor and sarcasm prevail.

Treatment

• You may wish to perform this material as a stand-up comedy routine. It certainly is appropriate for cabaret shows or nightclub acts. If you choose to treat it as a comedy routine, keep in mind that the primary intention should be to entertain.

• I have also seen actors build real characters from this material. The character is obvious: a frustrated middle-class housewife who longs to be upwardly mobile and respected. The humor lies in her *failure* to get the things she wants.

Aunt Erma's Cope Book by **Erma Bombeck** (not reproduced here)

Hardcover edition: McGraw-Hill Book Company, 1979 (also available in paperback: Crest/Fawcett)

Chapter 9: "The Complete Book of Jogging"

Begins: Page 75: "Jim Fixit's legs were the first thing I saw every morning and the last thing I saw every night."

Ends: Page 83: "Easy for Mr. Fixit."

Suggested age and gender: Broad age range; male or female

Recommended for: SS, DT

Summary

One can hardly call Aunt Erma a physical fitness enthusiast. Mere contemplation of such activities makes her wince. Eventually she is plunged into the world of jogging by family and friends and endures their boasts of blisters, shin splints, back pains and Achilles tendonitis. They speak "fluent jogging" (e.g., "euphoria," "building up lactic acid") while she cringes at the very thought of the sport.

It was only a matter of time before her "inner peace had brought out her outer fat." With a $65.00 pink velour warm-up suit in hand, she joins the masses and converts.

Treatment

See Treatment from *The Grass Is Always Greener Over the Septic Tank.*

The Art of Ruth Draper: Her Dramas and Characters
    by Morton Dauwen Zabel
Hardcover edition: Doubleday, Inc., 1960
"A Scottish Immigrant at Ellis Island."
Begins: Page 136: "Goodbye, Annie. Goodbye. . ."
Ends: Page 139: "Sandy! My Sandy. . .I'm here!"
Suggested age and gender: Young (19–27); female
Recommended for: DS

Summary

Leslie MacGregor is a young girl from the Highlands of Scotland who has just arrived at Ellis Island in New York harbor, the point of entry for immigrants coming to the United States. Leslie has come to meet her prospective husband whom she has not seen for three years.

Excerpt

Good morning, sir—good morning. . .My name?. . .Leslie MacGregor. . .Leslie. . .L-E-S-L-I-E. . .That's all. . .It is. My only name. . .Just Leslie. It's a Scottish name. . .I come from Crianlarich. . .Crianlarich. It's a small place—it's part way between Loch Katrine and Loch Awe in the Highlands of Scotland. . .Spell it?. . .Ye spell it C-R-I-A-N-L-A-R-I-C-H. Crianlarich. . .

I'm twenty-one years old. . .I have come oot to mary. . . Oh, he's here. . .Oh, yes. I know 'im. . .His name?. . .His name is Mr. Alexander MacAllister. . .

Well, d'ye see—he left home three years ago, and when he had enough, he was to send for me. So now I have come. . .Aye, he knows I'm coming. . .He'll be here the day to meet me. I'm sure he will. . .I beg your pardon?. . .Polygamist—am I a polygamist? What ever is that?. . .Am I mar-

51

ried?. . .Oh, no, Sir—I'm not married. . .Anarchist? Is that a religion?. . .I am a Presbyterian. . .In prison? Have I been to prison? No, Sir—we have no prison in Crianlarich. . .Asylum? De ye mean where the puir daft people go?. . .No, Sir—we have no asylum in Crianlarich. . .Contagious diseases? Well, I had a cold on the steamer coming over, but it's gone now—would that be a contagious disease?. . .No, Sir—I've never been ill; only in the wintertime, sometimes I have a wee cold! Come out under contract?. . .No contract—only to Mr. MacAllister!

Treatment

• It would be both appropriate and effective to use a stage dialect with this character. As I note in the audition guidelines (see Dialects, page 00), you should rehearse the piece in your own speech, tagging the dialect on last. Perhaps this selection is best suited for an exercise in an acting or voice class. To help build this character, ask yourself the following questions:

1. Where have I come from? (her past)
2. What are my expectations about America?
3. What are my expectations of Alexander MacAllister?
4. How do you pronounce "Crianlarich"?

• You may wish to stage this speech as a scene rather than a monologue. To capture Leslie MacGregor's innocence, excitement, and confusion, it could be helpful to have the clerk present.

The Art of Ruth Draper: Her Dramas and Characters
    by Morton Dauwen Zabel

Hardcover edition: Doubleday, Inc., 1960

"The German Governess"

Begins: Page 165: "Quiet, please, children!. . .And go to your
    places. . ."

Ends: Page 168: ". . .*Ich kann's nicht langer aushalten*. . ."

Suggested age and gender: Middle-aged; female

Recommended for: DS

Summary

"She sits in a straight chair before her pupils in the classroom of their family home. . .worn and harassed by her years
of teaching, and nervously aware of her unruly charges."

Excerpt

Now, children, I am going to read you a beautiful little
poem!. . .One minute! Harry—get up from under the desk
there! What have you got in your blouse?. . .What?. . .Guinea
pigs?. . .Those baby guinea pigs?. . .Children, where do you
get these ideas? There is absolutely nothing funny about it—it
is outrageous! Cruelty to animals!. . .Now, children, please
turn to page sixty-six. You will enjoy this. It is a very famous
poem called "Die Lorelei."

Ich weiss nich, was soll es bedeuten,
Dass ich so traurig bin;
Ein Marchen aus alten Zeiten,
Das kommt mir nicht aus dem Sinn.

Who threw this dead fly? Who threw it?. . .Children—I
can't stand it any longer! I come here every morning—I give

you my life and my time. I try so hard to make you happy, and I have only insults. I will control myself, now—but mind you—you will hear of this again. It is by no means the end— your parents shall hear of it! It's outrageous!"

Treatment

See Treatment from: *The Art of Ruth Draper:* "Scottish Immigrant."

California and Other States of Grace by Phyllis Theroux

Hardcover edition: William Morrow & Company, Inc., 1980 (also available in paperback: Fawcett Books)

Chapter V

Begins: Page 94: "When I turned nine and it was discovered that I needed glasses, Hollywood and stardom were not in my line of vision."

Ends: Page 103: "All my glossies would be accompanied by personal, handwritten notes."

Suggested age and gender: Young; female

Recommended for: REP, OB, SS, DT, DS, A

Summary

Struggling with childhood self-doubts and determined to escape a life of "lukewarm obscurity," the author finds in her idol, Margaret O'Brien, a Hollywood fantasy that eases the growing pains.

In this selection, she reflects upon those childhood memories.

Excerpt

When I turned nine and it was discovered that I needed glasses, Hollywood and stardom were not in my line of vision. I vaguely knew about Margaret O'Brien (my parents had taken me to see *Little Women* for my eighth birthday), but it was not until the day I sat waiting for my eyes to dilate in a doctor's office and listened to my mother read aloud from a book entitled something like "Margaret O'Brien's Very Own Diary"— not until that moment did I realize what stale doughnuts I had been eating all those years. My God, what a life that girl was leading. . .!

My heart stretched with envy. That I should be wearing dresses from Macy's Chubette Department and be 3,000 miles from an Automat. That I should be holding soggy tomato sandwiches in a hot schoolyard while Margaret was holding press conferences and getting toy Collies from unknown admirers. What kind of God was this who would visit astigmatism and flyaway hair upon the head of one nine-year-old and bestow twenty-twenty vision and a set of shiny black braids upon another? In one moment which extended for the next several years, I decided that Margaret O'Brien did not deserve her life. Wondering why I fixated upon Margaret O'Brien and not Shirley Temple, I think the reason was twofold: Shirley Temple was too treacly for my tastes. Secondly, Margaret O'Brien might be easier to knock off.

Treatment

• See Treatment from *Even Cowgirls Get the Blues*, *Working* (Conrad Swibel), and *American Dreams: Lost and Found*.

In addition: This speech is a child's fantasy—delicate and heartwarming. The insecurity and confusion which accompanies adolescence is an important part of the piece. The character yearns to be someone else ("my heart stretched with envy"), certain her own life is insignificant and mundane.

• Like so many monologues in this book, *California and Other States of Grace* is a stroll down memory lane. It is only in retrospect that the memories are humorous. While they were being lived, they were painful and frightening.

The Portable Dorothy Parker (revised and enlarged edition) (not reproduced here)

Paperback edition: Viking Press, 1973

"The Waltz"

Begins: Page 47: "Why, thank you so much. I'd adore to."

Ends: Page 51: "I'd simply adore to go on waltzing."

Suggested age and gender: Broad age range; female

Recommended for: REP, OB, SS, DT, DS, A

Summary

Here we are at the dance. The character cringes at the prospect of being asked to dance by a gentleman she suspects is an idiot. It turns out he is graced with the dancing skills of "Mrs. O'Leary's cow."

"What can you say, when a man asks you to dance with him? 'I most certainly will NOT dance with you, I'll see you in hell first. Why, thank you, I'd like to awfully, but I'm having labor pains. Oh, yes, do let's dance together—it's so nice to meet a man who isn't a scaredy-cat about catching my beri-beri!"

Reluctantly she accepts his invitation. Her inner monologue continues while waltzing with the gentleman, who by this time has managed to kick her in the shins, crush her instep and shove her against the wall.

Treatment

• As with all the writings of Dorothy Parker, her prose is humorous, bright, and sharp-edged. The characters are pathetic little creatures who blame God (and everyone else) for life's injustices. ("Why can't he let me lead my own life? I ask so little—just to be left alone in my quiet corner of the table, to do my evening brooding over all my sorrows.")

• While developing these characters, take note of their two contrasting levels. On the surface, they are witty, charming, and sincere. ("Oh, yes, it's a waltz. Mind? Why, simply thrilled. I'd love to waltz with you.") These niceties are cover-ups for the character's real feelings and needs. Anger and frustration lie beneath the surface and reveal the true identities of these women. ("I'd love to waltz with you, I'd love to have my tonsils out, I'd love to be in a midnight fire at sea.")

• It should be easy to connect and identify with these characters since their problems are universal. We (especially women) have experienced these predicaments at least once in our lives. Perhaps this is the attraction of Dorothy Parker's characters.

The Portable Dorothy Parker (revised and enlarged edition) (not reproduced here)

Paperback edition: Viking Press, 1973

"The Little Hours"

Begins: Page 254: "Now what's this? What's the object of all this darkness all over me?"

Ends: Page 259: ". . .Till the next ten o'clock, if I feel like it."

Suggested age and gender: Broad age range; male or female

Recommended for: REP, OB, SS, DT, DS, A

Summary

"At the time when all decent people are just going to bed, I must wake."

At four-thirty A.M. we find the character in "The Little Hours" plagued with insomnia. She (or he) takes us on a journey of frustrating attempts to drift back to sleep. When reading fails, she tries counting sheep. "I hate sheep. . .I can tell the minute one's in the room. They needn't think that I am going to lie here in the dark and count their unpleasant little faces for them."

When counting sheep fails, she finally decides to make a list of beautiful and profound quotations: "To thine own self be true." "If winter comes, can spring be far behind?" "Mrs. Porter and her daughter wash their feet in soda water." Et cetera.

The prose in "The Little Hours" abounds with wit and sarcasm. It is quite appropriate for either sex.

Treatment

See Treatment from *The Portable Dorothy Parker:* "The Waltz."

The Portable Dorothy Parker (revised and enlarged edition) (not reproduced here)

Paperback edition: Viking Press, 1973

"Sentiment"

Begins: Page 354. "Oh, anywhere, driver, anywhere—it doesn't matter. Just keep driving."

Ends: Page 359. "Driver, what street is this? Sixty-Fifth? Oh. No. nothing, thank you. I—I thought it was Sixty-Third. . ."

Suggested age and gender: Broad age range; female

Recommended for: REP, OB, SS, DT, DS, A

Summary

In an attempt to mend a broken heart, Rosalie seeks refuge in a taxi cab (where the entire scene takes place). She has no particular destination and instructs the driver to "just keep driving." It's better than walking. If she was walking she might catch a glimpse of her former lover in the crowded street: "Someone with his swing of the shoulders, his slant of the hat."

As she continues to be driven aimlessly throughout the city she talks herself through the stages of their now ill-fated romance. These thoughts are soon interrupted when she screams to the driver not to ride through a particular street. "This was our street, this is the place of our love and laughter." Rosalie proceeds to crouch down below the back seat with her hands tightly covering her eyes. "Oh why can't I be let to die as we pass through?"

As in "The Little Hours" and "The Waltz," "Sentiment" is deliciously witty and sarcastic.

Treatment

See Treatment from: "The Waltz," page 57.

Les Liaisons Dangereuses by Choderlos de Laclos
Letter 97
1782, Paris
This piece appears in its entirety.
Suggested age and gender: Broad age range; female
Recommended for: REP, OB, DS

Summary

Les Liaisons Dangereuses is a series of letters (175) which describes two ruthless aristocrats, the Marquise de Merteuil and the Vicomte de Valmont and their scheme to seduce a young girl, Cécile Volanges.

In this scene, Cécile tells Madame de Merteuil the guilt and shame felt after Monsieur de Valmont seduced her. She blames herself for not protesting the act and allowing him to return the next evening. "I was so very agitated! If it is always as difficult as this to defend oneself, one needs a good deal of practice!"

LETTER 97: CÉCILE VOLANGES TO THE
MARQUISE DE MERTEUIL
OH God, Madame, how heavy-hearted, how miserable I am! Who will console me in my distress? Who will advise me in my difficulties? This Monsieur de Valmont . . . and Danceny? No: the very thought of Danceny throws me into despair. . . . How shall I tell you? How shall I say it? . . . I dont' know what to do. But my heart is full . . . I must speak to someone, and in you alone can I, dare I confide. You have been so kind to me! What shall I say? I do not want you to be kind. Everyone here has offered me sympathy to-day . . . they have only increased my wretchedness: I was so very much aware that I did not deserve it! Scold me instead; give me a good scolding, for I am very much to blame. But then save me. If you will not have the kindness to advise me I shall die of grief.

Know then . . . my hand trembles, as you see. I can scarcely write. I feel my cheeks on fire. . . . Oh, it is the very blush of shame. Well, I shall endure it. It shall be the first punishment for my fault. Yes, I shall tell you everything.

You must know, then, that Monsieur de Valmont who hitherto has delivered Monsieur Danceny's letters to me, suddenly found it too difficult to continue in the usual way. He wanted a key to my room. I can certainly assure you that I did not want to give him one: but he went so far as to write to Danceny, and Danceny wanted me to do so. I am always so sorry to refuse him anything, particularly since our separation which has made him so unhappy, that I finally agreed. I had no idea of the misfortune that would follow.

Last night Monsieur de Valmont used the key to come into my room as I slept. I was so little expecting this that he really frightened me when he woke me. But as he immediately began to speak, I recognized him and did not cry out; then, too, it occurred to me at first that he had come to bring me a letter from Danceny. Far from it. Very shortly afterwards he attempted to kiss me; and while I defended myself, as was natural, he cleverly did what I should not have wished for all the world. . .but first he wanted a kiss. I had to: what else could I do? The more so since I had tried to ring, but besides the fact that I could not, he was careful to tell me that if someone came he would easily be able to throw all the blame on me; and, in fact, it would have been easy on account of the key. After this he budged not an inch. He wanted a second kiss; and, I don't know why, but this time I was quite flustered and afterwards it was even worse than before. Oh, really, it was too wicked. Then, after that. . .you will spare my telling you the rest, but I am as unhappy as anyone could possibly be.

What I blame myself for most, and what, nevertheless, I must tell you about, is that I am afraid I did not defend myself as well as I was able. I don't know how that happened. I most certainly am not in love with Monsieur de Valmont, quite the contrary: yet there were moments when it was as if I were. . . .As you may imagine, this did not prevent me from saying no all the time: but I knew quite well that I was not doing as I said: it was as if I could not help it. And then, too, I was so very agitated! If it is always as difficult as this to defend oneself, one needs a good deal of practice! It is true that Monsieur de Valmont has a way of saying things so that one is hard put to it to think of a reply: at all events, would you believe that when he left I was almost sorry, and was weak enough to agree to his returning this evening? That is what horrifies me more than all the rest.

Oh, in spite of all, I promise you I shall stop him coming. He had scarcely left when I knew for certain that I had been very wrong to promise him anything. What is more, I spent the rest of the night in tears. It was Danceny above all who haunted me! Every time I thought of him my tears came twice as fast till they almost suffocated me, and I thought of him all the time. . . .I do even now, and you see the result: my paper quite sodden. No, I shall never be consoled, if only on his account. . . .At length I could cry no more, and yet could not sleep for a minute. And when I woke this morning and looked at myself in the mirror, I frightened myself, I was so changed.

Mamma noticed it as soon as she saw me, and asked me what was wrong. I began at once to cry. I thought she was going to scold me, and perhaps that would have hurt me less: but quite the contrary. She spoke to me kindly! I scarcely deserved it. She told me not to distress myself like that! She did not know what I had to be distressed about. She said that I would make myself ill! There are moments when I should like to be dead. I could not restrain myself. I threw myself sobbing into her arms, crying 'Oh, Mamma your daughter is very unhappy!' Mamma could not help crying a little herself, and that only increased my misery. Fortunately she did not ask why I was unhappy, or I would not have known what to say.

I beseech you, Madame, write to me as soon as you can and tell me what I must do; for I have not the courage to think of anything and can do nothing but suffer. Please address your letter to Monsieur de Valmont; but if you are writing to him at the same time, I beg you not to mention that I have said anything to you.

I have the honour to be, Madame, ever with the most sincere friendship, your very humble and obedient servant. . . .I dare not sign this letter.

Château de—
1 October 17—

Treatment

• The background of this book is rather interesting. When it was first published in 1782 French society was outraged and it caused quite a scandal. It is said that "young ladies would retire with it behind locked doors." It was later found in the library of Marie-Antoinette.

In 1824, the government condemned it to be a work of "revolting immorality, a book to be admired and execrated."

• The piece easily transforms into a monologue. The young girl does not have to be writing a letter to Madame de Merteuil. You can change the situation to suit your needs. i.e. Cécile pays a visit to the home of Madame and begins the speech there. This seems a more "actable" choice than writing a letter and allows for more physical movement and interaction with another character.

• The piece runs a bit long and you will most likely have to edit. See Chapter I, "How to Use This Book," to help in the process.

• There are 175 letters to choose from in *Les Liaisons Dangereuses* which are spoken by characters other than Cécile Volanges. The letters of Valmont, Merteuil, and Danceny (male) adapt well to monologue form.

Sophie's Choice by William Styron

Paperback edition: Bantam Books, 1980 (by arrangement with
   Random House, Inc.)

Chapter 13

This selection appears in its entirety.

Suggested age and gender: Broad age range; female

Recommended for: REP, OB

Summary

Wanda is a prisoner in the women's compound at
Birkenau during the Nazi Occupation. In this scene she finds her
way to Sophie's side and "through a tumultuous outpouring" fills
Sophie with hope about her son Jan and the possibility that he
is safe and well.

Wanda passionately pleads with Sophie to *use* her position as translator-stenographer to the German Commandant, Ru-
dolph Höss, to liberate her son and further the cause of the Resistance.

Excerpt

I knew I had to see you when I heard about you through the
grapevine. We hear everything. I've so wanted to see you anyway all these months, but this new job of yours made it absolutely necessary. I've risked everything to get here to see you—if
I'm caught I'm done for! But nothing risked, nothing gained
in this snakepit. Yes, I'll tell you again and believe me: Jan is
well, he's as well as can be expected. Yes, not once—three times
I saw him through the fence. I won't fool you, he's skinny as
I am. It's lousy in the Children's Camp—everything's lousy at
Birkenau—but I'll tell you another thing. They're not starving
the children as badly as some of the rest. Why, I don't know,

it can't be their conscience. Once I managed to take him some apples. He's doing well. He can make it. Go ahead and cry, darling, I know it's awful but you mustn't give up hope. And you've got to try to get him out of here before winter comes. Now, this *Lebensborn idea may sound bizarre but the thing really exists—we saw it happening in Warsaw, remember the Rydzón child?—and I'm telling you that you simply must make a stab at using it to get Jan shipped out of here. All right, I know there's a good chance that he might get lost if he's sent to Germany, but at least he'll be alive and well, don't you see? There's a good chance that you'll be able to keep track of him, this war can't last forever.

Listen! It all depends on what kind of relationship you strike up with Höss. So much depends on that, Zosia darling, not only what happens to Jan and yourself but to all of us. You've got to *use* that man, work on him—you're going to be living under the same roof. Use him! For once you've got to forget that priggish Christer's morality of yours and use your sex for all it's worth. . .Listen, underground intelligence knows all about that man, just as we've learned about Lebensborn. Höss is just another susceptible bureaucrat with a blocked-up itch for a female body. Use it! And use him! It won't be any skin off his nose to take one Polish kid and have him committed to that program—after all, it'll be another bonus for the Reich. And sleeping with Höss won't be collaboration, it'll be espionage—a fifth column! Zosia, this is your chance! What you do in that house can mean everything for the rest of us, for every Pole and Jew and misbegotten bundle of misery in this camp—*everything*. I beg of you—don't let us down!

Treatment

Wanda's character is well described in this excerpt from *Sophie's Choice*:

". . . .She had a vivacity, a luminous intensity which sometimes transformed her in a spectacular way; she glowed, she

---

*The wholesale kidnapping of foreign children to add to the breeding stock of the Third Reich. On Heinrich Himmler's orders children with Aryan-looking features were selected in mass examinations, brought to Germany for placement in indoctrination centers, and then put up for adoption by "racially trustworthy" German families.

became all sparks and fire (Sophie often thought of the word *fougueuse*) like her hair.

. . . .Sophie never believed that such violent patriotism could dwell within a human breast, even in a land of throbbing patriots. Wanda was the reincarnation of the young Rosa Luxemburg, whom she worshipped. She seldom mentioned her father, nor did she ever try to explain why she had rejected so completely the German part of her heritage; Sophie only knew that Wanda breathed, drank and dreamed of a free Poland—most radiantly, a liberated Polish proletariat after the war—and such a passion had turned her into one of the most unbudgingly committed members of the Resistance. She was sleepless, fearless, clever—a firebrand."

For the Term of His Natural Life by Marcus **Clarke**

Lloyd O'Neil Pty. Ltd. Victoria, Australia (also published in London, America, and Germany)

1869

Book Four, chapter 67: "Diary of the Rev. James North"

This piece appears in its entirety.

Suggested age and gender: Broad age range; male

Recommended for: REP, DS

Summary

In 1846, James North spent 7 years as the Protestant chaplain of a penal colony off the coast of Sydney, Australia. He was assigned the post to establish order and discipline amongst the prisoners of the colony.

He once thought of himself as a college-hero, prizeman, poet, and man of deep religious ideals. Rev. North comes to realize he is no longer the man he once was. In this scene he struggles with his conscience and begs God to forgive him for having sinned. He has been tempted by love and lust for a woman and cannot bear the guilt and shame.

He makes a final plea to be pitied and forgiven or else be allowed to die.

Excerpt

EXTRACTED FROM THE DIARY OF
THE REV. JAMES NORTH

December 7th.—I have made up my mind to leave this place, to bury myself again in the bush, I suppose, and await extinction. I try to think that the reason for this determination is the frightful condition of misery existing among the prisoners; that because I am daily horrified and sickened by scenes of torture and infamy, I decide to go away; that, feeling myself powerless to save others, I wish to spare myself. But in this journal, in which I bind myself to write nothing but truth, I am forced to confess that these are *not* the reasons. I will write the reason plainly: "I covet my neighbour's wife." It does not look well thus written. It looks hideous. In my own breast I find numberless excuses for my passion. I said to myself, "My neighbour does not love his wife, and her unloved life is misery. She is forced to live in the frightful seclusion of this accursed island, and she is dying for want of companionship. She feels that I understand and appreciate her, that I could love her as she deserves, that I could render her happy. I feel that I have met the only woman who has power to touch my heart, to hold me back from the ruin into which I am about to plunge, to make me useful to my fellows—a man, and not a drunkard." Whispering these conclusions to myself, I am urged to brave public opinion, and make two lives happy. I say to myself, or rather my desires say to me—"What sin is there in this? Adultery? No; for a marriage without love is the coarsest of all adulteries. What tie binds a man and woman together—that formula of license pronounced by the priest, which the law has recognised as a 'legal bond'? Surely not this only, for marriage is but a partnership—a contract of mutual fidelity—and in all contracts the violation of the terms of agreement by one of the contracting persons absolves the other. Mrs. Frere is then absolved, by her husband's act. I cannot but think so. But is she willing to risk the shame of divorce or legal offence? Perhaps. Is she fitted by temperament to bear such a burden of contumely as must needs fall upon her? Will she not feel disgust at the man who entrapped her into shame? Do not the comforts which surround her compensate for the lack of affection?" And so the torturing catechism continues, until I am driven mad with doubt, love, and despair.

Of course I am wrong; of course I outrage my character as a priest; of course, I endanger—according to the creed I teach—my soul and hers. But priests, unluckily, have hearts and passions as well as other men. Thank God, as yet I have never expressed my madness in words. What a fate is mine! When I am in her presence I am in torment; when I am absent from her my imagination pictures her surrounded by a thousand graces that are not hers, but belong to all the women of my dreams—to Helen, to Juliet, to Rosalind. Fools that we are of our own senses! When I think of her I blush; when I hear her name my heart leaps, and I grow pale. Love! What is the love of two pure souls, scarce conscious of the Paradise into which they have fallen, to this maddening delirium? I can understand the poison of Circe's cup; it is the sweet-torment of a forbidden love like mine! Away gross materialism; in which I have so long schooled myself! I, who laughed at passion as the outcome of temperament and easy living—I, who thought in my intellect to sound all the depths and shoals of human feeling—I, who analysed my own soul—scoffed at my own yearnings for an immortality—am forced to deify the senseless power of my creed, and believe in God, that I may pray to Him. I know now why men reject the cold impersonality that reason tells us rules the world—it is because they love. To die, and be no more; to die and, rendered into dust, be blown about the earth; to die, and leave our love defenceless and forlorn, till the bright soul that smiled to ours in smothered in the earth that made it! No! To love is life eternal. God, I believe in Thee! Aid me! Pity me! Sinful wretch that I am, to have denied Thee! See me on my knees before Thee! Pity me, or let me die!

Treatment

• Background information: *For the Term of His Natural Life* is an outstanding novel of the early settlement of Australia. It depicts the horror and suffering of the penal colonies and the system under which many convicts vanished without a trace. In 1869, Marcus Clarke visited Tasmania and wrote his account of convict times. Much of his writing is based on actual records and dramatized into the story of its main protagonist, Rufus Dawes. It shares the timeless qualities of *Wuthering Heights*, *Great Expectations* or other works about the darkness of human behavior.

• This selection will need careful editing. Refer to Chapter I, "How to Use This Book."

• The scene is set with Rev. North writing these thoughts in his diary. This may be too passive a structure for an audition situation and you may wish to change it to suit your needs.

"The Diary of a Rent Striker"

New York Herald Tribune, 1964

Suggested age and gender: Broad age range; female

Recommended for: OB, DS

Summary

This piece is the diary of Innocencia Flores, mother of four, living in a decaying tenement in New York's East Harlem.

At the time this diary was written, she had just organized a rent strike with other tenants in her building.

Diary

WEDNESDAY, FEB. 5—I got up at 6:45. The first thing to do was light the oven. The boiler was broke so not getting the heat. All the tenants together bought the oil. We give $7.50 for each tenant. But the boiler old and many things we don't know about the pipes, so one of the men next door who used to be superintendent is trying to fix. I make the breakfast for the three children who go to school. I give them orange juice, oatmeal, scrambled eggs, and Ovaltine. They have lunch in school and sometimes they don't like the food and won't eat, so I say you have a good breakfast. Miss Christine Washington stick her head in at 7:30 and say she go to work. I used to live on ground floor, and she was all the time trying to get me move to third floor next door to her because this place vacant and the junkies use it, and she scared the junkies break the wall to get into her place and steal everything because she live alone and go to work. I'm glad I come up here to live because the rats so big downstairs. We all say, "The rats is big as cats." I had a baseball bat for the rats. It's lucky me and the children never got bit. The children go to school and I clean the house and empty the pan in the bathroom that catches the water dripping from pipe in the big hole in the ceiling. You have to carry umbrella to the bathroom sometimes. I go to the laundry place this afternoon and I wash again on Saturday because I change my kids' clothes every day because I don't want them dirty to attract the rats. . . .

THURSDAY, FEB. 6—I wake up at six o'clock and I went to the kitchen to heat a bottle for my baby. When I put the light on the kitchen I yelled so loud that I don't know if I disturbed the neighbors. There was a big rat coming out from the garbage pail. . . .

FRIDAY, FEB. 7—. . . .The baby woke up at five o'clock. I went to the kitchen but this time I didn't see the rat. After the girls left for school, I started washing the dishes and cleaning the kitchen. I am thinking about their school. . . . My girl take Spanish in junior high school, and I said to her, "Tell your teacher I'm going to be in school one day to teach him Spanish because I don't know where he learns to teach Spanish, but it ain't Spanish.". . .

I'm pretty good woman. I don't bother anyone. But I got my rights. I fight for them. I don't care about jail. Jail don't scare me. If have to go to jail, I go. I didn't steal. I didn't kill nobody. There's no record for me. But if I have to go, I go.

SATURDAY, FEB. 8—. . . .a tenant called me and asked me what was new in the building. She wanted to know about the junkies. . . .I'm not ascared of the junkies. I open the door and I see the junkies, I tell them to go or I call the police. Many people scared of them, but they scared of my face. I got baseball bat for the rats and for the junkies. . . .I know my rights and I know my self-respect. . . .

MONDAY, FEB. 10—. . . .At 9:30 a man came to fix the rat holes. He charged me only $3!. . .

TUESDAY, FEB. 11—. . . .We had no steam, the boiler is not running good. I feel miserable. . . .Living in a cold apartment is terrible. . . .

WEDNESDAY, FEB. 12—. . . .It still so cold the children trembling. You feel like crying looking your children in this way.

I think if I stay a little longer in this kind of living I'm going to be a dead duck. . . .My only weapon is my vote. This year I *don't vote* for nobody. . . .At least I clean my house and you could eat on the floor. The rest of the day I didn't do nothing. I was so mad all day long. I cooked a big pot of soup. . . .

FRIDAY, FEB. 14—. . . .I didn't write this about Friday in my book until this Saturday morning, because Friday night I sick and so cold. . . .

. . .It is really hard to believe that this happens in New York and richest city in the world. But such is Harlem and hope. Is this the way to live? I rather go to the Moon in the next trip.

Treatment

• See Treatment from *Even Cowgirls Get the Blues* and *Catcher in the Rye.* In addition:

• A typical week in the life of Innocencia Flores is characterized by frustration and unhappiness. Somehow she manages to cope. She survives a battle against junkies, rats, hostile landlords, and building inspectors by fighting back. "I see junkies, I tell them to go or I call the police. Many people scared of them, but they scared of my face. I got baseball bat for the rats and for the junkies. . .I know my rights and I know my self-respect."

• It is important to sense the *routine* of her life. Her circumstances never change but her reactions to them do. Some days she appears hopeful while other days she is discouraged and bitter.

• I have seen this selection work well as a scene—the other actor playing the role of interviewer.

Children in Jail by **Thomas J. Cottle**

Paperback edition: Beacon Press, 1977

Chapter 22: "I'm Crying 'Cause They Took Away My Future."

Begins: Page 35: "First thing I realized, man, I didn't know the time."

Ends: Page 38: "So I don't know."

Suggested age and gender: Broad age range; male

Recommended for: REP, OB, DS, A

Summary

Fernall Hoover had brains, charm, and good looks. Lacking the proper support system (an insensitive mother, absentee father) to help channel those attributes into a positive life style, he ended up going to prison at an early age. He was sentenced to five years for breaking and entering and carrying a gun.

In this piece he describes his prison experience.

As with the other selection from *Children in Jail*, the book provides detailed background material about Fernall Hoover's life.

Excerpt

. . .I'm crying in there, man, like I was this little boy or something. I'm really crying. I ain't shitting you. I'm crying 'cause I ain't got no future. I'm like my little brother used to get when we'd take away his toy or this blanket he carried around everywhere. Sitting on the floor crying so loud, you know, no one could shut him up. I'm crying 'cause they took away my future. I try to pull myself together, man. I say, "Okay, man, hold on, pull yourself together. Forget about this long future, this rest of your life stuff. You just be calm now, stop crying and start thinking about tomorrow." That's how I'm talking to myself. Just like that. So I try to settle down. "Forget the future," I say to myself. "Just tomorrow." Then, man, like it started raining or something, I'm crying all over again.

Treatment

See Treatment from *Even Cowgirls Get the Blues* (section on images) and *Catcher in the Rye* (final paragraph). In addition:

• All the selections are contemporary and deal with controversial issues of today.

• Language is descriptive and powerful.

• All of these men and women want desperately to be heard. Whether in the form of a confession or a remembrance, they struggle to express their thoughts and feelings.

• Life gave all of these characters an unfair shake at a very early age. We can assume they want to *mend* their situations—change their role(s) as life's protagonists. They search for peace of mind, forgiveness, freedom, and if they can get it—happiness.

• Make specific decisions regarding who you are talking to and what you need from that person.

Children in Jail by Thomas J. Cottle

Paperback edition: Beacon Press, 1977

Chapter 1: "That Kid Will End Up Killing Somebody"

Begins: Page 16: "I'd never been sick before."

Ends: Page 20: "I'm getting to think it really is only a matter of time."

Suggested age and gender: Broad age range; male or female

Recommended for: REP, OB, DS, A

Summary

Thomas Cottle's *Children in Jail* provides extensive background material on Bobbie Dijon. Her life of crime began at the age of thirteen, when she perpetrated such misdemeanors as fighting and shoplifting. It was only a matter of time before she was put behind bars to await trial for the murder of a neighbor. Here she recounts in remarkable detail her experiences in prison.

Excerpt

. . . That time I was vomiting? They said I was faking. . .They said that the vomit was real but I was sticking my finger down my throat to make myself vomit. You believe that? Can you see me having this conversation with a matron about whether or not I vomit 'cause I really have to or 'cause I'm sticking my finger down my throat so I can get a little attention? It's ridiculous. . .It's like that time in court when all these big shots were talking about the murder of that slob, Ben Colsey, and all I could think about was how stupid a name Arnold is. . . .I'm crying most of the time too, feeling sorry for myself like an old dog. But inside my head I'm saying, "Boy, this is terrific. I don't have to be in school anymore talking about mathematics or the Middle Ages. . .Now I get to talk to a matron, a real live woman who gets paid by the state, about vomiting.

Treatment

See Treatment from *Children in Jail* (Fernall Hoover).

Raging Bull by Jake La Motta with Joseph Carter and Peter Savage

Paperback edition: Bantam Books, Inc., 1980

Chapter 1

Begins: Page 1: "I was sixteen and a hard core, what they now call a juvenile delinquent."

Ends: Page 3: "Back then you knew that all you would ever get would be what you could steal."

Suggested age and gender: Broad age range; male

Recommended for: REP, OB, DS, A

Summary

The American public came to know Jake La Motta as a rapist, murderer, thief, and convict. He emerged from this sordid life to become a "hero of the slums" and finally the middleweight boxing champion of the world.

In this selection, he remembers his youth—memories of indigence and repression while growing up in a Bronx tenement.

Excerpt

Now, sometimes, at night, when I think back, I feel like I'm looking at an old black-and-white movie of myself. Why it should be black-and-white I don't know, but it is. Not a good movie, either, jerky, with gaps in it, a string of poorly lit sequences, some of them with no beginning and some with no end. No musical score, just sometimes the sound of a police siren or a pistol shot. And almost all of it happens at night, as if I lived my whole life at night.

. . .What I remember about the tenement as much as anything else is the smell. It's impossible to describe the smell of a tenement to someone who's never lived in one. You can't just put your head in the door and sniff. You have to live there, day and night, summer and winter, so the smell gets a chance to sink into your soul. There's all the dirt that the super never really manages to get clean even on the days when he does an hour's work, and this dirt has a smell, gray and dry and, after you've smelled it long enough, suffocating. And diapers. The slobs who live in tenements are always having kids, and naturally they don't have the money for any diaper service, so the old lady is always boiling diapers on the back of the stove and after a while the smell gets into the walls.

Treatment

See Treatment from *Children in Jail* (Fernall Hoover).

These two pieces are taken from the Memphis Police Department Sex Crime Squad's *1973 Rape Investigations Report.*

Suggested age and gender: Broad age range; female

Recommended for: REP, OB, DS

These two selections (see following page) are both testimonies from young rape victims. They appear in their entirety and can conceivably be edited into one piece.

I.

Okay, I was 14 years old at the time. School had let out, and I was walking home because I didn't have enough money for carfare. This guy saw me on the street or I saw him, and he said, "Hey, are you looking for a job?" Wow, I thought to myself, how did he know I was looking for a job? So I said, "Yeah, why?" And he said, "Because I know someone, a friend of mine, who's looking for someone to work part-time in his office." So I said, "Where's your friend's office?" and he said, "I'm not doin' anything, I'll walk you over there right now." I told him my mother was expecting me home. I said, "Why don't you just tell me where it is?" He said it would be better if he went with me because he had the connections. He said, "Why don't you call your mother and tell her you'll be home later?" We walked to a phone booth and this guy gave me a dime. He actually gave me a dime to call my mother. I called and said, "Ma, I got a job. I'm going over there right now."

He walked me over to this building and then he told me to wait downstairs and he'd go up and see if his friend was in. I thought that was a little odd, I didn't see why I had to wait downstairs, but I waited around and in a while he came back and said we could go upstairs. We went into this place and there was nothing in it but a dirty mattress. The guy locked the door real quick and then I knew what was happening. I started to cry. I was a virgin. I pleaded with him not to touch me, but he did. It hurt. He hurt me. I was crying a lot.

Afterward he gave me twenty cents to get home. He had the nerve to ask for my phone number so he could call me again. He wanted to ask my mother if he could date me. I gave him the wrong number and a phony name. All I could think of was that I had to go home and face my family, right? I had to go home, have dinner, smile and pretend nothing was wrong.

At dinner my ma kept asking, "What about your new job?" I said, "I don't want to talk about it, leave me alone. It didn't work out."

II.

I took a ride from a truck driver. I always thought truck drivers were good people to get rides from. My father used to drive trucks when he was young, and my cousin was a truck driver—they must be good people to take rides from, you know?

I got in the truck and he said to me, "Aren't you kind of young to be hitchhiking?" Right away I got scared. Then he told me that he'd have to pull off the highway and go to—I think it was Greenwich, or some other town. I thought, Oh God, he's going to pull off the highway and drive into the woods and rape me or stab me—because there had been a case I had just read about. I thought, My God, I have to jump out. I think he realized that this was on my mind because at that moment—we were on the highway—he started to attack me while he was driving. He started to beat me down and he started to rip off my blouse.

In the meantime the truck is swerving back and forth, I said—"Well, we're both going to die now." I remember at one point I was thinking, Why don't I just take the wheel and just swerve the fucking truck off the highway and end it? That was the only way I coud end it, but I didn't want to die. I don't know if this is what I imagine now, but I think there was some type of understanding between us that if I gave him all he wanted, he would let me go.

Treatment

See Treatment from *Children in Jail* (Fernall Hoover).

In Cold Blood by Truman Capote

Hardcover edition: Random House, Inc., 1965 (also available in
    paperback: NAL/Signet)

Final chapter: "The Corner"

Begins: Page 287: "There's nobody much I can talk to."

Ends: Page 287: "Dick was the best natured little kid."

Suggested age and gender: Middle-aged; female

Recommended for: REP, OB, DS, A

Summary

Mrs. Hickock is the mother of Richard Hickock, who sav-
agely murdered four members of the Clutter family in Holcomb,
Kansas on November 15, 1959. He was hanged for his crime on
a gallows in a warehouse in the Kansas State Penitentiary. Unable
to control her anguish during his trial, Mrs. Hickock had to be
led out of the courtroom by a woman reporter. In the scene she
reminisces about her own life and that of her son Richard's. "But
he was sweet, Dick was the best natured little kid."

Excerpt:

There's nobody much I can talk to. I don't mean people haven't
been kind, neighbors and all. . . .Everybody here has gone out
of their way to be friendly. The waitress over at the place where
we take our meals, she puts ice cream on the pie and don't
charge for it. I tell her don't, I can't eat it. Used to be I could
eat anything didn't eat me first. . . .It seems to me like people
are looking at me and thinking, well she must be to blame
somehow. The way I raised Dick. Maybe I did do something
wrong. Only I don't know what it could have been; I get head-
aches trying to remember.

Treatment

• There is a gentle, bittersweet quality about this speech and its speaker. Confused and tired, Mrs. Hickock traces the memories of her life in an attempt to understand what went wrong.

• Since this speech is so well written, many clues to the character are built into the text. Attack your work in the simplest, most obvious way.

• Note that this speech takes place in the ladies' room. This environment suggests Mrs. Hickock's need to escape the drama inside the courtroom, and be alone with her thoughts.

Sacco and Vanzetti

Taken from transcripts of the Public Record of the Trial of Sacco and Vanzetti in the courts of Massachusetts and subsequent proceedings, 1927–29

Suggested age and gender: Broad age range; male

Recommended for: REP, OB, DS

Summary

Sacco and Vanzetti were electrocuted on August 23, 1927 for the murder of two shoe factory employees. In these speeches, both men make a final plea of not guilty to spectators and members of the jury.

Both selections appear in their entirety and can conceivably be edited as one.

BARTOLEMEO VANZETTI

This is what I say: I would not wish to a dog or to a snake, to the most low and misfortune creature of the earth—I would not wish to any of them what I have had to suffer for things that I am not guilty of. I am suffering because I am a radical, and indeed I am a radical; I have suffered because I was an Italian, and indeed I am an Italian; I have suffered more for my family and for my beloved than for myself; but I am so convinced to be right that you could execute me two times, and if I could be reborn two other times I would live again to do what I have done already. I have finished; thank you.

NICOLA SACCO: I AM NEVER GUILTY

Yes sir, I am not an orator. It is not very familiar with me, the English language, and as I know, as my friend has told me, my comrade, Vanzetti will speak more long, so I thought to give him the chance.

I never know, never heard, even read in history anything so cruel as this court. After seven years prosecuting they still consider us guilty. And these gentle people here are arrayed with us in this court today.

I know the sentence will be between two classes, the oppressed class and the rich class, and there will be always collision between one and the other. We fraternize the people, tyrannize over them and kill them. We try the education of people always. You try to put a path between us and some other nationality that hates each other. That is why I am here today on this bench, for having been the oppressed class. Well. You are the oppressor.

You know it, Judge Thayer. You know all my life. You know why I have been here, and after seven years, we that you have been persecuting, me and my poor wife, and you still today sentence us to death. I would like to tell all my life, but what is the use? You know all about what I say before, and my friend—that is, my comrade—will be talking because he is more familiar with the language, and I will give him a chance.

My comrade, the kind man, the kind man to all the child, you sentence him two times, in the Bridgewater case and the Dedham case, connected with me, and you know he is innocent. You forget all this population that has been with us for seven years, to sympathize and give us all their energy and all their kindness. You do not care for them.

Among the peoples and the comrades and the working class there is a big legion of intellectual people which have been with us for seven years, not to commit the iniquitous sentence, but still the Court goes ahead. And I think I thank you all, you peoples, my comrades who have been with me for seven years, with the Sacco-Vanzetti case, and I will give my friend a chance.

I forgot one thing which my comrade remember me. As I said before, Judge Thayer know all my life, and he know that I am never guilty, never—not yesterday, nor today nor for ever.

Treatment

• The primary endeavor in this speech is to convince a judge and jury of your innocence. It may be helpful to recall a time in life when you felt very deeply about an issue and tried desperately to convince someone you were right. Crystallize that memory for yourself, then sprinkle it with energy, passion, and eloquence—qualities necessary to make this speech work.

• Since Sacco and Vanzetti were real people, you have the opportunity to research a role based on facts rather than assumptions. There is an abundance of background material available (including photographs) to assist you.

In particular:

Justice Crucified by Roberta Strauss Feuerlicht, New York: McGraw-Hill Book Co., 1977.

The Burning Bed by Faith McNulty

Hardcover edition: Harcourt Brace Jovanovich, 1980 (also available in paperback: Bantam Books)

Begins: Page 5: "Well, I don't know how it started or anything, but he began hitting me."

Ends: Page 7: "Just leave everything and never, never turn back."

Suggested age and gender: Broad age range; female

Recommended for: REP, OB, DS

Summary

Francine Hughes was an "ordinary" wife and mother from a small town in Michigan. By the age of twenty-nine, she had endured thirteen traumatic years of marriage to Mickey Hughes. He terrorized her with continual bouts of physical and mental violence. On March 9, 1977 she killed him.

This excerpt is from her testimony delivered during the trial later that year. Her speech taps a wide range of emotions: fear, sympathy, and outrage.

Excerpt

The kids were at the front door hollering they were hungry. And they were cold. I let the kids in. I just tried to stay quiet. Move quietly. Not say anything. Walking on eggs, because I didn't want him to start up again. I had the kids wash and we sat down to eat. None of us had eaten all day. I remember the salt on the food stinging my split lip where he'd hit me. The kids were trying to be quiet and I was trying to be quiet. Then Mickey came into the kitchen. He got a beer from the freezer and started yelling at me all over again. He pounded the table and the kids' milk spilled. It was dripping on the floor. The kids jumped up and started crying. Mickey made the kids go upstairs. Then he picked up the plates and dumped all the food on the floor. (*Witness is crying.*)

Treatment

See Treatment from *Sophie's Choice* (Sophie), "Diary of a Rent Striker," and *Even Cowgirls Get the Blues.*

In addition: You may wish to treat this piece as a scene rather than a monologue. Experiment with both possibilities.

Dispatches by Michael Herr

Paperback edition: Avon Books, 1978

Chapter I, Part II: "Breathing In"

Begins: Page 31: "One afternoon I mistook a bloody nose for a headwound."

Ends: Page 33: "I never went back to that outfit again either."

Suggested age and gender: Broad age range; male

Recommended for: REP, OB, DS

Summary

Dispatches is a war correspondent's personal journal of the Vietnam War. In this piece he experiences how he would have behaved had he actually been wounded in combat.

Excerpt

When we fell down on the ground, the kid in front of me put his boot into my face. I didn't feel the boot, it got lost in the tremendous concussion I made hitting the ground, but I felt a sharp pain in a line over my eyes. . .Some hot stinking metal had been put into my mouth, I thought I tasted brains there sizzling on the end of my tongue, and the kid was fumbling for his canteen and looking really scared. . .and somewhere in there I got the feeling that it was him, somehow he'd just killed me.

Treatment

See Treatment from *Nam*.

Nam: The Vietnam War in the Words of the Men and Women Who Fought There by Mark Baker

Hardcover edition: William Morrow & Company, Inc., 1981

Begins: Page 91: "I didn't know shit about Vietnam or war."

Ends: Page 95: "That scared the shit out of me."

Suggested age and gender: Broad age range; male

Recommended for: REP, OB, DS, A

Summary

As the title suggests, *Nam* is the assembled memoirs of Vietnam veterans. What separates this selection from other pieces of its kind is the tender age of the character narrating. He was eighteen years old when he joined the Marines. We learn about the Vietnam experience through the eyes of a teenager. The "men" he describes were still chewing bubble gum and blowing bubbles while acting out a "cops and robbers" fantasy. . ."When I saw what was happening in Nam, I really wanted to cash in on it. Why not? It was like being invited to play with the big kids."

Excerpt

"You try to have fun with things. Ambush was fun. It's supposed to be professional, but it's not.

"Oh boy, here he comes. I got that one."

"This one is mine."

"Nah, I got this one. You got the last one."

"Man, this one's for me. Get your own."

"He's mine."

"Is not."

"Is too."

"Is not."

I loved flying helicopters because you went fast. It's power, like having a Corvette. I got to do something I'd wanted to do since I was a kid, which was touch clouds. When we went up high and there were clouds around, I'd dangle out the door and try to grab them, just to say I did it.

Treatment

• *Dispatches* and *Nam* are monologues which share a common theme: war. The very nature of this subject produces similar conditions and emotional levels in each character: anxiety, panic, fatigue. In addition:

• As with so many monologues in this book, it is important to create someone to talk to and decide what you need from that person. The text does not provide this information; therefore, you must invent it.

• See notes on "images" from *Even Cowgirls Get the Blues*. Keep in mind, not all actors need to substitute *other* images to recreate the reality of a speech. This is simply *one* way to work. Some actors are able to connect and respond to the images which are provided in the text, while others must go the substitution route.

• All of these scenes take place *outdoors*. The actor has to be aware of the physical aspects of this environment and incorporate that sensory information into the character.

• You can use material from several literary sources to build a show that centers on a common theme, such as war. The show can take the form of a compilation of scenes, a variety hour, or a one-man (-woman) show. Hopefully, this will tempt you to look further into material which expands on a given subject.

First Person America by Ann Banks
Paperback edition: Vintage Books, 1981
"Testifying": Lloyd Green
Begins: Page 250: "I'm in New York, but New York ain't in me."
Ends: Page 252: "I drinks to think."
Suggested age and gender: Middle-aged; male
Recommended for: REP, OB, DS

Summary

Lloyd Green is a Pullman porter from New York City. He is also a drunk. Just off from work, we find him at Eddie's Bar on St. Nicholas Avenue in Harlem, sharing his mixed feelings about New York City, then and now.

Excerpt

I'm in New York, but New York ain't in me. You understand? I'm in New York, but New york ain't in me. What do I mean? Listen. I'm from Jacksonville, Florida. Been in New York twenty-five years. I'm a New Yorker! But I'm in New York and New York ain't in me. Yuh understand? Naw, naw, you don't get me. What do they do? Take Lenox Avenue. Take Seventh Avenue. Take Sugar Hill! Pimps. Numbers. Cheating these poor people outa what they got. Shooting, cutting, backbiting, all them things. Yuh see? Yuh see what I mean? I'm in New York, but New York ain't in me! Don't laugh, don't laugh. I'm laughing but I don't mean it; it ain't funny.

Treatment

• Obviously Lloyd Green is intoxicated in this speech. There is a rule of thumb to follow when called on to play a drunk.

Drunkenness is simply a condition, another obstacle which you have to negotiate to get your point across. Once you establish drunkenness, forget about it and fight to be coherent. Your action is to *overcome* the drunkenness so you can communicate the words.

• An actor is so often asked to prepare two contrasting pieces for his/her audition. Lloyd Green could be very effective if performed along with a more conventional, upper-class character such as Henry Higgins.

Spoon River Anthology by Edgar Lee Masters (not reproduced
    in its entirety)
Macmillan Publishing Company, Inc.
"Plymouth Rock Joe"
Suggested age and gender: Broad age range; male
Recommended for: OB, DS

Summary

As with the next piece ("Elizabeth Childers") from *Spoon
River Anthology*, this selection is in the form of a confessional
monologue.
Plymouth Rock Joe has accused the men and women in
his town of having led lives of insignificance and pretense.

Be chivalric, heroic, or aspiring,
Metaphysical, religious, or rebellious,
You shall never get out of the barnyard
Except by way of over the fence
Mixed with potato peelings and such into the trough!

Despite the angry, facetious quality of his speech, an underly-
ing layer of humor seems to emerge. He takes pleasure in saying
the things he does. After a lifetime of quietly observing these people, he is, at last, liberated.

Treatment

• The most suitable occasion for these two selections
(second selection on following page) from *Spoon River Anthology*, would be acting class. They force an actor to make
choices about a character where minimal background information is provided. Within the "confessional monologues" of Ply-

mouth Rock Joe and Elizabeth Childers lies the potential to create fully realized characters out of one's own imagination. Poems of this nature are excellent vehicles for learning the process of building a role.

• There are 244 characters to choose from in *Spoon River Anthology*. Here are a few other suggestions which my own students have successfully adapted to dramatic form: Zenas Witt, Russian Sonia, Lois Spears, Fiddler Jones, Dora Williams, and Yee Bow.

Spoon River Anthology by **Edgar Lee Masters** (not reproduced
in its entirety)

Macmillan Publishing Company, Inc.

"Elizabeth Childers"

Suggested age and gender: Broad age range; female

Recommended for: DS, OB

Summary

The poetry of Edgar Lee Masters' characters describes the
spiritual and physical disintegration of a small American town
and its inhabitants. All are confessional monologues of tragic
existence.

In this piece, Elizabeth Childers laments the loss of her
child who died at birth. She comforts herself by realizing death
may very well be better than life.

> It is well, my child. For you never traveled
> The long, long way that begins with school days,
> When little fingers blur under the tears
> That fall on crooked letters.
> And the earliest wound, when a little mate
> Leaves you alone for another.

Treatment

See Treatment from *Spoon River Anthology* ("Plymouth
Rock Joe").

Growing Up Southern* edited by Chris Mayfield

Hardcover edition: Pantheon Books, 1981 (also available in paper-
    back: Pantheon Books)

Chapter 4: "Born for Hard Luck" by Allen Tullos Arthur "Peg
    Leg Sam" Jackson

This piece appears in its entirety.

Suggested age and gender: Broad age range; male

Recommended for: REP, OB, DS, A

Summary

In the author's own words:

Arthur 'Peg Leg Sam' Jackson took a fancy to playing the har-
monica and riding freight trains. One longtime friend remembers that Arthur, upon hearing an approaching train, once left
his mule harnessed in the field and ran for the railroad tracks.
He was gone for months.

Peg's stories of hoboing, wandering, and odd jobbing re-
construct the plight of countless creative Southern men who
could find few satisfactory outlets in their lives.
Peg Leg Sam is a character equipped with a sense of humor
and the courage to persevere.

I rode more freight trains than days I got to live. All around
through Florida, Alabama, Georgia, Louisiana, Texas. What
got away with me one time was that Southern Pacific. I caught
it out of Louisiana one night—they called it the Sunset Limited. And it never did stop for nothing out through the sandy
desert. I was hungry, my God! Stomach thought my throat
was cut. When it got to Los Angeles, the first garbage can I
seen, I rushed to it, heels went over my head.

    *This article originally appeared in *Southern Exposure* Magazine, Volume
III, no. 4, winter, 1976.

I know every hobo jungle. From Alexandria, Virginia—with the ice cars. We'd drink rubbing alcohol there. Sometime we'd kill a pig or a cow. Four or five of us would carry him back and boy we had a ball that night. Hoboes telling lies and I was in there with 'em. Up there in Toledo, Ohio—the biggest hobo convention in the world. We had a sign hanging up, "When you eat, wash the pan and hang it up again. Another hobo, our friend, may come in."

Oh, I had a good living. Didn't have no home, always followed the season. I'd go down in Florida when it got cold, sleep outdoors. I slept outdoors half my life.

When I had two good feet I could catch the trains making forty miles an hour. When I lost my foot, I'd catch them making twenty-five miles an hour. I hoboed more after I got it cut off. Never caught the front car, always the back car so it would whup me up behind it.

I lost my leg in Raleigh. I was coming out of Richmond. I had gone uptown and bummed some of those ends they cut off meat. I got me some ends and come on back down near the tracks and laid down, I was right tired. My buddy shook me and said, "Train coming." That's all I remember. I caught it but I don't know how I fell off. I believe my head bumped under that bridge. You seen them things hanging down at bridges? That's to warn you before you get to it. I believe I caught it that way, half asleep when I caught it.

When I found myself, I was laying down on the rails. I thought, "My old leg done gone to sleep." And I got up, looked down, and my shoe was cut off my foot. Shoe split wide open. I said, "Mhnn, mhnn." Never felt bad till then. I fell back down on the railroad and yonder come the yard master. "Hoboing was you?" I says, "Sho was." "Let me see what I can do for you." He called the ambulance. About that time about a thousand people were up on the bridge looking down on me. They lifted me out of there and carried me to St. Agnes Hospital. They might be done changed the name now. That's been about forty-six years ago.

You look at me, you look at a man that was born for
    hard luck.
I was born on the thirteenth day, on Friday, bad luck day.
I was born the last month of the year.
I was born the last week in the month.
I was born the last day in the week.
I was born the last hour in the day.

I was born the last minute in the hour.
I was born the last second of the minute.

To show you that I am in hard luck,
If I go up the street walking fast, I run over something.
If I go up the street walking slow, something runs over
  me.
I'm in such hard luck, if I'm sitting down, I'm in every-
  body's way.
I'm in such hard luck, that if it's raining down soup at this
  very minute,
Everybody would be standing there with a spoon, why I'd
  have a fork.
I'm in such hard luck that if my daddy was to die,
They'd make a mistake and bury me.
I'm in such hard luck,
If I was to die they'd make me walk to the cemetery.
I was born for hard luck.

—Arthur "Peg Leg Sam" Jackson

Treatment

• Who are you addressing in this speech? Create someone to talk to and make a decision about what you need from
them; otherwise the speech will seem vague and insignificant.

• Resist the urge to go the sympathetic route with this
character. Emotional recollections of painful memories could
lead you down the wrong path. I do not think Peg indulges
himself in sorrow and self-pity. He describes his experiences
(hoboing, losing a leg) in a very matter-of-fact way. Hoboing
is his job and he accepts the hazards of his profession. He almost seems excited and proud of his escapades.

• Peg's memory is sharp. He recollects his experiences in
great detail, double-checking the facts to get the story right.

• For further reading see the original articles from *Southern Exposure* Magazine, Volume III, no. 4, winter, 1976.

Hillbilly Women by Kathy Kahn

Paperback edition: Doubleday & Company, Inc., 1972

Part Three: "I'm Proud To Be A Hillbilly."

Begins: Page 112: "My mother worked in the cotton mill here, where they made the gauze wrapping for Kotex."

Ends: Page 120: "I want a man that's as big as I am. . . .When I find him, I don't care if he digs outhouse holes for a living, I'm going to live with him."

Suggested age and gender: Broad age range; female

Recommended for: REP, OB, DS

Summary

Donna Redmond grew up in a cotton mill town in Southern Appalachia. She spent years trying to make it there and, when it became impossible, migrated to Atlanta. She now works as a receptionist in an insurance agency. Though her life is not really a success story, she has managed to survive and support herself and her two children. She is bright, compassionate, and outspoken.

Excerpt

One girl VISTA told me recently that I don't know anything about life because I had never been to college, never been to New York City. Said I didn't know anything about what's really going on, like campus riots and all that crap. I may live in my own little world, but as far as knowing anything about life, that's a bunch of bull. Cause you just don't get pregnant, get married at fifteen, get divorced, work to support your kids and yourself without knowing a little bit about where it's really at. . . .

I really have this thing with these VISTA's, them coming in here with this idea that we're a bunch of poor ignorant hillbillies. I'm proud to be a hillbilly. And if you don't like the way I talk, then, damn it, go home! And don't make fun of my Southern accent, and if I want to eat grits for breakfast. . .dang straight, I think grits are the greatest thing that come along. . . .

They've all come from upper-middle-class families, all had Mama and Daddy handing them everything they ever wanted, ever needed. And as for their college educations, take your college education and shove it.

Treatment

I watched an actress perform these two selections (second piece follows) from *Hillbilly Women* and took a few notes:

1. The actress performed the entire speech sitting on a log in an empty room, rising *once* to lace her work boots and light a cigarette. This simple approach on a simple set worked very well.

2. Her choice and execution of a "mountain dialect" (a harsh, gutteral sound) was both appropriate and effective.

3. Both selections were well edited. (See Chapter 1, "How to Use This Book," for tips on editing a lengthy piece.)

4. Quite clearly, Shirley Sommerour and Donna Redmond are tough, courageous women. What impressed me about this particular performance was the actress's ability to uncover those qualities which are less apparent: sensitivity, femininity, and a sense of humor. You have to dig a little deeper to find these levels but your efforts will be worth the trouble. The reward is a lively, three-dimensional character.

Hillbilly Women by Kathy Kann

Paperback edition: Doubleday & Company, Inc., 1972

Part Three: "My Grandpa Always Taught Me to Fight."

Begins: Page 101: At one time Auraria was better known for gold then even California."

Ends: Page 109: "Later, I found out from a doctor that the little white pill was LSD."

Suggested age and gender: Broad age range; female

Recommended for: REP, OB, DS

Summary

Shirley Sommerour is a hard-working hillbilly woman from Southern Appalachia. Ostracized from family and community because of her illegitimacy, Shirley has had to fight a constant struggle for survival. Her pride, strength, and courage assist that struggle.

Excerpt

I went to work at Pine Tree Carpet Mills when I'd just hit my nineteenth birthday. . . .

One thing that happens in the mill is women are getting a lot of gas from the two machines where the men are operating machines run on butane gas. Women that sits behind these machines have almost passed out from the gas those machines throw off. That gas is bad. It burns us in our eyes and we have to breathe it in. . . .

There are pills being used by women in the mill. . . .The pills can be got by just snapping your fingers. You can get them through the black market here. One pill they use is the "green heart" and another is the "speckled bird.". . .

Once, when I was feeling real bad, a woman come to me with a little bitty white pill. Well, I wasn't too sure about the pill so I only took half of it. . . .Then about three weeks later I began having nightmares. I'd see the most terrible monsters you'd ever imagined. Later, I found out from a doctor that the little white pill was LSD.

Treatment

See Treatment from *Hillbilly Women:* "Donna Redmond."

"Weary with Toil" by William Shakespeare

1596

Suggested age and gender: Broad age range; male or female

Sonnet 27

Weary with toil, I haste me to my bed,
The dear repose for limbs with travel tired.
But then begins a journey in my head,
To work my mind, when body's work's expired.
For then my thoughts, from far where I abide,
Intend a zealous pilgrimage to thee,
And keep my drooping eyelids open wide,
Looking on darkness which the blind do see.
Save that my soul's imaginary sight
Presents thy shadow to my sightless view,
Which, like a jewel hung in ghastly night,
Makes black night beauteous and her old face new.
    Lo, thus by day my limbs, by night my mind,
    For thee and for myself no quiet find.

"That Time of Year" by William Shakespeare

1598

Suggested age and gender: Middle-aged; male or female

Sonnet 73

That time of year thou mayst in me behold
When yellow leaves, or none, or few, do hang
Upon those boughs which shake against the cold,
Bare ruined choirs where late the sweet birds sang.
In me thou see'st the twilight of such day
As after sunset fadeth in the west,
Which by and by black night doth take away,
Death's second self, that seals up all in rest.
In me thou see'st the glowing of such fire,
That on the ashes of his youth doth lie
As the deathbed whereon it must expire,
Consumed with that which it was nourished by.
   This thou perceivest, which makes thy love more strong,
   To love that well which thou must leave ere long.

"Let Me Not to the Marriage of True Minds" by William Shakespeare

1598

Suggested age and gender: Broad age range; male or female

Sonnet 116

Let me not to the marriage of true minds
Admit impediments. Love is not love
Which alters when it alteration finds,
Or bends with the remover to remove.
Oh no! It is an ever-fixed mark
That looks on tempests and is never shaken.
It is the star to every wandering bark,
Whose worth's unknown, although his height be taken.
Love's not Time's fool, though rosy lips and cheeks
Within his bending sickle's compass come.
Love alters not with his brief hours and weeks,
But bears it out even to the edge of doom.
    If this be error and upon me proved,
    I never writ, nor no man ever loved.

The Common Muse: An Anthology of Popular British Ballads and Poetry (XVth–XXth Centuries)

Edited by V. de Sola Pinto and A. E. Rodway

Philosophical Library, Inc., 1957

"My Thing is My Own"

Suggested age and gender: Broad age range; female

Note: If you audition for a classical theatre company and are asked to sing, this selection as well as the two which follow can easily be set to a simple tune. They are a wonderful departure from the usual Broadway fare and better suited to accompany your classical audition since they are similar in period and style.

I a tender young Maid have been courted by many,
Of all sorts and Trades as ever was any:
A spruce Haberdasher first spake me fair,
But I would have nothing to do with Small ware.
    My thing is my own, and I'll keep it so still,
    Yet other young Lasses may do what they will.

A sweet scented Courtier did give me a Kiss,
And promis'd me Mountains if I would be his,
But I'll not believe him, for it is too true,
Some Courtiers do promise much more than they do.
    My thing is my own, and I'll keep it so still,
    Yet other young Lasses may do what they will.

A fine Man of Law did come out of the Strand,
To plead his own Cause with his Fee in his Hand;
He made a brave Motion but that would not do,
For I did dismiss him, and Nonsuit him too.
    My thing is my own, and I'll keep it so still,
    Yet other young Lasses may do what they will.

Next came a young Fellow, a notable Spark,
(With Green Bag and Inkhorn, a Justice's Clark)
He pull'd out his Warrant to make all appear,
But I sent him away with a Flea in his Ear.

My thing is my own, and I'll keep it so still,
Yet other young Lasses may do what they will.

A Master of Musick came with an intent,
To give me a Lesson on my Instrument,
I thank'd him for nothing, but bid him be gone,
For my little Fiddle should not be plaid on.
    My thing is my own, and I'll keep it so still,
    Yet other young Lasses may do what they will.

An Usurer came with abundance of cash,
But I had no mind to come under his Lash,
He profer'd me Jewels, and great store of Gold,
But I would not Mortgage my little Free-hold.
    My thing is my own, and I'll keep it so still,
    Yet other young Lasses may do what they will.

A blunt Lieutenant surpriz'd my Placket,
And fiercely began to rifle and sack it,
I mustered my Spirits up and became bold,
And forc'd my Lieutenant to quit his stong hold.
    My thing is my own, and I'll keep it so still,
    Yet other young Lasses may do what they will.

A Crafty young Bumpkin that was very rich,
And us'd with his Bargains to go thro' stitch,
Did tender a Sum, but it would not avail,
That I should admit him my Tenant in tayl.
    My thing is my own, and I'll keep it so still,
    Yet other young Lasses may do what they will.

A fine dapper Taylor, with a Yard in his Hand,
Did profer his Service to be at Command,
He talk'd of a slit I had above Knee,
But I'll have no Taylors to stitch it for me.
    My thing is my own, and I'll keep it so still,
    Yet other young Lasses may do what they will.

A Gentleman that did talk much of his Grounds,
His Horses, his Setting-Dogs and his Grey-hounds,
Put in for a Course, and us'd all his Art,
But he mist of the Sport, for Puss would not start,
    My thing is my own, and I'll keep it so still,
    Yet other young Lasses may do what they will.

A pretty young Squire new come to the Town,
To empty his Pockets, and so to go down,
Did profer a kindness, but I would have none,
The same that he us'd to his Mother's Maid Joan.
  My thing is my own, and I'll keep it so still,
  Yet other young Lasses may do what they will.

Now here I could reckon a hundred and more,
Besides all the Gamesters recited before,
That made their addresses in hopes of a snap
But as young as I was I understood Trap.
  My thing is my own, and I'll keep it so still,
  Until I be marryed, say Men what they will.

The Common Muse: An Anthology of Popular British Ballads and Poetry (XV th–XXth Centuries)
Edited by V. de Sola Pinto and A. E. Rodway
Philosophical Library, Inc., 1957
"They're Shifting Father's Grave"
Suggested age and gender: Broad age range; male

They're shifting father's grave to build a sewer
They're shifting it regardless of expense
They're shifting his remains to make way for ten-inch drains
To suit some local high-class residents.

Now what's the use of having a religion
If when you die your bones can't rest in peace.
Because some high-born twit wants a pipeline for his s____t
They will not let poor father rest in peace.

But father in his life was ne'er a quitter
I don't suppose he'll be a quitter now.
He'll dress up in a sheet and he'll haunt that s____thouse
    seat
And never let those bastards s____t nohow.

Now won't there be an age of constipation
And won't those bastards howl, and rant, and rave
But they'll have got what they deserve, 'cause they had the
    bleeding nerve
To desecrate a British workman's grave.

The Common Muse: An Anthology of Popular British Ballads and Poetry (XVth–XXth Centuries)
Edited by V. de Sola Pinto and A. E. Rodway
Philosophical Library, Inc., 1957
"The Lass of Lynn's New Joy, for Finding a Father for Her Child"
Suggested age and gender: Broad age range; male or female

Come listen, and hear me tell
   the end of a Tale so true,
The Lass that made her Belly Swell,
   with *Marry and thank ye too.*

With many hard Sobs and Throws,
   and Sorrow enough (I wot)
She had wept Tears, the whole Town knows,
   could fill a whole Chamber-pot.

For Pleasure with Pain she pays,
   her Belly and Shame to hide
So hard all day she Lac'd her Stayers,
   as pinch'd both her Back and Side.

Oh! were not my Belly full,
   a Husband I'de have to Night;
There's *George* the *Tapster* at the *Bull,*
   I'm sure I'm his whole Delight.

This day on his Knees he Swore
   he Lov'd me about his Life,
Were not my Pipkin Crackt before,
   I vow I would be his Wife.

Her Mother that heard her, spoke,
   O take him at's word, said she,
A Husband, Child's, the only Cloak
   to cover a Great Belly.

Her Mother she show'd the way,
   and straight without more ado,
She took him to the Church next day,
   and *Marry'd and thank'd him too.*

111

But Oh! when he came to Bed,
    the saddest news now to tell ye;
On a soft place his hand he laid,
    and found she'd a Rising Belly.

At which he began to Roar,
    Your Fancy it has been Itching;
By th'Meat in your Pot, I find, you Whore,
    you've had a Cook in your Kitchin.

O fie, my dear Love, said she,
    what puts you into this Dump?
For what tho' Round my Belly be,
    it is only Fat and Plump.

Good Flesh it is all, ye Chit,
    besides, the plain truth to tell,
I've eat so much, the Sack-Posset
    has made my poor Belly Swell.

Nay, then I've wrong'd thee, he crys,
    I beg thy sweet pardon for't;
I'll get thee a Son before we rise,
    and so he fell to the Sport.

No, the Boy it was got before,
    the Midwife soon wisht him Joy;
But, Oh! e're full five Months were o're,
    she brought him a lusty Boy.

My Wife brought to Bed, says *George*,
    I hope she has but Miscarry'd;
A Boy! says he, how can that be,
    when we are but five Months Marry'd.

Five Months! has the man lost his Wits?
    crys Midwife, what does the Fool say?
Five months by Days, and five by Nights,
    sh'has gone her full time to a day.

The Child's all your own, by my truth,
    the pritty Eyes do but see,
Had it been spit out of your Mouth,
    more like you it could not be.

Nay then, my kind Gossips all,
    says George, let us Merry make;

I'll Tap a Barrel of stout Ale,
  and send for a Groaning-Cake.

The Gossips they Laugh'd and Smil'd,
  and Mirth it went round all through;
She'd found a Father for her Child,
  Hye, Marry and thank him too.

"Corinna's Going A-Maying" by Robert Herrick

1648

Suggested age and gender: Broad age range; male

Get up, get up for shame, the blooming morn
Upon her wings presents the gold unshorn.
  See how Aurora throws her fair
  Fresh-quilted colors through the air:
  Get up, sweet slug-a-bed, and see
  The dew bespangling herb and tree.
Each flower has wept and bowed toward the east
Above an hour since: yet you not dressed;
  Nay; not so much as out of bed?
  When all the birds have matins said
  And sung their thankful hymns, 'tis sin,
  Nay, profanation, to keep in,
Whenas a thousand virgins on this day
Spring, sooner than the lark, to fetch in May.

Rise, and put on your foliage, and be seen
To come forth, like the spring-time, fresh and green,
  And sweet as Flora. Take no care
  For jewels for your gown or hair:
  Fear not; the leaves will strew
  Gems in abundance upon you:
Besides, the childhood of the day has kept,
Against you come, some orient pearls unwept;
  Come and receive them while the light
  Hangs on the dew-locks of the night:
  And Titan on the eastern hill
  Retires himself, or else stands still
Till you come forth. Wash, dress, be brief in praying:
Few beads are best when once we go a-Maying.

Come, my Corinna, come; and, coming, mark
How each field turns a street, each street a park
  Made green and trimmed with trees; see how
  Devotion gives each house a bough
  Or branch; each porch, each door ere this
  An ark, a tabernacle is,

Made up of white-thorn, neatly interwove;
As if here were those cooler shades of love.
  Can such delights be in the street
  And open fields and we not see't?
  Come, we'll abroad; and let's obey
  The proclamation made for May:
And sin no more, as we have done, by staying;
But, my Corinna, come, let's go a-Maying.

There's not a budding boy or girl this day
But is got up, and gone to bring in May.
  A deal of youth, ere this, is come
  Back, and with white-thorn laden home.
  Some have despatched their cakes and cream
  Before that we have left to dream:
And some have wept, and wooed, and plighted troth,
And chose their priest, ere we can cast off sloth:
  Many a green-gown has been given;
  Many a kiss, both odd and even:
  Many a glance too has been sent
  From out the eye, love's firmament;
Many a jest told of the keys betraying
This night, and locks picked, yet we're not a-Maying.

Come, let us go while we are in our prime;
And take the harmless folly of the time.
  We shall grow old apace, and die
  Before we know our liberty.
  Our life is short, and our days run
  As fast away as does the sun;
And, as a vapor or a drop of rain,
Once lost, can ne'er be found again,
  So when or you or I are made
  A fable, song, or fleeting shade,
  All love, all liking, all delight
  Lies drowned with us in endless night.
Then while time serves, and we are but decaying,
Come, my Corinna, come, let's go a-Maying.

"The Solitary Reaper" by William Wordsworth

1807

Suggested age and gender: Broad age range; male

Behold her, single in the field,
  Yon solitary Highland Lass!
Reaping and singing by herself;
  Stop here, or gently pass!
Alone she cuts and binds the grain,
And sings a melancholy strain;
O listen! for the vale profound
Is overflowing with the sound.

No nightingale did ever chaunt
  More welcome notes to weary bands
Of travellers in some shady haunt,
  Among Arabian sands:
A voice so thrilling ne'er was heard
In spring-time from the cuckoo-bird,
Breaking the silence of the seas
Among the farthest Hebrides.

Will no one tell me what she sings?—
  Perhaps the plaintive numbers flow
For old, unhappy, far-off things,
  And battles long ago:
Or is it some more humble lay,
Familiar matter of to-day?
Some natural sorrow, loss, or pain,
That has been, and may be again?

Whate'er the theme, the maiden sang
  As if her song could have no ending;
I saw her singing at her work,
  And o'er the sickle bending;—
I listened, motionless and still;
And, as I mounted up the hill,
The music in my heart I bore,
Long after it was heard no more.

"Ode to the West Wind" by Percy Bysshe Shelley

1819

Suggested age and gender: Broad age range; male

O Wild West Wind, thou breath of Autumn's being,
Thou from whose unseen presence the leaves dead
Are driven like ghosts from an enchanter fleeing,

Yellow, and black, and pale, and hectic red,
Pestilence-stricken multitudes! O thou
Who chariotest to their dark wintry bed

The wingèd seeds, where they lie cold and low,
Each like a corpse within its grave, until
Thine azure sister of the Spring shall blow

Her clarion o'er the dreaming earth, and fill
(Driving sweet buds like flocks to feed in air)
With living hues and odours plain and hill;

Wild Spirit, which art moving everywhere;
Destroyer and preserver; hear, O hear!

II

Thou on whose stream, 'mid the steep sky's commotion,
Loose clouds like earth's decaying leaves are shed,
Shook from the tangled boughs of heaven and ocean,

Angels of rain and lightning! there are spread
On the blue surface of thine airy surge,
Like the bright hair uplifted from the head

Of some fierce Maenad, even from the dim verge
Of the horizon to the zenith's height,
The locks of the approaching storm. Thou dirge

Of the dying year, to which this closing night
Will be the dome of a vast sepulchre,
Vaulted with all thy congregated might

Of vapours, from whose solid atmosphere
Black rain, and fire, and hail will burst: O hear!

Thou who didst waken from his summer dreams
The blue Mediterranean, where he lay,
Lull'd by the coil of his crystalline streams,

Beside a pumice isle in Baiae's bay,
And saw in sleep old palaces and towers
Quivering within the wave's intenser day,

All overgrown with azure moss, and flowers
So sweet, the sense faints picturing them! Thou
For whose path the Atlantic's level powers

Cleave themselves into chasms, while far below
The sea-blooms and the oozy woods which wear
The sapless foliage of the ocean, know

Thy voice, and suddenly grow grey with fear,
And tremble and despoil themselves: O hear!

IV

If I were a dead leaf thou mightest bear;
If I were a swift cloud to fly with thee;
A wave to pant beneath thy power, and share

The impulse of thy strength, only less free
Than thou, O uncontrollable! If even
I were as in my boyhood, and could be

The comrade of thy wanderings over heaven,
As then, when to outstrip thy skiey speed
Scarce seem'd a vision—I would ne'er have striven

As thus with thee in prayer in my sore need.
O! Lift me as a wave, a leaf, a cloud!
I fall upon the thorns of life! I bleed!

A heavy weight of hours has chain'd and bow'd
One too like thee—tameless, and swift, and proud.

V

Make me thy lyre, even as the forest is:
What if my leaves are falling like its own?
The tumult of thy mighty harmonies

Will take from both a deep autumnal tone,
Sweet though in sadness. Be thou, Spirit fierce,
My Spirit! Be thou me, impetuous one!

Drive my dead thoughts over the universe,
Like wither'd leaves, to quicken a new birth;
And, by the incantation of this verse,

Scatter, as from an unextinguish'd hearth
Ashes and sparks, my words among mankind!
Be through my lips to unawaken'd earth

The trumpet of a prophecy! O Wind,
If Winter comes, can Spring be far behind?

"Ulysses" by Alfred, Lord Tennyson

1842

Suggested age and gender: Broad age range; male

It little profits that an idle king,
By this still hearth, among these barren crags,
Matched with an agèd wife, I mete and dole
Unequal laws unto a savage race,
That hoard, and sleep, and feed, and know not me.

I cannot rest from travel: I will drink
Life to the Lees: All times I have enjoyed
Greatly, have suffered greatly, both with those
That loved me, and alone; on shore, and when
Through scudding drifts the rainy Hyades
Vext the dim sea: I am become a name;
For always roaming with a hungry heart
Much have I seen and known,—cities of men
And manners, climates, councils, governments,
Myself not least, but honored of them all;
And drunk delight of battle with my peers,
Far on the ringing plains of windy Troy.
I am a part of all that I have met;
Yet all experience is an arch wherethrough
Gleams that untraveled world, whose margin fades
For ever and for ever when I move.
How dull it is to pause, to make an end,
To rust unburnished, not to shine in use!
As though to breathe were life! Life piled on life
Were all too little, and of one to me
Little remains; but every hour is saved
From that eternal silence, something more,
A bringer of new things; and vile it were
For some three suns to store and hoard myself,
And this grey spirit yearning in desire
To follow knowledge like a sinking star,
Beyond the utmost bound of human thought.

This is my son, mine own Telemachus,
To whom I leave the scepter and the isle—

Well-loved of me, discerning to fulfil
This labor, by slow prudence to make mild
A rugged people, and through soft degrees
Subdue them to the useful and the good.
Most blameless is he, centered in the sphere
Of common duties, decent not to fail
In offices of tenderness, and pay
Meet adoration to my household gods,
When I am gone. He works his work, I mine.

There lies the port; the vessel puffs her sail:
There gloom the dark, broad seas. My mariners,
Souls that have toiled, and wrought, and thought with
    me—
That ever with a frolic welcome took
The thunder and the sunshine, and opposed
Free hearts, free foreheads—you and I are old;
Old age hath yet his honor and his toil.
Death closes all; but something ere the end,
Some work of noble note, may yet be done,
Not unbecoming men that strove with Gods.
The lights begin to twinkle from the rocks;
The long day wanes; the slow moon climbs; the deep
Moans round with many voices. Come, my friends,
'Tis not too late to seek a newer world.
Push off, and sitting well in order smite
The sounding furrows; for my purpose holds
To sail beyond the sunset, and the baths
Of all the western stars, until I die.
It may be that the gulfs will wash us down;
It may be we shall touch the Happy Isles,
And see the great Achilles, whom we knew.
Though much is taken, much abides; and though
We are not now that strength which in old days
Moved earth and heaven, that which we are, we are:
One equal temper of heroic hearts,
Made weak by time and fate, but strong in will
To strive, to seek, to find, and not to yield.

"The Song of the Shirt" by Thomas Hood

1843

Suggested age and gender: Broad age range; female

With fingers weary and worn,
   With eyelids heavy and red,
A woman sat, in unwomanly rags,
   Plying her needle and thread—
Stitch! stitch! stitch!
   In poverty, hunger, and dirt,
And still with a voice of dolorous pinch
   She sang the 'Song of the Shirt.'

'Work! work! work!
   While the cock is crowing aloof!
And work—work—work,
   Till the stars shine through the roof!
It's Oh! to be a slave
   Along with the barbarous Turk,
Where woman has never a soul to save,
   If this is Christian work.

'Work—work—work,
   Till the brain begins to swim;
Work—work—work,
   Till the eyes are heavy and dim!
Seam, and gusset, and band,
   Band, and gusset, and seam,
Till over the buttons I fall asleep,
   And sew them on in a dream!

'Oh, Men, with Sisters dear!
   Oh, Men, with Mothers and Wives!
It is not linen you're wearing out
   But human creatures' lives!
Stitch—stitch—stitch,
   In poverty, hunger, and dirt,
Sewing at once, with a double thread,
   A Shroud as well as a Shirt.

'But why do I talk of Death?
  That Phantom of grisly bone,
I hardly fear its terrible shape,
  It seems so like my own—
It seems so like my own,
  Because of the fasts I keep;
Oh, God, that bread should be so dear,
  And flesh and blood so cheap!

'Work—work—work!
  My labour never flags;
And what are its wages? A bed of straw,
  A crust of bread—and rags.
That shattered roof—this naked floor—
  A table—a broken chair—
And a wall so blank, my shadow I thank
  For sometimes falling there!

'Work—work—work!
  From weary chime to chime,
Work—work—work,
  As prisoners work for crime!
Band, and gusset, and seam,
  Seam, and gusset, and band,
Till the heart is sick, and the brain benumbed,
  As well as the weary hand.

'Work—work—work!
  In the dull December light,
And work—work—work,
  When the weather is warm and bright—
While underneath the eaves
  The brooding swallows cling
As if to show me their sunny backs
  And twit me with the spring.

'Oh! but to breathe the breath
  Of the cowslip and primrose sweet—
With the sky above my head,
  And the grass beneath my feet;
For only one short hour
  To feel as I used to feel,
Before I knew the woes of want
  And the walk that costs a meal.

'Oh! but for one short hour!
  A respite however brief!
No blessèd leisure for Love or Hope,
  But only time for Grief!
A little weeping would ease my heart,
  But in their briny bed
My tears must stop, for every drop
  Hinders needle and thread!'

With fingers weary and worn,
  With eyelids heavy and red,
A woman sat, in unwomanly rags,
  Plying her needle and thread—
Stitch! stitch! stitch!
  In poverty, hunger, and dirt,
And still with a voice of dolorous pitch,—
Would that its tone could reach the Rich!—
  She sang this 'Song of the Shirt'!

"The Raven" by Edgar Allan Poe

1845

Suggested age and gender: Broad age range; male

Once upon a midnight dreary, while I pondered, weak and
weary,
Over many a quaint and curious volume of forgotten
lore—
While I nodded, nearly napping, suddenly there came a
tapping,
As of some one gently rapping, rapping at my chamber
door.
" 'Tis some visitor," I muttered, "tapping at my chamber
door—
      Only this and nothing more."

Ah, distinctly I remember it was in the bleak December,
And each separate dying ember wrought its ghost upon
the floor.
Eagerly I wished the morrow;—vainly I had sought to
borrow
From my books surcease of sorrow—sorrow for the lost
Lenore—
For the rare and radiant maiden whom the angels name
Lenore—
      Nameless here for evermore.

And the silken sad uncertain rustling of each purple
curtain
Thrilled me—filled me with fantastic terrors never felt
before;
So that now, to still the beating of my heart, I stood
repeating:
" 'Tis some visitor entreating entrance at my chamber
door—
Some late visitor entreating entrance at my chamber door;
      This it is and nothing more."

Presently my soul grew stronger; hesitating then no longer,
"Sir," said I, "or Madam, truly your forgiveness I implore;
But the fact is I was napping, and so gently you came
    rapping,
And so faintly you came tapping, tapping at my chamber
    door,
That I scarce was sure I heard you"—here I opened wide
    the door;—
            Darkness there and nothing more.

Deep into that darkness peering, long I stood there
    wondering, fearing,
Doubting, dreaming dreams no mortals ever dared to
    dream before;
But the silence was unbroken, and the stillness gave no
    token,
And the only word there spoken was the whispered word,
    "Lenore!"
This I whispered, and an echo murmured back the word,
    "Lenore!"—
            Merely this and nothing more.

Back into the chamber turning, all my soul within me
    burning,
Soon again I heard a tapping something louder than be-
    fore.
"Surely," said I, "surely that is something at my window
    lattice;
Let me see, then, what thereat is, and this mystery
    explore—
Let my heart be still a moment, and this mystery
    explore;—
            'Tis the wind and nothing more.

Open here I flung the shutter, when, with many a flirt and
    flutter,
In there stepped a stately Raven of the saintly days of
    yore.
Not the least obeisance made he; not a minute stopped or
    stayed he,
But, with mien of lord or lady, perched above my
    chamber door—
Perched upon a bust of Pallas just above my chamber
    door—
            Perched, and sat, and nothing more.

Then this ebony bird beguiling my sad fancy into smiling,
By the grave and stern decorum of the countenance it
    wore,
"Though thy crest be shorn and shaven, thou," I said, "art
    sure no craven,
Ghastly grim and ancient Raven wandering from the
    Nightly shore—
Tell me what thy lordly name is on the Night's Plutonian
    shore!"
                  Quoth the Raven, "Nevermore."

Much I marvelled this ungainly fowl to hear discourse so
    plainly,
Though its answer little meaning—little relevancy bore;
For we cannot help agreeing that no living human being
Ever yet was blessed with seeing bird above his chamber
    door—
Bird or beast upon the sculptured bust above his chamber
    door,
              With such name as "Nevermore."

But the Raven, sitting lonely on that placid bust, spoke
    only
That one word, as if his soul in that one word he did
    outpour.
Nothing farther then he uttered; not a feather then he
    fluttered—
Till I scarcely more than muttered: "Other friends have
    flown before—
On the morrow *he* will leave me as my Hopes have flown
    before."
              Then the bird said, "Nevermore."

Startled at the stillness broken by reply so aptly spoken,
"Doubtless," said I, "what it utters is its only stock and
    store,
Caught from some unhappy master whom unmerciful
    Disaster
Followed fast and followed faster till his songs one burden
    bore—
Till the dirges of his Hope that melancholy burden bore
              Of "Never—nevermore.'"

But the Raven still beguiling all my sad soul into smiling,
Straight I wheeled a cushioned seat in front of bird and
    bust and door;

Then, upon the velvet sinking, I betook myself to linking
Fancy unto fancy, thinking what this ominous bird of
    yore—
What this grim, ungainly, ghastly, gaunt, and ominous
    bird of yore
                Meant in croaking "Nevermore."

This I sat engaged in guessing, but no syllable expressing
To the fowl whose fiery eyes now burned into my bosom's
    core;
This and more I sat divining, with my head at ease
    reclining
On the cushion's velvet lining that the lamp-light gloated
    o'er,
But whose velvet violet lining with the lamp-light gloating
    o'er
                She shall press, ah, nevermore!

Then, methought, the air grew denser, perfumed from an
    unseen censer
Swung by Seraphim whose foot-falls tinkled on the tufted
    floor.
"Wretch," I cried, "thy God hath lent thee—by these
    angels he hath sent thee
Respite—respite and nepenthe from thy memories of
    Lenore!
Quaff, oh quaff this kind nepenthe and forget this lost
    Lenore!"
                Quoth the Raven, "Nevermore."

"Phophet!" said I, "thing of evil!—prophet still, if bird or
    devil!—
Whether Tempter sent, or whether tempest tossed thee
    here ashore,
Desolate, yet all undaunted, on this desert land
    enchanted—
On this home by Horror haunted,—tell me truly, I
    implore—
Is there—*is* there balm in Gilead?—tell me—tell me, I
    implore!"
                Quoth the Raven, "Nevermore."

"Prophet!" said I, "thing of evil!—prophet still, if bird or
    devil!
By that heaven that bends above us—by that God we both
    adore—

Tell this soul with sorrow laden if, within the distant
  Aidenn,
It shall clasp a sainted maiden whom the angels name
  Lenore—
Clasp a rare and radiant maiden whom the angels name
  Lenore."
            Quoth the Raven, "Nevermore."

"Be that word our sign of parting, bird or friend!" I
  shrieked, upstarting—
"Get thee back into the tempest and the Night's Plutonian
  shore!
Leave no black plume as a token of that lie thy soul hath
  spoken!
Leave my loneliness unbroken!—quit the bust above my
  door!
Take thy beak from out my heart, and take thy form
  from off my door!"
            Quoth the Raven, "Nevermore."

And the Raven, never flitting, still is sitting, still is sitting
On the pallid bust of Pallas just above my chamber door;
And his eyes have all the seeming of a demon's that is
  dreaming,
And the lamp-light o'er him streaming throws his shadow
  on the floor;
And my soul from out that shadow that lies floating on
  the floor
            Shall be lifted—nevermore!

Sonnets from the Portuguese by Elizabeth Barrett Browning
"I Lift My Heavy Heart Up Solemnly"
1846
Suggested age and gender: Broad age range; female

I lift my heavy heart up solemnly,
As once Electra her sepulchral urn,
And, looking in thine eyes, I overturn
The ashes at thy feet. Behold and see
What a great heap of grief lay hid in me,
And how the red wild sparkles dimly burn
Through the ashen greyness. If thy foot in scorn
Could tread them out to darkness utterly,
It might be well perhaps. But if instead
Thou wait beside me for the winds to blow
The grey dust up. . . .those laurels on thine head,
O my beloved, will not shield thee so,
That none of all the fires shall scorch and shred
The hair beneath. Stand further off then! go.

Sonnets from the Portuguese by **Elizabeth Barrett Browning**

"Belovèd, My Belovèd"

1846

Suggested age and gender: Broad age range; female

Belovèd, my Belovèd, when I think
That thou wast in the world a year ago,
What time I sat alone here in the snow
And saw no footprint, heard the silence sink
No moment at thy voice, but, link by link,
Went counting all my chains as if that so
They never could fall off at any blow
Struck by thy possible hand—why, thus I drink
Of life's great cup of wonder! Wonderful,
Never to feel thee thrill the day or night
With personal act or speech—nor ever cull
Some prescience of thee with the blossoms white
Thou sawest growing! Atheists are as dull,
Who cannot guess God's presence out of sight.

"I Felt a Funeral in My Brain" by Emily Dickinson

1861

Suggested age and gender: Broad age range; female

I felt a Funeral, in my Brain,
And Mourners to and fro
Kept treading—treading—till it seemed
That Sense was breaking through—

And when they all were seated,
A Service, like a Drum—
Kept beating—beating—till I thought
My Mind was going numb—

And then I heard them lift a Box
And creak across my Soul
With those same Boots of Lead, again,
Then Space—began to toll,

As all the Heavens were a Bell,
And Being, but an Ear,
And I, and Silence, some strange Race
Wrecked, solitary, here—

And then a Plank in Reason, broke,
And I dropped down, and down—
And hit a World, at every plunge,
And Finished knowing—then—

"I Like to See It Lap the Miles" by Emily Dickinson

1862

Suggested age and gender: Broad age range; female

I like to see it lap the miles,
And lick the valleys up,
And stop to feed itself at tanks;
And then, prodigious, step

Around a pile of mountains,
And, supercilious, peer
In shanties by the sides of roads;
And then a quarry pare

To fit its ribs,
And crawl between,
Complaining all the while
In horrid, hooting stanza;
Then chase itself down hill

And neigh like Boanerges;
Then, punctual as a star,
Stop—docile and omnipotent—
At its own stable door.

*The Bab Ballads** by W. S. Gilbert

1869

"The Pantomime 'Super' to His Mask"

Suggested age and gender: Broad age range; male

Vast, empty shell!
Impertinent, preposterous abortion:
 With vacant stare,
 And ragged hair,
And every feature out of all proportion!
Embodiment of echoing inanity,
Excellent type of simpering insanity,
Unwieldy, clumsy nightmare of humanity,
 I ring thy knell!

Tonight thou diest,
Beast that destroy'st my heaven-born identity!
 Twelve weeks of nights
 Before the lights,
Swamped in thine own preposterous nonentity,
I've been ill-treated, cursed, and thrashed diurnally,
Credited for the smile you wear externally—
I feel disposed to smash thy face, infernally,
 As there thou liest!

I've been thy brain:
I've been the brain that lit thy dull concavity!
 The human race
 Invest *my* face
With thine expression of unchecked depravity:
Invested with a ghastly reciprocity,
I've been responsible for thy monstrosity,
I, for thy wanton, blundering ferocity—
 But not again!

The Bab Ballads were later to be part of the vast repertoire of operettas by Gilbert and
Sullivan.

'Tis time to toll
Thy knell, and that of follies pantomimical:
A twelve weeks' run,
And thou hast done
All thou canst do to make thyself inimical.
Adieu, embodiment of all inanity!
Excellent type of simpering insanity!
Unwieldy, clumsy nightmare of humanity!
Freed is thy soul!

(*The Mask respondeth.*)

Oh! master mine,
Look thou within thee, ere again ill-using me.
Art thou aware
Of nothing there
Which might abuse thee, as thou art abusing me?
A brain that mourns *thine* unredeemed rascality?
A soul that weeps at *thy* threadbare morality?
Both grieving that *their* individuality
Is merged in thine?

The Bab Ballads by W. S. Gilbert
1869
"They'll None of 'Em Be Missed"
Suggested age and gender: Broad age range; male or female

As some day it may happen that a victim must be found,
   I've got a little list—I've got a little list
Of social offenders who might well be underground,
   And who never would be missed—who never would be
   missed!
There's the pestilential nuisances who write for
   autographs—
All people who have flabby hands and irritating laughs—
All children who are up in dates, and floor you with 'em
   flat—
All persons who in shaking hands, shake hands with you
   like *that*—
And all third persons who on spoiling *tête-à-têtes* insist—
   They'd none of 'em be missed—they'd none of 'em
   be missed!

There's the banjo serenader, and the others of his race,
   And the piano organist—I've got him on the list!
And the people who eat peppermint and puff it in your
   face,
They never would be missed—they never would be
   missed!

Then the idiot who praises, with enthusiastic tone,
All centuries but this, and every country but his own;
And the lady from the provinces, who dresses like a guy,
And who "doesn't think she waltzes, but would rather like
   to try";
And that *fin-de-siècle* anomaly, the scorching motorist—
   I don't think he'd be missed—I'm *sure* he'd not be
   missed!

And that *Nisi Prius* nuisance, who just now is rather rife,
   The Judicial humorist—I've got *him* on the list!
All funny fellows, comic men, and clowns of private life—

They'd none of 'em be missed—they'd none of 'em be missed!

And apologetic statesmen of the compromising kind,

Such as—What-d'ye-call-him—Thing'em-Bob, and like-
wise—Never-mind,

And 'St—'st—'st—and What's-his-name, and also—You-
know-who—

(The task of filling up the blanks I'd rather leave to *you*!)

But it really doesn't matter whom you put upon the list,
For they'd none of 'em be missed—they'd none of 'em be
missed!

"Thirty Bob a Week" by John Davidson
1895
Suggested age and gender: Middle-aged; male

I couldn't touch a stop and turn a screw,
    And set the blooming world a-work for me,
Like such as cut their teeth—I hope, like you—
    On the handle of a skeleton gold key;
I cut mine on a leek, which I eat it every week:
    I'm a clerk at thirty bob as you can see.

But I don't allow it's luck and all a toss;
    There's no such thing as being starred and crossed;
It's just the power of some to be a boss,
    And the bally power of others to be bossed:
I face the music, sir; you bet I ain't a cur;
    Strike me lucky if I don't believe I'm lost!

For like a mole I journey in the dark,
    A-travelling along the underground
From my Pillar'd Halls and broad Suburban Park,
    To come the daily dull official round;
And home again at night with my pipe all alight,
    A-scheming how to count ten bob a pound.

And it's often very cold and very wet,
    And my missis stitches towels for a hunks;
And the Pillar'd Halls is half of it to let—
    Three rooms about the size of travelling trunks.
And we cough, my wife and I, to dislocate a sigh,
    When the noisy little kids are in their bunks.

But you never hear her do a growl or whine,
    For she's made of flint and roses, very odd;
And I've got to cut my meaning rather fine,
    Or I'd blubber, for I'm made of greens and sod:
So p'r'aps we are in Hell for all that I can tell,
    And lost and damn'd and served up hot to God.

I ain't blaspheming, Mr. Silver-tongue;
    I'm saying things a bit beyond your art:

Of all the rummy starts you ever sprung,
    Thirty bob a week's the rummiest start!
With your science and your books and your the'ries about
    spooks,
    Did you ever hear of looking in your heart?

I didn't mean your pocket, Mr., no:
    I mean that having children and a wife,
With thirty bob on which to come and go,
    Isn't dancing to the tabor and the fife:
When it doesn't make you drink, by Heaven! it makes you
    think,
    And notice curious items about life.

I step into my heart and there I meet
    A god-almighty devil singing small,
Who would like to shout and whistle in the street,
    And squelch the passers flat against the wall;
If the whole world was a cake he had the power to take,
    He would take it, ask for more, and eat it all.

And I meet a sort of simpleton beside,
    The kind that life is always giving beans;
With thirty bob a week to keep a bride
    He fell in love and married in his teens:
At thirty bob he stuck; but he knows it isn't luck:
    He knows the seas are deeper than tureens.

And the god-almighty devil and the fool
    That meet me in the High Street on the strike,
When I walk about my heart a-gathering wool,
    Are my good and evil angels if you like.
And both of them together in every kind of weather
    Ride me like a double-seated bike.

That's rough a bit and needs its meaning curled.
    But I have a high old hot un in my mind—
A most engrugious notion of the world,
    That leaves your lightning 'rithmetic behind
I give it at a glance when I say 'There ain't no chance,
    Nor nothing of the lucky-lottery kind.'

And it's this way that I make it out to be:
    No fathers, mothers, countries, climates—none;
Nor Adam was responsible for me,
    Nor society, nor systems, nary one:

A little sleeping seed, I woke—I did, indeed—
    A million years before the blooming sun.

I woke because I thought the time had come;
    Beyond my will there was no other cause;
And everywhere I found myself at home,
    Because I chose to be the thing I was;
And in whatever shape of mollusc or of ape
    I always went according to the laws.

I was the love that chose my mother out;
    I joined two lives and from the union burst;
My weakness and my strength without a doubt
    Are mine alone for ever from the first:
It's just the very same with a difference in the name
    As 'Thy will be done.' You say it if you durst!

They say it daily up and down the land
    As easy as you take a drink, it's true;
But the difficultest go to understand,
    And the difficultest job a man can do,
Is to come it brave and meek with thirty bob a week,
    And feel that that's the proper thing for you.

It's a naked child against a hungry wolf;
    It's playing bowls upon a splitting wreck;
It's walking on a string across a gulf
    With millstones fore-and-aft about your neck;
But the thing is daily done by many a one;
    And we fall, face forward, fighting, on the deck.

Through the Looking-Glass and What Alice Found There
by Lewis Carroll
1896
Chapter VIII: "The White Knight's Song"
Suggested age and gender: Broad age range; male

I'll tell thee everything I can;
   There's little to relate.
I saw an aged aged man,
   A-sitting on a gate.
"Who are you, aged man?" I said.
   "And how is it you live?"
And his answer trickled through my head
   Like water through a sieve.

He said "I look for butterflies
   That sleep among the wheat:
I make them into mutton-pies,
   And sell them in the street.
I sell them unto men," he said,
   "Who sail on stormy seas;
And that's the way I get my bread—
   A trifle, if you please."

But I was thinking of a plan
   To dye one's whiskers green,
And always use so large a fan
   That they could not be seen.
So, having no reply to give
   To what the old man said,
I cried "Come, tell me how you live!"
   And thumped him on the head.

His accents mild took up the tale:
   He said "I go my ways,
And when I find a mountain-rill,
   I set it in a blaze;
And thence they make a stuff they call
   Rowland's Macassar-Oil—

Yet twopence-halfpenny is all
    They give me for my toil."

But I was thinking of a way
    To feed oneself on batter,
And so go on from day to day
    Getting a little fatter.
I shook him well from side to side,
    Until his face was blue:
"Come, tell me how you live," I cried,
    "And what it is you do!"

He said "I hunt for haddocks' eyes
    Among the heather bright,
And work them into waistcoat-buttons
    In the silent night.
And these I do not sell for gold
    Or coin of silvery shine,
But for a copper halfpenny,
    And that will purchase nine.

"I sometimes dig for buttered rolls,
    Or set limed twigs for crabs;
I sometimes search the grassy knolls
    For wheels of Hansom-cabs.
And that's the way" (he gave a wink)
    "By which I get my wealth—
And very gladly will I drink
    Your Honour's noble health."

And now, if e'er by chance I put
    My fingers into glue,
Or madly squeeze a right-hand foot
    Into a left-hand shoe,
Or if I drop upon my toe
    A very heavy weight,
I weep, for it reminds me so
Of that old man I used to know—
Whose look was mild, whose speech was slow,
Whose hair was whiter than the snow,
Whose face was very like a crow,
With eyes, like cinders, all aglow,
Who seemed distracted with his woe,
Who rocked his body to and fro,

And muttered mumblingly and low,
As if his mouth were full of dough,
Who snorted like a buffalo—
That summer evening long ago
   A-sitting on a gate.

INDEX

Jaine,

Happy Hiking
& Yoga-ing!

Nicole Tsong

YOGA *For* HIKERS

YOGA *For* HIKERS

HOW TO STRETCH, STRENGTHEN, *and* HIKE FARTHER

NICOLE TSONG
PHOTOGRAPHY BY ERIKA SCHULTZ

MOUNTAINEERS
BOOKS

TO MY PARENTS, PETER AND JOANNA, WHO HAVE ALWAYS
LOVED AND SUPPORTED ME TO BE MY BEST SELF

**MOUNTAINEERS
BOOKS**

Mountaineers Books is the publishing division of
The Mountaineers, an organization founded in 1906
and dedicated to the exploration, preservation, and
enjoyment of outdoor and wilderness areas.

1001 SW Klickitat Way, Suite 201 • Seattle, WA 98134
800.553.4453 • www.mountaineersbooks.org

Copyright © 2016 by Nicole Tsong
Photos copyright © 2016 by Erika Schultz

Printed in China
Distributed in the United Kingdom by Cordee, www.cordee.co.uk
First edition, 2016

Copy editor: Nancy Waddell Cortelyou, Saffron Writes
Design and layout: Heidi Smets Graphic Design
Additional layout: Jennifer Shontz, www.redshoedesign.com
Illustrator: Anna-Lisa Notter, www.annalisanotter.com

Cover photograph: *Mountain Pose*
Frontispiece: *Tree pose*

Library of Congress Cataloging-in-Publication Data
Names: Tsong, Nicole, author.
Title: Yoga for hikers: how to stretch, strengthen, and hike farther /
   Nicole Tsong ; photography by Erika Schultz.
Description: Seattle, WA : Mountaineers Books, 2016. | Includes
   bibliographical references and index.
Identifiers: LCCN 2015033250| ISBN 9781594859939 (paperback) |
   ISBN 9781594859946 (ebook)
Subjects: LCSH: Hatha yoga. | Hikers. | Endurance sports—
   Training. | Exercise.
Classification: LCC RC1220.Y64 T76 2016 | DDC 613.7/046—dc23
   LC record available at http://lccn.loc.gov/2015033250

Mountaineers Books titles may be purchased for corporate,
educational, or other promotional sales, and our authors are
available for a wide range of events. For information on special
discounts or booking an author, contact our customer service
at 800-553-4453 or mbooks@mountaineersbooks.org.

ISBN (paperback): 978-1-59485-993-9
ISBN (ebook): 978-1-59485-994-6

CONTENTS

ACKNOWLEDGMENTS

THIS BOOK IS THE culmination of a big soul goal, and there are many people and communities whose generosity of spirit and big love helped me arrive here.

To my parents, Joanna and Peter, for their unconditional love and support. To my sister, Ingrid, for her love and patient listening through all iterations of this project.

To my teacher Baron Baptiste, who inspired me to teach yoga and whose methodology remains the source for my teaching. To my mentor Susanne Conrad, for teaching me to see and embrace who I am and why I am on the planet.

To Michel Spruance, for giving me my first yoga job, for reading early drafts, and for listening and being an inspiring, dear friend. To Tina Templeman, for being a tremendous support on anatomy and a big yes for all elements of this project.

To my yoga models—Tina, Michel, Brian Charlton, Austin Carrillo, Genevieve Alvarez, Paul Javid, Christine Bachman, and Taylor Moravec. You all are remarkably skillful at balancing on rocks and logs. To Gaylinyet Roberts, for bringing out our inner beauty.

To my friends and Be Luminous Yoga, Shakti, igolu, and Baptiste communities—you are the best.

To the staff at Mountaineers Books, especially editor in chief Kate Rogers, for seeing the possibility in this collaboration. To all my teachers and the wise people who contributed their knowledge and expertise to me and this book. To Kathy Triesch, Kathy Andrisevic, and the staff at *Pacific NW* magazine at the *Seattle Times*—thank you for the best gig ever with "Fit for Life."

To Karen B., for forging the way with your first book and being an incredible resource and friend.

To my photographer, Erika Schultz, for her extraordinary collaboration and incredible talent.

Finally, to my above-the-line guy and favorite hiking partner, Chris, for being hilarious and direct, and always holding me to my best self. I love you.

INTRODUCTION

WHEN I STARTED PRACTICING yoga, I saw little connection between my yoga mat and the woods. I had recently moved from Anchorage, Alaska, to Seattle. It was summer, and I chose yoga to cope with the new obstacles of traffic and living at a latitude where the sun faded away at 9 p.m. rather than at midnight.

Until that time, I was active, but I lacked endurance. I spent nearly four years in Alaska's outdoor playgrounds. I built strength during the summer hiking and in the winter skiing several times a week, but the first ski or hike of each season was always agony. I knew using the elliptical machine during the off-seasons (either waiting for snow to melt or dump copiously on ski trails) was not enough, but I didn't have a solution beyond half-hearted attempts with a personal trainer.

In Seattle I became irritable without easy access and much-needed time outdoors to decompress from traffic and work. I needed something to sustain me. I dabbled in yoga in Alaska, but only practiced once a week—at most. After I moved, I decided to take yoga more seriously.

I dove headfirst into a heated power flow practice; I had never sweated so much in my life. I loved feeling my legs burn while holding poses, even as I mentally begged the teacher to let us release out of the pose. I adored the little snooze I snuck in during the final rest at the end of each class. Each time, I felt rinsed out, and I had let go of stress from work. I was exhausted in the best way.

Back then, I would give myself a day or two to recover, and return to my mat. One teacher said if your heart rate was up, it was proof you were building cardiovascular strength. She looked buff, and she only did yoga. I wanted to believe her claim. But as much as I loved yoga, I was skeptical.

That winter, on my first trip to the cross-country ski trails outside Seattle, instead of pausing halfway up every hill, I made it all the way to the top. On every single hill. I was panting each time, sure, but I had done it. I was astonished. Until that point, I only knew a world where I had to stop during the first climb of the season, gasping for air to fuel my burning legs. In the past it had usually taken me at least a month to skate ski up to about 4 miles in one go without pause—and here I was practically bolting up the hills the first day.

But I still didn't give yoga credit. Other people encouraged me to run or add more cardio. I was obsessed with yoga. But off my mat, I fretted about my conditioning.

During that spring, waiting for the snow to melt, I worried hiking was going to be painful. But on the first hike of the season, my legs felt strong. My breathing was heavy, but steady, even during the steepest elevation gain. More than once, I announced to my friends how good I felt. I wondered aloud if people (me) needed to give yoga more credit for building strength and endurance. My answer is yes.

Since then, through regular yoga practice, I've become even stronger. I can bear my own body weight and more: I have core strength and a deeper body awareness. My endurance for long hikes and skis has increased—and I recover faster. The experience also made me excited to try new physical activities, from kickboxing and learning to row a single scull, to swing dancing.

More importantly, it showed me a different path to achieve an experience of freedom and peace that once required an elevation gain of at least 3000 feet. On a yoga mat in a warm room deep in the heart of a bustling city, I learned to push myself physically, to breathe in a new way, and to feel that same sense of grounding and serenity I feel when hiking up to the clouds.

A regular yoga practice—by which I mean two to three times a week—is a reliable way to enhance your physical strength in the woods, regardless of your condition. It provides additional stability in your ankles to prevent injury on the trail, increases core strength and overall durability for long physical days, and will stretch out tight hip flexors, hamstrings, and glutes after an epic hike.

Yoga also teaches you to listen to your body and understand when you can push and when you need to take your intensity down a notch. You may find you can focus on your breath and make it farther up a steep incline with greater ease.

Above all, a yoga practice—with its focus on the breath—creates the ease and connection to a meditative mindset that so many hikers feel on the trail. Yoga gives you access to an experience of rest, quiet, and solitude when you can't make it out to the wilderness.

The connection between my mat and the woods is obvious to me now. Hikers live to summit a coveted peak, to hear the crunch of undergrowth on a quiet trail, or to tax themselves physically via distance. A yoga practice can support all of those goals and surprise you with some additional benefits, including the deeper understanding of why you love being out in nature.

YOGA HAS EXPLODED IN popularity since I started practicing more than ten years ago. *Yoga Journal*, the leading national yoga magazine, and Yoga Alliance, a national trade association, recently released a study that showed more than thirty-six million Americans practice yoga. More than eighty million Americans—or thirty-four percent of the population—say they are likely to practice yoga in the next twelve months for reasons including flexibility, stress relief, and fitness. Yoga has emerged from being a trend in the early 2000s to a mainstream activity for active Americans.

Athletes of all types now tout yoga as part of their training. Snowboard Slopestyle 2014 Olympic gold medalist Jamie Anderson and basketball superstar LeBron James are among the high-profile athletes who speak about the benefits of a regular yoga practice. The Seattle Seahawks famously meditated on their path to the 2014 Super Bowl championship.

Throughout this book, athletes and hiking enthusiasts share what the practice of yoga has done for their physical health and how it has honed their mental focus. But you don't have to be a professional athlete to benefit. Many outdoor lovers are interested in or already practice yoga. Get ready to see how a regular yoga practice connects with your passion for hitting the trail.

HOW TO USE THIS BOOK

Yoga for Hikers is intended to be a general guide to the practice of yoga, providing a new perspective and deeper understanding of your body—and how you are affected when hiking. There are directions for nearly 70 poses with mix-and-match opportunities in 3 complete sequences (see chapter 4). As you work your way through this book, you will start to recognize some of the foundational poses. In chapter 3, you will learn about poses that can support the specific stresses your body experiences during a hike, organized by body part and presented as stand-alone poses. In chapter 4, you will discover the benefits of adding a yoga practice to your routine, from developing strength to recovering post-hike, with sequences for each. And in chapter 5, you can apply what you have learned on the trail itself. In chapters 4 and 5, the poses are presented in sequences (building strength, post-hike recovery, mid-hike grounding, and pinnacle practice) within a flow from one pose to the next. These sections also provide more detailed information about how to deepen or modify poses, as well as common challenges and where to focus your attention.

All of these practices are designed for daily use and also for recovery post-hike. In this book you will also learn ways of supporting yourself off the trail, including starting a meditation practice, bringing mindfulness to what you eat, managing injury, and approaching your health from a holistic perspective. You'll read through personal stories and hear about research, giving you a deeper understanding of the cultural challenges we all face in taking care of our bodies.

The practice of yoga in the Western world encompasses many styles and philosophical approaches. If you are looking to expand your yoga practice beyond what I share in this book, you will find tips on finding a local yoga class and style suited to you—as well as a yoga community—to continue to bring the benefits of yoga into not only your hiking life, but your whole life.

With your purchase of this book, you also get access to our easy-to-use, downloadable cheat sheets for each of the three sequences featured in chapter 4! • Go to our website: www.mountaineersbooks.org/YogaHike. • Download the PDF. • When you open the document on your computer, enter the code "Tw1st13!" when prompted. It's our way of thanking you for supporting Mountaineers Books and our mission of outdoor recreation and conservation.

CHAPTER 1
AN INTRODUCTION TO YOGA

YOU HAVE PRACTICED YOGA, even if you didn't know it. You experience yoga when silenced by a sunset—layers of gold, tangerine, and pink streaking across the sky. You feel it when you climb past the last false peak to the summit, and look up from your muddy boots to see what was unknowable on the way up—a view of crystal blue sky and soaring, tree-topped peaks, a cascade of water tumbling down massive boulders and an azure alpine lake below. You light up with yoga when held by someone you love deeply, be it a child, friend, or lover—so close and connected you do not need words.

The word *yoga* means "union," a yoking of body and mind; it is a state of being, a state of unity. Yoga is an ancient, internal practice most widely known for the physical practice of yoga poses, or asana (AH-sah-na). The goal of yoga is to achieve consciousness, or awakening, and the way to do so is in the present moment. How do you get there? Through your physical body, you discover yourself. In yourself, you learn all the answers you have ever needed.

It starts simply, with the connection to the sole of your foot on the floor, to your breath, to your spine. In those moments of awareness of your body, your mind arrives in the present. You may find after practicing, you notice how tight your hips are or you become aware of an ache in your lower back. The more you practice, the easier it will be to determine what feels good physically, and what doesn't. You'll learn to differentiate

YOGA EQUIPMENT

With a few basic tools, you can practice anywhere—at home or on the road. Props are essential to supporting your practice; experienced yogis rely on them.

» **Mat:** Yoga mats are widely available, ranging from affordable to higher end; the latter tend to offer more padding and grip and are likely to last for years. Mats vary in weight. Most higher-end manufacturers produce lighter mats for travel.
» **Yoga block:** A basic foam or cork block supports your alignment in poses. It also is helpful for seated postures. Note that a block can be used at three different heights.
» **Strap:** A six- or eight-foot strap is useful for multiple poses. For tight shoulders, you can use a strap to bind your hands. A strap can be used to support full relaxation or to intensify some poses.
» **Blanket:** A cozy covering is helpful for a meditation setup and for keeping you warm during savasana, or final rest.
» **Bolster:** A soft bolster is a nice alternative to a block during seated postures.
» **Comfortable, stretchy clothes:** Wear comfortable, stretchy clothes to keep from feeling restricted during your practice.

between pain and intensity. You'll understand if you tend to give up when you could instead push yourself—or discover that you're the type to push yourself into injury.

Through poses, your awareness of your body expands: You notice when you struggle to keep your gaze focused (*drishti*). You see when your mind cries out for you to get out of an intense pose like Frog, a deep hip opener. You find you can last far longer in Warrior 2 than you originally thought—and you realize you think a lot in this quiet standing power pose!

A YOGA PRACTICE IS a path of exploration, with as many soaring summits and curious valleys as any trail you may encounter. Be playful as you practice, just as you are when you hike. Laugh if you fall over in a balance pose, just like the day you fell off a log into a stream. Or slow down to appreciate your own strength, just as you pause at the sound of a squeaking marmot. See your body for what it is—a powerful vessel to carry you in life and the best teacher you'll ever know.

A BRIEF HISTORY OF YOGA

The spiritual and life-instructive elements of yoga can be found in ancient Indian teachings dating back 5000 years. Patañjali formalized these teachings into the *Yoga Sūtras* about 2000 years ago, creating the seminal text that remains the foundation for yoga. Author Chip Hartranft writes in *The Yoga-Sūtra of Patañjali*, the work "stands as a testament to heroic self-awareness, defining yoga for all time."

Modern yoga bears little resemblance to yoga during Patañjali's time, when postures were focused on seated ones, rather than the athletic poses practiced in gyms and yoga studios today.

Yet the study of the Eight Limbs as written in the *Yoga Sūtras* is the root for modern yoga practice, even as the physical practice and presentation has evolved with Western culture. The teachings of yoga, or union, are still alive because the ancient teachings apply to—and are perhaps needed even more urgently—in modern life.

BUT THERE ARE MANY elegant ways to approach other elements of the Eight Limbs, as shared by Hartranft. You practice some of them on the hiking trail. **Concentration**, for example, shows up when you focus on putting one foot in front of the other or listen to the sound of birds as you walk up the trail.

The first four limbs, which include **poses** and **breath work**, emphasize behavior, the physical body, and developing energetic awareness. The five **external disciplines**, or the **yamas**, include nonharming, truthfulness, nonstealing, right use of energy (including sexual), and being nonacquisitive. You can practice being truthful at any time, by being honest with yourself on a hike, knowing when you can take on a particularly tough trail, for example, or listening to your body,

CREATING A SPACE FOR YOGA AT HOME

....

Create a calm, peaceful environment for yourself at home.

» Use a quiet space that is empty of distrac-
  tions—no television.
» Shut the door, if you can.
» Let others know not to interrupt you for a
  set period of time.
» Turn off your cell phone.
» Commit to a set period of time to practice,
  no matter how short, and stick to it.
» If you prefer to practice with music, keep it
  in the background.

say a nagging knee injury, to know when you need to rein it in. Another limb encompasses the five **internal disciplines**, or the **niyamas**—purity, contentment, intense discipline, self-study, and devotion to pure awareness, or god. You may have experienced contentment when taking off your

hiking boots and sweaty socks at the end of a long day, and wiggling your toes, with a sigh of great satisfaction.

The latter four limbs address the mind and a higher state of consciousness. You may have also accessed the practice to **withdraw the senses**, focusing on one step at a time without attachment to distance, elevation, weather, or how you feel. During 100-mile races, ultra marathoner Buzz Burrell says yoga has helped him stay present and focused. "You really don't want to fall off the cliff or in the river," he says. "Yet you're going on for long periods of time. You have to be relaxed and aware at the same time for hours and hours. Yoga trains you to do that, no question."

There is a limb focused on a meditative experi-ence, or **absorption**, that you may have felt when you have fallen into a steady rhythm on the trail. You do not have to think to navigate a stream. Your body relaxes, your thoughts melt away, and your attention is immersed in the continuous move-ment forward. Then there is the limb **samadhi**, the practice of experiencing no distance between you and what is around you, whether it's people or nature. You are at one with everything around you, with no separation in your mind from your physical surroundings or other people. It's one reason so many of us head for the hills.

Yoga poses, or **asana**, and breath work, or **pranayama**, occupy their own limbs. As you focus on poses and breath work, observing your body in new ways, also notice how the practice relates back to all of the Eight Limbs. The practices are a road map for the way you approach any aspect of life—the next hike, an upcoming project at work, or even whether you express appreciation for the people you love. Through the exploration of your body and your mind, compassion, gentleness, or joy may arise. Observe the shifts, and see what else is possible.

"How can you move toward something that, like Divinity, is already by definition everywhere? A better image might be that if we tidy and clean our houses enough, we might one day notice that Divinity has been sitting in them all along."

—B. K. S. Iyengar, *Light on Life*

THE EIGHT LIMBS
ADAPTED FROM HARTRANFT'S *YOGA-SŪTRAS OF PATAÑJALI*

....

1. Yamas (five external disciplines, or ethical standards)
   » ahimsa (nonharming)
   » satya (truthfulness)
   » asteya (nonstealing)
   » bramacharya (right use of energy, including sexual)
   » aparigraha (being nonacquisitive)
2. Niyamas (five internal disciplines)
   » saucha (purity)
   » santosha (contentment)
   » tapas (intense discipline or zeal)
   » svadhyaya (self-study)
   » isvara pranidhana (devotion or surrender to pure awareness, or god)
3. Asana (sitting postures)
4. Pranayama (breath regulation)
5. Pratyahara (withdrawal of the senses)
6. Dharana (concentration)
7. Dhyana (meditation or absorption)
8. Samadhi (bliss, self-realization)

YOGA FUNDAMENTALS

Yoga starts with awareness. The first layer is the physical one. Through awareness of how your body does basic functions like breathe or balance upright during yoga poses, you begin to practice the Eight Limbs.

BREATH

Sometimes, on the steepest stretch of a trail, your breath announces itself. You realize sweat is dripping down your back, your legs are burning, and you are panting heavily. You pause, take a deep breath in and out, and swallow some water. Onward.

Breath is an automatic body function: respiration happens all day long, whether you are awake or asleep. Breath also is a natural filtration system. When you inhale, you draw in fresh air and oxygen; when you exhale, you release carbon dioxide and other toxins.

You don't *need* to pay attention to your breath. But what happens when you do? Even right now, you may have started to notice your breath. When you do intentional breath work, you connect your conscious mind to a primitive function. In doing so, you activate your parasympathetic nervous system, slowing your heart rate, among other internal functions.

Try it for a moment. Take a deep full breath in, pause, then exhale all the air out. Do it three times. You may notice stress or anxiety dissipating. Your heart rate slows; your body relaxes. Breathing clears your mind.

Breath (pranayama) is a fundamental element in yoga. The main breath practice is an ancient one known as *ujjayi* (oo-JAI), or victorious breath. As well-known anatomy expert Leslie Kaminoff writes in *Yoga Anatomy*, "If you take care of the exhalation, the inhalation takes care of itself."

ELEMENTS OF UJJAYI

Enter any room where people are practicing yoga and you will hear ujjayi breath. It's a low, lovely background sound to a practice. The technique requires you to breathe through your nose while constricting your throat. It creates a sound akin to the lapping of ocean waves at the beach. The sound keeps you focused on breathing—if it goes away, you've let go of your breath. Ujjayi also physically directs your breath into the ribs in your back, stretching the intercostal muscles that connect your ribs. Engaging your core lock—addressed later in this chapter—also supports your ujjayi breath.

Breathing is an energetic practice. You can direct it more by breathing in an energy or intention that supports you, such as joy or calm, and exhaling what you don't need, like stress or anxiety.

Ujjayi contracts the muscles in your throat and helps you control the speed and depth of your breath—and generates heat. Controlling your breath helps you breathe deeper and more fully. When you first learn ujjayi, you may find either your exhalation or your inhalation is longer than the other. During the practice below, focus on evening out your inhales and exhales.

Breath Practice

» Find a comfortable seated position, either in a chair or on the floor atop a cushion.
» Sit up straight, and pull your belly button in toward your spine.
» Lift your shoulders up to your ears, then relax them down.

BUZZ BURRELL
Ultramarathon runner | Boulder, Colorado

Q: Why did you start practicing yoga?
A: I was young, and yoga was cool.

Q: Why do you still do yoga?
A: I stuck with it because I am a very physical person, and I am a mind-body person. Yoga has that mind-body aspect. For me, doing yoga and hiking and running go hand in hand.

Q: What's been hard for you about the practice?
A: What I've always been challenged by in yoga is lack of movement, or minimal movement. That was the real learning experience and the growing edge for me because movement is a way of not being with ourselves. Running or hiking, you're moving.

Q: How has yoga helped you with races or other outdoor pursuits?
A: There's the internal one, which I call poise—being comfortable, balanced, and present with what you're doing right now. If you're running a mile, it's not like that at all. You're looking at that finish line. Yoga asana is intended to help you be in that moment. I think that's a terrific practice.

- » Place your hands around your ribs (fingers in front), circling the front and back of your body.
- » Take a deep breath in through your nose until you feel your ribs expand, open your mouth and exhale with an extended "haaaaa" sound. Keep your belly engaged as you exhale.
- » Take another deep breath in through your nose. This time, keeping your mouth closed for the exhale, repeat the "haaaaa" sound (it will come from your throat) and keep your core engaged. This is ujjayi breath.
- » Repeat. Don't force your breath; let the sound be a whisper, while still breathing deeply into your lungs.
- » If you need to, gently smooth out your breath until you are breathing evenly in and out. Count to five for each round of inhale and exhale. Do this for one minute.
- » Sit quietly, and observe any shifts in what you feel in your body or your state of mind.

YOUR UJJAYI BREATH IN PRACTICE

For new practitioners, breathing through your nose consistently may be challenging. When you exert yourself and find it difficult to stay upright in a pose—let alone breathe—you may revert to old breathing patterns and pant through your mouth. Close your mouth! And try again. Or, if you notice you are unable to recover your ujjayi breath, relax into Child's Pose: close your mouth and breathe through your nose until you recover enough to come back to your practice.

"Pranayama is thus the science of breath. It is the hub round which the wheel of life revolves."

—B. K. S. Iyengar, *Light on Yoga*

FOUNDATION

Your feet carry you many thousands of steps a day—even more so on a hike. Your concern for your feet may only go as far as avoiding blisters from a new pair of boots. But there is so much more to be discovered. Focusing on your feet in your yoga practice will not only strengthen your body, it also opens a new appreciation for the connection points between you and the earth.

A yoga practice builds from the ground up. Since many poses start from standing, that means your feet. Yogis practice barefoot to keep the connection of feet to the floor. Notice how sensitive your feet are to sensation by paying attention to the texture of your mat or the floor under the soles of your feet. By practicing barefoot and challenging your balance through various placements of your feet in poses, you will strengthen the muscles deep in your feet and gain more balance and stability.

Wiggle your toes on the floor or inside your shoes. Notice how it brings your attention to your feet. When you do the same with your feet in a yoga practice, standing tall in Mountain Pose, your entire posture changes. You activate new muscles in your legs, and become strong and connected in your lower body. Keep applying the same intention and focus to every part of your body, and you'll soon build up a strong and centered Mountain Pose, the foundational pose of all yoga poses.

In a yoga practice, you spend a significant amount of time on your hands. Your hands are sensitive, with a concentrated number of nerve endings. Connecting your hands to the ground creates grounding and ensures good alignment in poses. In Downward-Facing Dog, for example, when you flatten your palms and connect the knuckles at the base of your pointer and middle fingers to the floor, your arms straighten and take the stress of the pose out of your elbow joints. It's a small move with a big effect.

Bring one of your hands in front of you. Stretch out your fingers. Notice the space between your fingers. Look at your palm. Look at the back of your hand. Put this book down for a moment and bring your palms together. Press your knuckles at the base of your fingers together, and tune in to the sensitivity of your fingertips. Observe the warmth of your skin. Are your palms rough or smooth? Your body senses all of these things without needing your thoughts.

Your hands and feet need time to develop strength. Culturally, most people wear shoes, and spend little time putting weight on their hands. Your yoga practice strengthens your hands, wrists, ankles, and feet, and from there, creates a strong foundation for your poses and your hikes. Pay attention to your hands and feet throughout the practice, connect them to the ground, and restore their natural energy and strength.

» Set a timer for one minute, and walk barefoot. Walk mindfully, noticing every part of your foot that comes into contact with the floor. Pay attention to which part of your foot strikes the floor first. Does the entire sole of your foot touch the floor with each step? Observe your toes and how they keep you from falling forward. Notice how your feet hold you up, how sensitive they are to every step. Feel the texture of the floor under your feet. Do your feet tend to rotate in or out? Does your stride change when you pay close attention?

» After one minute, stop and stand with your feet hip-width apart and flat on the floor. Bend from your hips, knees soft, and bring your hands to your feet.

» Press your fingertips on top of the knuckle at the base of your big toe. Do the same for your little toe knuckle.

» Lift the arch of your foot up toward your shins without overpronating onto the outer edge of your foot. Press down into the solidness of your heels.

» Lift your toes up and stretch them out as wide as possible; notice what it feels like to stretch your toes and toe knuckles.

» Keeping space between your toes, settle them back down on the floor. Stand for a moment. Note the texture of the floor, and how the soles of your feet feel.

» Set a timer again. Walk again for one minute with active feet. Observe shifts in your body as you walk.

CORE

Your core muscles are your silent buddies on a hike. They hold your upper body upright against gravity as you head up the trail, and connect down to your legs and hips, which tend to chatter loudly about how much work they are doing on long treks. Your torso (trunk) holds its own for hours at a time, so building endurance will help with stability, mobility, and injury avoidance on the trail.

Luckily, a yoga practice addresses your core strength basically throughout the entire practice. In yoga, *uddhiyana bandha*, or "upward-lifting lock," is used in all poses in the practice. Using your

CORE AND ROOT LOCK

To engage your Core Lock, pull your belly button in like you are buttoning a tight pair of pants. Now, lift your belly upward toward your back ribs until your chest lifts. Keep breathing and shift your focus to your front ribs. If the muscles where your front ribs meet are not engaged, your front ribs will pop out. Imagine a little kid sticking their belly forward—cute, but not what you want. When you flare your ribs, you also drop into your middle and lower back.

Wrap your hands around your front rib cage. Pull your fingertips toward each other until the front tips of your ribs squeeze toward each other. Keep your core engaged, and lift your chest up toward the ceiling again. Notice your posture and energy when your belly muscles are fully engaged.

Another less visible action when engaging your core is a lock known as *mula bandha*, your root lock. It is your pelvic floor, and it supports the lift of your core. Essentially, you lift your anus in toward your body in sync with the action you take to keep from wetting your pants when you really have to go. Try to lift it without squeezing your inner thighs or butt cheeks. (No one said it was easy.)

Mula bandha lifts from the base of your pelvis, pulling in toward the centerline. Since it works from the bottom of your pelvis, the body's fulcrum, it creates stability energetically and physically, with a calming effect on your nervous system. Like your core lock, engage root lock throughout your practice.

core lock (pulling your belly in toward your spine and up toward your shoulder blades—see the core and root lock sidebar above) supports your lower back, elevates your spine, and engages your back muscles. When using uddhiyana bandha throughout a yoga practice, you are conditioning your belly muscles. Get your core used to engaging, and it will be quicker to activate on the trail.

UDDHIYANA BANDHA ALSO SUPPORTS a deep breath practice. If you are having trouble with your ujjayi breath, engage your core and focus again, extending your inhales and your exhales and breathing into your back ribs.

As the central connecting point in your body, your trunk transfers force from your lower to upper body. Your core works from all sides to protect your spine. If you are struggling with injuries, your trunk is a vital area to take a look. Specific poses will strengthen your trunk. Your oblique muscles along the sides of your abdomen grow stronger in Plank; your lower back and spine builds in belly backbends and your mid-back muscles develop during twists. If you suffer from a sore lower back, a yoga practice will strengthen key muscles in your trunk to help alleviate pain. And no matter how strong your core gets, you will always feel it in poses like Boat!

Core Strength Practice

» Position yourself on your hands and knees to set yourself up for a push-up. Stack your hands right under your shoulders with your fingers spread and your index finger pointed toward the front of your mat.
» Keep your hips just below the height of your shoulders. Pull your belly button in toward your spine. Press your hands into the floor. Tuck your toes under, and press your heels firmly away from your body.
» Squeeze your thigh muscles and glutes. Stretch your chest forward akin to sitting up straight. Roll your shoulder blades toward your spine. Lift your gaze toward the front of your mat so that your head is even with your spine. To modify, keep your knees on the floor and lower your hips so your body is level from shoulders to knees.
» Set a timer. Build up to holding for sixty seconds at a time.

CENTERLINE

Your body has a plumb line that keeps you centered when you walk. Your body uses this centerline to navigate its balance. When you wear a heavy pack, your body adjusts to balance itself with this additional weight making your centerline shift—sometimes for the worse when you hopscotch across a stream.

During your yoga practice, your body recalibrates balance and strength, according to the shape of each pose. Becoming aware of and understanding your centerline will give you more access to stability and the natural alignment of each pose. Most of the cues for the poses move your body toward your centerline and your spine to hug your bones in toward your midline. Your spine is where stability lives in your body. The more you access the centerline, the more ease you'll experience in your practice and out in the wilderness.

Centerline Practice

EQUIPMENT: TWO BLOCKS
» Come to your knees on a mat.
» Turn a block to the narrowest width and put it between your inner thighs up as high as you can toward your pelvis.
» Place the other block on the floor in front of you, wide and flat. Bring your thumbs to the bottom edge of the block, and put the corners of the block into the crease between your thumb and index finger. Your index fingers will point straight ahead.

» Come to Plank (see pose instructions on p.74), keeping your hands in place at the block. Lift your legs off the floor. Lower your hips just under your shoulders. Ground your palms into the mat. Lift your head so it's even with your shoulders. Set your gaze in front of your block on the floor.

Experience Centerline

» Sag your hips and soften your legs, almost to the point of dropping the block. Notice what happens when you lose your centerline.
» Lift your hips again just below your shoulders. Squeeze your block between your inner thighs firmly. Hug your hands and upper arm bones in toward the block on the floor. Notice the shift in energy through your core and leg when you hug in toward the center. Do your limbs feel lighter, more aligned, and in sync with your body?

GAZE

For three years, I've taught yoga to kids at the White House Easter Egg Roll. Every year, it feels like more kids say they do yoga at school, or know breathing techniques they learned from their teachers. One year, another yoga teacher filmed a conversation with a kid named Elijah, who said his teachers taught him to practice looking at one spot for one minute at a time. She asked him why he does that. "It helps you concentrate on stuff," he replied. "Like when you're with your friends and you're trying to do your homework. You have to concentrate on your homework."

Well said, Elijah. The same applies to a hike. Have you ever walked along a wooded path, the weather crisp and clear with a light breeze sending puffy clouds scudding across the sky? All trail reports are a go. You're with your favorite people in one of your favorite places. But you are thinking about an email you forgot to send at work. You think seriously about pulling out your phone to send that message right now. Suddenly, a half hour has passed and you don't remember a single curve of the trail.

Western culture is one of constant distraction—from kids, partners, or coworkers, by the television, or by cell phones. Focus and concentration require practice.

Yoga poses rely on *drishti* (a simple, focused gaze) to keep your concentration in a pose. Gaze is a foundational part of a yoga practice, and a powerful way to bring concentration into your day. Setting your gaze over and over is a reminder to stay in the present.

You will see cues for your drishti throughout the poses found in this book. Get specific—look at one unmoving spot on the wall or ground. By adding drishti and concentration into your life, you may become more productive, plus your mindfulness and your ability to stay present while in conversation may grow exponentially. When combined with breath, drishti also offers release from stress and anxiety.

Drishti Candle Practice

» Light a candle. Set a timer for one minute. Set your gaze on the flame and stay with it. Notice the movement of the flame, what affects it, how it flickers, flares, and settles. Soften your eyes. Stay focused. Notice if you are tempted to move, and keep your drishti in one spot.

VINYASA FLOW

Vinyasa is the combination of breath and poses, moving in a flow and rhythm with the body. When you connect poses to an inhale or an exhale, you can notice how the inhale supports lengthening and the exhale connects you to the empty space in your lungs and body. Like your drishti, staying focused on your breath requires a certain amount of rigor and discipline.

I love simple Sun Salutations A and B to open my practice. When I first connect to my breath and my body, I often feel tired, and I move slowly. But as my body warms up, my focus sharpens. I tune into my core, my hands on my mat, and the sound of my breath. In this way, it's much like a hike. For the first steep uphill, I notice my body adapting to the terrain. I sometimes feel terribly stiff and wonder if I was a little too ambitious when choosing the hike. But as I walk, I warm up and get into the rhythm of my feet pounding against the earth. I move with the trail's flow, shortening my stride when it gets steep, picking up my pace when it evens out, and moving smoothly around roots and rocks.

A flow practice builds heat. Moving through poses in a vinyasa builds strength and also reminds your muscles of the last time you did these same poses. The flow often requires you to notice when you are lagging with your breath or adding in superfluous movements that take away from the essential combination of pose, inhale, and exhale.

For new practitioners, the art of linking movement and breath can feel elusive. Not all yoga styles include flow, and if you are new to it, vinyasa can feel messy. It may lead to uncertainty about whether you are doing the alignment properly when holding each pose for "one breath," or if you are flowing in sync. It takes time to develop the breath work and the physical strength to move through the poses with alignment and coordination. Be playful with it, notice when you are trying too hard to perfect your moves. Stay in the intention of moving with your breath. It will come eventually.

Once you get accustomed to a flow practice, a quiet rhythm and peace will come with vinyasa. Your breath begins to enhance each pose. Inhales create space in your physical body, allow you to deepen into your core, and focus on alignment.

They are timed for poses that lengthen the spine or expand your energy out like Halfway Lift or stretching your fingers to the ceiling in Warrior.

An exhale creates space by pushing the air out of your lungs for a Forward Fold or to sustain your focus on your Core Lock (see sidebar above). Exhales also allow you to soften and deepen into a pose, supporting your body so that you can stay in a challenging pose longer. In vinyasa, focus on how your body moves with your breath.

Basic Vinyasa Practices

» **Seated Vinyasa:** Take a comfortable seat. Rest your hands in your lap. Inhale and circle your arms out wide and up to the ceiling until your palms touch. Exhale and draw your palms down through your centerline to your chest. Repeat this cycle for ten breaths.
» **Cat–Cow:** Come to all fours on your hands and knees. Stack your hands underneath your shoulders, with index finger pointing to the front of the mat and palms pressed flat into the floor (see photos and instructions on pp. 184–185). Stack your knees underneath your hips.

Seated Vinyasa

Pull your belly button in, engaging your core. On your inhale, slowly lift your chest forward and up. Tilt your tailbone up toward the ceiling and squeeze your shoulder blades toward each other, keeping your core engaged as your belly dips like a cow. On your exhale, round your spine and your shoulders, pulling your belly up toward the sky and lowering your head and gaze at the floor, like a cat. Move back to Cow on an inhale, and repeat Cat on an exhale. Do this sequence for ten breaths.

MOUNTAIN POSE

Growing up in the Midwest, I remember the first time I saw the stark peaks of the Rockies. I was in high school, and my parents took me to Colorado. I had never seen mountains like that. I couldn't believe the sheer size and height of the snowy peaks. I craned my neck out the car window, and experienced a scale I didn't know existed until that moment.

Mountain Pose is similar to the experience of realizing there is something so much bigger than yourself—it connects you to the scale and inspiration of your own physical form. Through the pose, you feel the foundation of your own feet, your strength, spine, and energy.

All poses wire your body up for healthy, neutral alignment, which supports you as you access your body's full potential. It makes you healthier for long hiking trips, alerts you to when your body isn't feeling right, and also gives you a better understanding of how to recreate a feeling of alignment and freedom. Like a long hike that pushes you to your edge, in Mountain Pose, you can tap into the experience that you are stronger than you can possibly know. You realize how amazing the human body is, and in particular, how strong and powerful you are.

Mountain Pose starts in your feet, stretched broadly on the floor. Once your feet are aligned in a neutral position, your legs connect in, strong and grounded. From there, observe the tilt of your pelvis. You now have a foundation to move it into neutral, with the front and back of your pelvis even. Your belly now has more space to squeeze in and lengthen your spine. Pull your shoulder blades toward your spine to lift your chest even higher. Your head can now reach up the same way a mountain peak juts into the clouds. Your breath has more room to expand into your lungs. Practice the pose to experience the shift in energy and perspective possible from such a simple, essential place.

Mountain Pose Practice

Each of the cues in this pose builds upon another; layer them in one by one.

» Stand on a mat with your bare feet directly under your hips, your arms loose by your sides.
» Point your toes straight ahead, and bring the outer edges of your feet parallel with the edges of your mat; this position may make you slightly pigeon-toed. Lift your toes and connect with the four corners of your feet to the mat. Soften your toes back to the floor.
» Lift the arches of your feet, and with your feet grounded, press your outer shins out until you feel your legs engage, then spiral your inner ankles toward the back of your mat. Energetically, drive your outer ankles down to the floor.
» Squeeze your thigh muscles to the bone. If your knees became stiff, soften the joints slightly.

Mountain Pose

- » Tilt your tailbone down toward the floor. Gently pull in your belly button to engage your core. Squeeze your front ribs toward each other.
- » Roll your shoulders up to your ears, then soften them down away from your ears. Pull your upper arm bones toward your shoulder blades to engage your shoulders.
- » Send breath into your ribs in your mid-back.
- » Let your hands relax by your sides, and spin your palms to face forward.
- » Lift the crown of your head up toward the sky to lengthen your neck. Soften your jaw.
- » Set your gaze on one point.
- » Take ten deep ujjayi breaths.
- » Observe what it feels like to ground your feet, and notice the rise of energy along your spine and center. Experience how it radiates from your center out through your fingers and up through the crown of your head. Note what it is like to connect to your physical body and the present moment through Mountain Pose.

MEDITATION FUNDAMENTALS

Meditation is a practice to train your mind to be present. There are many techniques, and meditation and contemplative practices are found in almost all spiritual traditions, including Christianity, Islam, and Judaism, although it is probably most closely associated with Buddhism.

Like yoga, meditation requires practice. The goal isn't necessarily to relax, but the benefits can be experienced that way. Studies have shown that when you meditate, you lower your blood pressure, blood cortisol levels, and your heart rate. You improve your blood circulation, sweat less, have less anxiety . . . the list goes on.

WHY MEDITATE?

More people than ever are curious about the benefits of a meditation practice. Meditation's growing popularity has led to robust scientific studies focused on the effect it has on the brain and the body. Various recent studies have shown it has cognitive and mental benefits. The magazine *Scientific American* devoted a cover story to the topic called "Mind of the Meditator" in November 2014. In it, the writers noted that brain scans of experienced meditators demonstrated that the practice has a noticeable effect on how their brains are wired. Like a person learning to play an instrument, experienced meditators are able to develop new areas of their brains. They can achieve a focused state of mind with little effort, much like an expert musician or athlete can become immersed in a performance with ease.

The studies discuss types of meditations—focused-attention meditation that brings awareness to a physical action like breath; mindfulness or open-awareness meditation that might focus on sight or sound, and not becoming attached to any particular perception or thought; and compassion meditation, when the meditator focuses on feelings of unconditional love and compassion toward others. Meditation has four distinct cycles identified by researchers—time when the mind wanders, a moment when you become aware of the distraction, a period when you reorient your attention, and then the period you resume focused attention.

A study on focused-attention meditators showed they were less likely to react or get distracted when interrupted; they were more able to stay vigilant. Those who focused on open-awareness meditation had improved perception, with depressed patients better managing negative thoughts or feelings and a reduced chance of relapse in some. The compassion meditation helped meditators share the feelings of other people without becoming emotionally overwhelmed, particularly helpful for people in caregiver roles.

Meditation also brings lasting change to brain function, from the levels of stress people experience and an ability to stay calm in the face of stress to an improved immune system and resilient brain cells. Observing an eight-week study of active meditators, Harvard researchers found that brain matter grew in regions of the brain associated with learning, cognition, memory, emotional regulation, empathy, and compassion.

LEARNING TO MEDITATE

A daily meditation practice is a powerful point of connection and is key to understanding some of the deeper qualities of yoga. In Patañjali's time, yoga was comprised of mostly seated poses, with a focus on meditation.

Be kind to yourself when starting out, and playful too. Start with five minutes in the morning as soon as you wake up, and sit for five minutes again

CREATING A SPACE
FOR MEDITATION

Creating a comfortable setup for your meditation practice is important for making it a routine. Find a quiet space in your home where you won't be disturbed. Set yourself up with the following props:

» **Meditation cushion:** There are many suppliers of meditation cushions, but you can use any cushion in your house. Use a large cushion for the base to support your ankles, with a smaller cushion set on top that elevates your hips above your knees and makes it easier to sit for longer stretches. You can sit with your legs crossed or with your shins on either side of your smaller cushion.

» **Chair:** If it is challenging for you to sit on a low cushion, sit on a chair. Sit on the front half of the chair away from the back in an upright posture. Prop your feet up if the chair cuts into the back of your legs. Place a cushion or other support behind your back as needed.

» **More props:** During meditation, you may prefer to fold your hands in your lap. One option is to place a cushion or blanket in your lap to keep your hands propped up comfortably. Wrap a blanket around your shoulders for warmth for longer meditations.

» **Altar:** Adding an altar can create a sense of ritual around your meditation practice. Use a small table or get creative. Place treasured items, such as small tokens from loved ones, a candle, or fresh flowers, on the altar.

before you go to bed. Once you are in the routine of bookending your day with meditation, increase the time up to thirty minutes morning and night. Give yourself thirty days to create a meditation practice and see the results.

When you start this practice, your mind will wander. That's OK. Part of the practice is to notice your thoughts. You will not empty your mind, per se. You will initially notice you are thinking. Meditation is a practice of return, and even when it does not feel like it is working, trust that it is.

Just as hiking gets easier through the summer as your endurance builds for longer excursions, the more frequently you sit in meditation, the more you will find you not only can sit, but that you experience greater ease, focus, and less reactivity throughout your day.

Lastly, do not underestimate the importance and clarity provided by the daily ritual of meditation. By creating and establishing a ritual to support your own health—and returning to the ritual even if you miss a day—you put your well-being first. Just as you must commit to experience a hike you have heard is awe-inspiring but have not experienced yourself, commit to the practice of meditation. Experience for yourself its effect on you and those around you.

"However beautifully we carry out an asana, however flexible our body may be, if we do not achieve the integration of body, breath, and mind, we can hardly claim that what we are doing is yoga. What is yoga after all? It is something that we experience inside, deep within our being."

—T. K. V. Desikachar, *The Heart of Yoga*

Breath Meditation Practice

» Sit on a cushion or in a chair. Set a timer for five minutes.
» Close your eyes. Note the feeling of your feet and ankles against the floor. Walk your awareness up your legs to your hips. Stack your vertebrae and sit up straight. Tilt your chin parallel to the floor to lengthen the back of your neck. Bring your awareness to your nose.
» Notice the in and out of your breath. Do not try to control your breath. Pay attention to the natural state of how your body breathes. Note how your breath may be cool on the way in and warm on the way out. Focus on the feeling of air passing through your nostrils.
» When you notice your mind wandering, note you have wandered and bring your attention back to your breath. Focus again on your breath coming in and out.

Walking Meditation Practice

If all this talk about sitting sounds uncomfortable, consider a walking meditation practice,

WHEN IS THE BEST TIME TO MEDITATE?

....

Meditation is traditionally practiced in the early morning right when you wake up, and in the evening before you go to bed. Meditating both morning and night bookends your day with a contemplative, quiet space. That said, if you need to squeeze it in, meditating midday is better than skipping out completely!

most closely associated with the Buddhist tradition. While you will be moving no farther than the distance across your living room, it is a powerful mindfulness practice. (Hint: It's also a practice you can layer into your next hike.)

» Find a spot in your home where you can walk ten paces in one direction without any obstacles. Set a timer for ten minutes.
» You can do this practice with or without shoes. Stand still for a moment and close your eyes. Feel the weight of your body over your feet. Notice the bones of your feet.

» Start to walk, focusing lightly on each step. Observe the muscles required for your body to take a step forward. Pay attention to your feet as you walk. Move slowly, feeling every part of your body as you go.
» When your mind wanders, bring it back to your feet. When you turn around, note what has to happen in your body to turn. Continue your mindful focus on walking.

Mantra Meditation Practice

In a mantra meditation, you focus your mind on a phrase. *So hum* is a basic mantra meditation—it means "I am that" in Sanskrit.

» Sit on a cushion or in a chair. Set a timer for five minutes.
» Close your eyes. For a five rounds of breath, notice the natural inhales and exhales of your breath.
» Focusing on your inhale, say the word "so" to yourself. On your exhale, say "hum." Repeat. Observe if your mind wanders to your body or other thoughts, and return to the mantra.

CHAPTER 2
THE BENEFITS OF YOGA

"Yoga says we must deal with the outer or most manifest first, i.e., legs, arms, spine, eyes, tongue, touch, in order to develop the sensitivity to move inward. This is why asana opens the whole spectrum of yoga's possibilities."

—B. K. S. Iyengar, *Light on Life*

AT ITS HEART, YOGA is a multidimensional and transformative practice. It has immense physical benefits, and those are the ones you learn first. Yoga poses help you become strong, flexible, and graceful. Your body awareness expands, while your endurance builds. Conveniently, you learn to balance on one foot, which is helpful when walking across a precarious log or balancing on rocks in a rushing stream.

The physical lessons also are the gateway to the deeper mental ones, which is what ultimately change lives. It's why I practice and teach yoga. In this chapter, you will learn more about the physical strength, balance, and stability available through a regular yoga practice, in addition to the ways it can support you mentally to sort through whatever challenges life decides to throw your way on a particular day. You'll learn new ways to look at injury and how a yoga practice can help you manage and prevent injury as well as rehabilitate.

THE PHYSICAL BENEFITS

A strong, focused practice can echo a long, arduous day backpacking and the reward of exhausted delight that comes from testing your body's physical limits. You may start your hike distracted, thinking about what time you'll get back, worried you won't make it home for that evening's commitments. But after hours of moving along uneven trails, stopping to listen to a burbling creek, or saying hi to strangers on the trail, you can feel your feet and your breath.

In yoga, your attention is similarly focused on the feeling of the mat under your feet, the experience of inhaling and exhaling, your drishti focused at one point. You can experience the potent mix of physical work and a sense of calm and connection to something bigger than yourself, much like the experience of being outdoors.

Yoga also more readily brings your attention to your thoughts. You notice you are babbling to yourself, and you rely on your breath, gaze, and physical alignment to turn your focus instead to the present.

The same way an epic day of backpacking taxes your body so deeply that you can focus on moving forward one step at a time, yoga deepens your awareness of how your body moves, how your poses are connected to your breath, and how to access a sense of space physically and mentally in that moment. You notice the days you wake up tired, tell yourself you are too tired to go, but still manage a challenging hike, or the days an injury is shouting loudly at you.

One key to staying healthy is using your body in all the ways it was meant to move. Moving in multiple directions challenges your body's limits and builds strength. When you are strong and mobile, with a deep understanding of how your body moves, you trust it more deeply. You can keep up with an eight-year-old all day. You can work in the garden. You feel excited to try something new, no matter your age.

Or, perhaps you live for multiday backpacks, carrying heavy loads of forty pounds or more. You love twenty-mile days. Effort is your middle name. And your body's aches and pains tell the story of every trip. Your body needs to rest and release too. Plus, it's hard to make it to the mountains *every* day. A yoga practice will teach you the importance of reducing physical intensity.

The following physical benefits range from the ones you may know, such as flexibility, to ones you haven't considered, like deeper body awareness.

THE HAZARDS OF SITTING

The first time I observed adults squatting was in Beijing, China. It was the mid-1990s, and people squatted everywhere—street corners, Tiananmen Square, the Great Wall of China. Their squat was deep, their heels stayed on the ground. They looked relaxed. My American friends and I tried to emulate them, but after just a few moments, we would grimace and stand up.

Many years of yoga and fitness later, I know the squat is a natural and essential resting position (and movement) for the human body. Observe toddlers. They squat to look at something on the ground, or to communicate with a friend—it doesn't occur to them that it is uncomfortable because for them, it is not.

Many Americans spend the day with their hips in a static 90-degree position, either in a chair or in a car. Once you hit your school years, where you spent the day at a desk, most of you lost your squat. That also may mean you lose some strength for standing up, and mobility in your hips and lower back. If you struggle to get out of a chair, you most likely end up staying there, a perpetual challenge as people age.

According to a report from the *Washington Post* about the health hazards of sitting, your brain function slows down when you don't have fresh blood moving through it from physical activity. Sitting leads to a strained neck, sore shoulders and back, tight chest, tight hip flexors, and a weak core and glutes. It can lead to a weak spine and bad back, to poor circulation and soft bones from a lack of activity. Extended sitting can lead to high blood pressure, a greater risk of heart disease, and an overproductive pancreas, which can lead to diabetes and a greater risk of colon, breast, and endometrial cancer. Are you convinced yet?

It's important to take breaks from sitting by standing periodically and changing position. Some people set timers every 20 to 30 minutes at work to remind them to stand up and get blood flowing back into their legs. It's also worth noting that your body is completely capable of reclaiming its squat. Follow the Thirty-Day Squat Challenge below!

THIRTY-DAY SQUAT CHALLENGE

Created by movement leader Ido Portal, this challenge is to bring back your squat. You don't need to do all ten minutes in one stretch, but set out to squat ten minutes a day for thirty days. (For detailed pose instructions, see pp. 64–65.) Set a timer to keep track. When it gets too intense, stand up. See how you feel about your body, mobility, and squat ability by the end of the month.

Note: If you have trouble getting into a full squat, you can practice lowering into a chair without sitting all the way onto the seat, hovering until you get strong and open enough to go into a full squat. Or place a mat or blanket under your heels.

MOBILITY

When I meet someone new and tell him I teach yoga, it often prompts a confession—he doesn't do yoga. Often, he will follow up with a second confession, brow furrowed, that he is terribly inflexible. I counter the confession with my own—I was barely able to touch my toes when I started practicing.

When you open up your body to its natural mobility, when your joints move in all the ways available to your body, and your muscles become more pliable, capable of movements including squats, twists, flexing, or extending to touch your toes. Access all of these directions, and you can crawl under logs, clamber through boulder fields, and perhaps even squat easily!

Certain kinds of repetitive movement naturally tighten up your body. Take hiking: It requires your body to move in the same direction for miles at a time. Your body largely moves in one plane of motion, and carrying a heavy pack for several nights in the wilderness intensifies the effects. If you don't vary the way you move, your hip flexors and hamstrings get tighter. Your lower back and hips take the brunt of your pack weight. Stress and anxiety accumulate in your body, showing up as tightness in your shoulders, and furthering issues with your lower back and hips.

More than that, if you don't challenge your body to do all it is capable of, you limit both your understanding of and your range of possibility. The goal with a yoga practice, or any kind of movement, should be to experience your body at its optimal, healthiest, and most energetic.

The key is listening to your body. If you're tight, that means being kind and working slowly into stretches. If you're very open, that means not becoming dependent on your flexibility in poses. You *can* overstretch, especially if you're stretching where the muscle begins, which pulls on tendons and other connective tissue. "Pay attention to stretch into the target muscle itself," says Leslie Kaminoff in *Yoga Anatomy*.

Mobility is key to restoring your body from a long day on a trail. A yoga practice supports multiple approaches to mobility. Most people associate flexibility with static stretching. During Half Pigeon, it takes a full minute before the muscles around the piriformis, a deep hip muscle, relax and the piriformis begins to lengthen, Kaminoff writes. The experience can bounce back and forth between intensity and a deep release.

Yoga poses also include active stretches, known as dynamic stretches, when you contract an opposing muscle to open your muscles safely. For example, engaging your thigh muscles will support flexibility in your hamstrings, opening them more effectively. You also lengthen your muscles by contracting in moves like lifting one leg off the floor while in a Downward-Facing Dog pose. In a vinyasa practice, when you repeatedly move through similar poses, muscles stretch over time as they warm up. Your body is doing constant active stretches at the beginning of practice, contracting some muscles to lengthen other tissue.

Many people experience some form of tightness in their hips and their shoulders. Sitting is a major factor for both. Also, if you primarily walk, hike, or run, your muscles become accustomed to that same motion and direction.

You may be surprised by how many parts of your body can open up. Your ankles become more flexible with Downward-Facing Dog and squats. Your ankles and feet strengthen during balancing poses. Your wrists get stronger in arm balances like Crow, and learn to relax and open during Plank and Downward-Facing Dog. Yoga poses also include many twists that relax tight muscles in your trunk and keep your spine healthy. Backbends open up your chest and heart area, teaching you to let go in your shoulders.

Your body can release tension through a regular breath practice, which ultimately allows your body to open up. When you work into mobility, you can experience the full freedom of a wide range of motion for hiking and life.

STRENGTH AND STABILITY

The physicality of a yoga practice offers you insight into where your strengths reside, and where you can focus to build needed strength. Holding poses, in particular, requires your body to adapt to what's happening in the moment. Holding Warrior strengthens stabilizer muscles around your hips, knees, and ankles, while pausing in Plank stabilizes your wrists, hands, shoulders, and your core.

Creating stability in a yoga practice begins at your foundation—your feet. Activate your feet, and your leg muscles will light up, stabilizing your knee and hip joints. Move into your core and shoulders, and you create stability everywhere. The more you practice and listen deeply to your body, the more you strengthen different muscles. Your body loves to cheat, and will depend upon the strongest muscle rather than engaging the proper muscle for good alignment. In the standing pose Warrior 2, for example, people often let their front knee cave in and hip jut out, allowing their stron-

ger thigh muscle to compensate for weak glutes. By centering your front knee over your ankle and pulling your front thigh bone into your hip socket, you strengthen your outer hip and butt muscles and create more stability around your hip.

All yoga poses call for core engagement throughout the practice, and doing so supports your lower back, elevates your spine, and engages your back muscles, all of which you use on a hike.

As you work into your body's strength and stability, you will see other benefits, like stronger bones and improved bone density from holding your body weight. As you get stronger in your core and shoulders, holding Plank—the beginning of a push-up—will not be as hard as it once was, though I can't promise it will ever be easy. You'll learn to access and stabilize your shoulders in a forward fold. You'll feel your ankles get stronger. You'll experience more freedom in your hands and wrists.

BALANCE

When a practitioner named Marie first came to me at age seventy-seven, she had trouble standing on one foot. During balancing poses, she would grit her teeth, a look of determination in her eyes.

She wanted to do them over and over, occasionally ignoring me when I gently suggested we move on. She taught me a thing or two about discipline— she stopped wearing shoes at home to help her feet get stronger; she practiced Tree while she brushed her teeth; she requested balancing poses every week so she could show me how much she was improving.

After a couple months of weekly yoga sessions combined with her daily regimen, she came in one day and told me that for the first time in years, she was able to pull her pants on, one leg at a time— while standing on one foot. The smallest triumphs can be the biggest breakthroughs, and it was huge for her.

Your body's ability to balance is based on an intricate system including vision, inner balance function in your ears, your core, and legs. Balance is a critical function that runs in the background all day. You don't notice, but your eyes take in the horizon, your ears calculate when your head moves, and your core and feet adjust to movement. Your brain is the coordinator, syncing all of this to keep you upright. It knows how to adjust when you heave on a heavy pack for a multiday trip.

If you don't challenge your body's ability to balance, you lose it, says Chris Morrow, a physical therapist. The older you get, the less likely you are to test your balance out of fear of falling; one-third of people older than sixty-five fall every year.

One simple strategy anyone can do to improve balance is to take away one of the essential systems, like sight, Morrow recommends. Another is to focus on the parts of your body that coordinate balance. Notice your feet. See what happens when you scrunch your toes, and your foot arches. Practice lifting all of your toes and setting them back on the floor. Rise up onto the balls of your feet and balance there, then walk. Walk on your heels. All of these small movements bring your attention to your feet, and you'll notice how the parts work together.

All of the poses I describe require you to pay attention to your foundation, typically your feet, although some of them include your hands. In standing poses, you place your feet on the ground at various distances to test your center of gravity. Many poses strengthen your butt muscles and outer hips, which play a major role in balance. Balancing poses where you stand on one leg, like

Tree in chapter 3, challenge you to stay upright on one foot. When your center of gravity moves, your body adapts, and you strengthen both your grounded foot and your core.

You might find your standing foot cramps as it relies on deeper ligaments and tendons that keep your foot stable. With different positions for your upper leg, torso, and arms, your body must figure out new ways to keep you upright.

You also can play with taking away sight in your yoga practice. Start out in a standing Mountain Pose, with your eyes closed. Notice how your body sways, adjusting to balance until your pelvis centers itself over your feet. Next, close your eyes in Warrior 2 (see Strength Practice I). Your awareness of your feet grows, and you notice how important it is to engage your core so you don't fall over.

Experiment with eyes closed during Tree pose, and see how much you rely on your eyes to stay upright. Stand in Mountain Pose and observe how your inner ear balance works by turning your head slowly side to side.The longer you practice and the more stable your balance becomes, the more playful you can be.

EASE AND RECOVERY

One of the essential yoga teachings is ease. In the *Yoga Sūtras*, there's a teaching called *sthira sukham asanam* (STEE-rah SOO-kum AH-sa-nam). Basically, it means combining steadiness and ease.

Fun and laughter is a surefire way to invoke ease, even when students are shooting me murderous glances during Warrior 2. I often tease my students for being Type A (it takes one to know one), and ask them to observe if they are being overzealous. I can spot those students from across the room—their arms and legs shake, their gaze is like a laser beam drilling a hole into the wall, and they avert their eyes when I suggest they soften their shoulders or jaw to relax into a pose.

But once those students learn to soften, they are often surprised. That is the moment when they can hold a pose longer than they thought. When you take a Chair pose, you can feel your feet, legs, hips, and core resisting gravity to keep you in the pose. You may still wish for nothing else on this earth but for the pose to end, and you also notice that it's possible to deepen your breath, set your gaze, and stay focused. Like when you reach the next false summit or are deep into a marathon,

PROPRIOCEPTION

Proprioception is your brain's understanding of where your body is in space. Your body learns balance by sensing where your body parts are in relation to each other and gauging strength and movement through muscles, tendons, and your joints.

When you learn a new skill, your body picks up new elements of movement. The more you ask of your body, the more your brain forms circuits between existing neurons to meet the new demands. Proprioception is what allows you to walk in the woods after dusk with a headlamp. It's how you can run without looking at your feet. It's why we feel awkward doing a new, unfamiliar activity.

Challenge your body's sense of space with new activities that are out of your comfort zone. If you don't dance, try a new dance class. If you're not a trained dancer, you might notice how tough it is to coordinate your hands, feet, and torso to the beat. It might feel nearly impossible. But if you keep going back to the class, and practicing the steps over and over, your body starts to learn them. Suddenly, the spin on one foot combined with the stomp of another, is possible. You have just built new circuits for your brain and body.

when you think you're almost there and then you realize you have miles to go. Instead of thinking grimly you'll never make it, you take a deep breath, let go of worrying about how much longer you have, and you keep going. You practice being present with your body.

The more you relax in a pose and the more your brain can focus on the muscles that hold you there, the better your body understands which muscles to engage and which ones to relax. You don't need to knit your eyebrows in *any* pose, trust me. This softer approach will serve you everywhere, particularly on a long hike. Think about if you spent the entire time hiking with your teeth gritted and without pause, never taking a break to shed layers, to drink water or catch your breath. You would tire out, your mind slowing, your ability to enjoy the hike crumbling. But if you stop, take a deep breath, remove a sweaty layer, eat a snack, and look around, you can appreciate your rich surroundings.

The next level of ease is supporting your body in release and recovery. If you spend most of your time in intense activity, your body stays in a constant state of stress and tension. Physical therapist Morrow advises that people take on calming exercises for overall health and balance. If your body feels happy, safe, and secure, rather than stressed and anxious, it will perform better.

Adding in a yoga practice dedicated to recovery is important for everyone. In practices designed to help your body relax and stretch out tight hips and shoulders, you may notice earlier if something is not working properly. Recovery and ease is the path to understanding your body and giving it space to heal for the next trail.

BODY AWARENESS

Understanding your body starts at the granular level—the sensation of your feet on the floor, the feeling of your ribs expanding and contracting while you breathe. The more you focus on feeling the sensations in your body, the more you will understand how your body moves in space, or proprioception (see sidebar earlier).

Yoga poses deepen your understanding of where your body is in space and how to maneuver on a microlevel of awareness. Alignment teaches you to feel the difference between pitching your pelvis, shaped like a bowl, forward and a neutral pelvis, where the front and back are even. You might notice you always stand with your pelvis tipped forward, your core slack, contributing to a sore lower back.

Kristin Hostetter, gear editor at *Backpacker* magazine, once broke four ribs during a ski fall. She credits a regular yoga practice and body awareness with preventing the injury from being worse. "I took such a bad tomahawking fall," she says. "Because I was strong and had awareness of limbs and where I was in space, I was able to protect myself a lot better than I would have been able to do otherwise."

THE BETTER YOU KNOW your body and how it moves in space, the deeper your understanding of poses and alignment will be, and the more it will serve you in life anywhere. Your ability to listen

KRISTIN HOSTETTER
Gear Editor, *Backpacker* magazine
Milton, Massachusetts

Q: What was your first yoga class like?
A: I was completely lost, trying to learn poses and the sequence, and quiet my mind, and do all the other things the instructor was talking about. I couldn't believe how hard it was. By the end, I was in love. I saw a really dramatic change in my body after practicing five days a week for two weeks. I loved the way it felt.

Q: How has yoga helped you physically?
A: I broke four ribs in a ski fall. It was just crippling for me. My yoga teacher had me doing classes, floor Pilates classes, six weeks after the fall, which was incredible. I couldn't believe what I could actually do. I would have been a lot worse off had I not had the core strength and the body awareness that yoga has taught me.

Q: Is there a connection for you between yoga and hiking?
A: Hiking is so important to me. I can't imagine ever having to choose between the two. They're very different on the outside. When you look at them from their root, they make you happy, bring you peace, and bring you joy. I feel lucky to have found two things that bring me all that.

Q: What type of pose speaks to you?
A: I love when I'm in a balancing pose and I have those few minutes of nothingness in my head where I realize I'm perfectly balanced, not only because my body is strong enough to hold me there but because my mind is not distracting me.

to your body will be greater. You'll notice which muscles are strong, and which ones could use some work. You'll trust your body to do what you ask it to do, essential for any athlete. You'll feel free to test your body on new hikes. You'll know how to keep your body healthy, safe, and strong.

A study by researchers at the University of Miami, Florida, discovered that instructors and advanced yoga practitioners engage different muscles from newcomers to yoga or even practitioners with three years of experience or more. In some poses, for example, instructors used their deltoid muscles in standing forward folds, Downward-Facing Dog, and in Warrior poses. Your deltoids stabilize your shoulders, and those with experience have learned over years of practice to engage while folding to deepen the fold. Newer practitioners struggled to use those muscles. More experienced yogis also were more likely to engage their thigh muscles in Plank, which stabilize your knees—an important area of strength for any hiker.

As you practice and focus on alignment, your body will understand how to connect to the bigger, stronger muscles that best support a pose. With deeper body awareness, you also will notice when something feels off and realize it's time to modify until your body heals, rather than pushing through. A consistent yoga practice teaches you the difference between pain and potential injury, and an intense, challenging practice pushes you to the edge of your strength.

MANAGING AND PREVENTING INJURY

An injury can happen before you know it. One of my biggest lessons happened at a rock climbing gym. I lifted my foot for the next hold, and my hip did a little pop. I ignored it—against my own intuition and everything I knew about moving in an integrated, stable way. I stepped onto the next hold and pressed down into my foot with all of my weight. The sudden pain in my groin shocked me. I spent one full week on the couch, barely moving. Even after a couple of weeks, I couldn't practice yoga. It took three weeks before I began to recover.

Injuries might happen frequently as you push your body's limits. Elite athletes in particular may push through pain that signals them to slow down. The real learning comes in how you handle the aftermath.

Deepening body awareness will help you prevent injury. But another important element in a yoga practice is learning the difference between intensity and pain. In an intense pose, your legs may tremble or you may want to give up. Instead, breathe deeply to build endurance. Sharp, shooting pain, a snap or a pop or feeling like you pulled something, however, indicates it is time to stop.

The first step in assessing your injury is to figure out exactly what part of the activity bothers you. Does it hurt when I push off my heel, or is it in my knee in a lunge or when I go down the stairs? Does it hurt every time, or only when I move in certain directions? Does it hurt when I'm not moving at all?

If you're really curious, you can go online and find out a common compensation for someone, say, in a lunge with knee pain. You might find out you're not using your butt muscles. If you can stop the compensation, you can come back from the injury once you let the acute injury heal, according to Seattle physical therapist Mark Trombold. If you are uncertain on any level about an injury, go see a professional.

Sometimes you may find that you're not injured, but instead facing a strength deficit. Injury comes from a weakness in your body, and it's a sign you need to focus on that area. Your body may compensate for a weakness, and that can cause an injury. Since the body likes to cheat, it will use the strongest muscles rather than the key muscles.

A yoga practice can help you discover your physical weaknesses. When you understand the deficit, you can target particular poses to work on. Once your injury feels better, gradually ease back into activity. Modify your poses or practice as you need to, and spend the time focusing on your breath and listening to your body to know if it's sharp, shooting pain or the shaky intensity that comes with building strength.

THE MENTAL BENEFITS

Many times, you are the one who chose the difficult hike. You know it will be challenging, but you tell yourself it will be worth it. You head out, excited for a beautiful day with your hiking buddies.

But then the hike itself shows up, and it is far harsher than you envisioned. The trail is relentlessly steep. You plod upward and scold yourself for underestimating the elevation. You spend your time wondering if you will make it, and say out loud maybe you should turn around. You get to the top, but despite a rest and lunch in view of a spectacular waterfall, you can't stop thinking about the pain of blisters on your heels. You spot the parking lot and realize you have dozens of grueling switchbacks ahead. You wonder if it might be better if you stopped and let a wild beast take you.

> "Problems are just places where we have been separated from our authentic selves. . . . When you change your focus from limitations to boundless possibilities, from doubt and fear to love and confidence, you open your world in entirely new ways. You stop worrying about fixing what's wrong with you and start living from all that's right within you."
>
> —Baron Baptiste, *Journey into Power*

The hike has become the opposite of joyful, the experience, the antithesis of why you go in the woods. But then something startles you, be it a chattering chipmunk or a vista you missed on the way up. You stop muttering to yourself about how miserable you are—you pause. You look around and notice the beauty of the landscape. You feel amazed at how far your two legs can take you. You realize you are strong enough to finish. Your mental state switches to gratitude. For the first time in hours, you sniff the rich scent of wildflowers. You swig some water, and you go on.

The trick is turning the trail into yoga. Some days it happens easily; some days it does not.

But yoga teaches you to notice when you have turned even your favorite pastime into a burden. It teaches you to shift your mindset regardless of hike, job change, or breakup. Yoga is a minute-by-minute practice, and when you do it every day, all day, it changes your life.

DISCOVER INNER STRENGTH

Every year, I lead a "40 Days to Personal Revolution" program, designed by my yoga teacher Baron Baptiste. Participants do yoga six days a week, meditate twice a day, and focus on nutrition. My studio includes a nutrition challenge for the program, and participants have the option to give up caffeine, alcohol, tobacco, or sugar for the six weeks. You can choose one—or all.

At the end of the program, one participant, Ellen, came up to me. In the first meeting, Ellen told the group she was giving up sugar, but she shared with me she also had secretly pledged to her program buddy that she would quit smoking.

Ellen had smoked off and on for twenty-one years. She gave up cigarettes when she was pregnant, but picked it up again once her kids were toddlers. Right before starting the "40 Days" program, she completed a yoga teacher training, smoking all the way through it. She started most days with a cigarette and lit one or two more at night.

At fifty-two, Ellen knew smoking was a sign of something amiss in her life. But she couldn't identify it. When she signed up for "40 Days," she knew she had the option to give up smoking, but she was undecided at that first meeting.

One theme in the first meeting is integrity, or keeping your word. I remind the students that they, not I, benefit from staying true to their word to practice yoga and meditation. It's the first moment in years some people have taken steps to prioritize their health and well-being over the needs of their kids, spouses, or careers. No matter how much they may want it, they are often resistant to changing their ingrained habits.

During that first meeting Ellen realized she had to quit smoking, if only to prove to herself she could. A regular yoga practice had already taught her she was physically stronger than she thought. She knew somewhere inside, she was mentally stronger than her cigarette habit.

The first two weeks were hard, she says. She was accustomed to looking forward to her evening cigarette when things got tough at work. The thought of that cigarette helped her hang on during the day. When she struggled, she had to find other ways to feel better. She would go to the bathroom at work and do deep breathing or cry as a release.

Ellen occasionally broke on sugar during the six weeks, and she missed some meditation practices. But she didn't light a cigarette. "It was acknowledging I was strong enough to be without," she told me.

During that period, Ellen realized what she had been stuffing down with cigarettes—her angst over her secure corporate job. She had known for years she was unhappy. Instead of making a change, she smoked. With smoking gone, she realized it was time to do something different. Three months after the end of "40 Days," Ellen gave notice at her job. She's taking a road trip, and she says she'll see what's next.

REDUCE STRESS AND ANXIETY

Yoga and meditation help combat stress, and give you more tools to listen to your body and improve your overall health. The majority of Americans live with moderate to high stress, the American

Psychological Association (APA) has found. The most common reason people don't do more to manage their stress is they say they are too busy. But estimates claim that seventy-five to ninety percent of all primary care doctor visits are stress-related.

Stress takes an immense toll on your body. Our bodies developed the fight-or-flight response to handle genuine emergencies, like an animal attacking. Even though many people no longer live in a dangerous environment, our bodies still experience the fight-or-flight response in reaction to ordinary challenges, like getting stuck in traffic, meeting a project deadline, or managing our finances, the APA says.

Basically, people often act like a bear is chasing them around. Any hiker knows that moment of panic when you encounter a bear, a snake, or another large wild animal—or even a sound—you think is dangerous. Your adrenal glands flood your body with stress hormones. Your muscles grow tense, your pupils dilate, your sense of smell and hearing heighten, your breathing and heart rate ramp up, and you start to sweat.

React like that every day, and the stress shows up in your body—in tight shoulders, tension in your jaw from grinding your teeth, or an aching in your lower back. The physical focus on strength and mobility in yoga helps you function day to day. But layered underneath those physical benefits are critical practices that lessen stress and anxiety, and help you to move through challenging situations.

A technique as simple as looking at a tree can reduce stress. A frequently cited study published in the journal *Science* in 1984 by environmental psychologist Roger Ulrich showed that hospital patients had shorter hospital stays, took fewer painkillers, and recovered more quickly overall from surgery when they could see a tree out their window. This study is a window into why people often feel more at ease in the wilderness: being outside reduces stress. That alone is good to know, but you can take it to another level by bringing a mindfulness practice to your hike. When you pause to gaze at layers of rock exposed by a steady, patient river, or halt in your tracks to spot an eagle soaring overhead, something in your mind and body shifts. You forget about your latest project at work, the bothersome neighbor, or long to-do list. Your mind clears. You are present.

Meditation, its own mindfulness practice, produces a state of restful alertness in your body, according to the Chopra Center, a wellness center founded by Deepak Chopra and David Simon. When you are in a state of restful response, your heart rate slows down, your blood pressure normalizes, your breathing calms down, and you sweat less, the Chopra Center says. Your body also produces less adrenaline and cortisol, your pituitary gland releases more growth hormone, and your immune function improves. A growing body of evidence suggests the amygdala, the area of the brain responsible for fight-or-flight, shrinks with just eight weeks of mindfulness training.

LEARN TO PAUSE

Studies have suggested yoga can have an effect on the brain similar to that of antidepressants and psychotherapy. One study by Duke University researchers published in *Frontiers in Psychotherapy* showed that yoga plays a role in treating depression, sleep challenges, and even in schizophrenia and attention deficit disorder (ADD). Your quality of life also may improve. Free safety Earl Thomas of the Seattle Seahawks told *Mindful*

magazine that a meditation and mindfulness practice has changed the way he looks at the world. "It's an inner thing," he said. "When you're quiet and don't say anything, you start to see the unseen. That's why people need to be observant and listen. When I turned my ears to listening, I improved personally and in everything."

I've seen it happen over and over. Take my student Brian. He came every Saturday to my yoga class, riding his bike no matter the weather and smiling a shy hello each week.

I later learned Brian was an alcoholic. He took up yoga at age thirty-one to help him with his sobriety. Yoga helped him feel better physically—and he can now touch his toes. An old shoulder injury healed, allowing him to throw a baseball again. His sciatica eased up. He met his girlfriend at the studio.

The practice was a window for him to understand why he smoked pot and drank so much—to numb his anxiety. "I had an incredible amount of tension," he says. "I doused it with alcohol."

Through yoga and breathing, he learned to be with his emotions. After class, his mind no longer raced, looping the same repetitive thoughts. He realized if he was feeling angry or stressed or irritable, he could zoom out of his head, ask himself what was going on, and realize that he didn't have to feel that way. In the early days, he got emotional during final rest. "Yoga in a lot of ways is about observing self and being with challenge, not necessarily trying to make it go away," he says.

Once you use the tools consistently, yoga filters into every layer of your life. New possibilities emerge through the practices of presence and listening.

TRANSFORMATION AND CHOICE

Yoga teaches you to observe yourself. Perhaps you're obsessed with backpacking because the wilderness is the only place you feel grounded, and you don't know how to access those feelings of peace at home. A yoga practice can help you figure that out.

At my first yoga teacher training, I sat across from another trainee and repeated my sob story over and over, crying as I talked: My editors at the newspaper had moved me from my dream job to one I didn't want. I listed all of my misery, including layoffs, departures of dear mentors, an unfruitful job search, and what I considered unreasonable demands at work.

Every time I told her the story, her job was to respond, "Blah blah, blah blah." The idea was to repeat the story until I no longer felt suffering. The first few times she blah-blah'd me, I felt anger through my tears. By the eighth telling, the words started to lose their meaning. By the twelfth, I could recount my tale without feeling intense pain, plus I noticed I'd created a lot of drama about my career. It was only a job.

At the training, I set a goal to leave the paper in a year to teach yoga. When I returned from the training, work felt OK. Nothing changed, on the surface. My responsibilities and requests from my editor didn't change. But I did. I went with the flow. I didn't take it personally when I was assigned a story or my editor gave me feedback. I sometimes worked late on deadline, but unlike before, I didn't get angry or resentful. I even thought cheerily for the next few months that I could teach yoga on the side and be content.

And for a few months, I was. But when I was honest with myself, I knew the truth—my best self was not thriving at the newspaper. I wasn't aligned with the work any more. I was practicing contentment (*santosha*), a yoga teaching, but I had not been honest (*satya*), another teaching. I was terrified about giving up health insurance and a retirement plan to run a business entirely dependent on one person—me. But those reasonable concerns were holding me back. I had to try a life teaching yoga.

I saved more money, plotted, and stressed constantly. A dear friend and mentor advised me to be less Western and deadline-oriented. "Set an intention," she said. Four months later—a year and four months after saying I would leave the newspaper to teach yoga full-time—I did.

When I wonder what I am supposed to do, who I am supposed to be with, what is next, or why am I here on this planet, I have learned that I must first stop spinning out on my thoughts. Anxiety, fear, and doubt feel heavy in my head, stomach, and face. When I am present, I am excited, energized, and ready for what's next. I let my intuition guide me.

I go to yoga, or I meditate, or I pause in the midst of what I am doing. I see what is true about myself and what I can do. Instead of questioning myself, I have gone on harder hikes than I give myself credit for. Instead of being afraid of the response, I said "I love you" first to my partner. When I wondered if I was certifiably insane each time I quit financially stable jobs to follow a dream, I still did it—first, to teach yoga, and second, to write a book.

You might now be hearing a little voice inside that says, "Wow, great for her, that won't happen for me." In the great words of my mentor, Susanne Conrad, "Stop it!" Don't listen to that voice. Get on your mat. Breathe. Meditate. Practice. Hike. The answer is already in you.

CHAPTER 3
YOGA POSES FOR HIKERS

DURING THE BEST MOMENTS of a hike while you are immersed in the landscape, the effort can feel like a side note. Heavy breathing becomes a backdrop to the panoramas of distant peaks that open up along the trail. You tune into the whistle of birdsong or the quick wooden thwack of a distant woodpecker hammering into a tree. Occasionally, your mind drifts to lunch and how much longer until you can dig in.

Then come the days you feel like nothing is harder than the hike at hand. Oblivious to the woodpecker, your attention tunes into the hammering thrum in your chest. Your glutes and calves scream—it's all you can do to move forward one grueling step at a time. Water, extra clothing layers, and your delicious lunch turn into weighted bricks in your pack. You wonder if you could have left something—anything—behind. On the return, your quads protest if you descend too quickly, begging for mercy. You look past every hairpin turn, hoping to see the elusive trailhead.

On a challenging hike, your body goes full tilt, sweat pouring down your back. Your leg muscles work overtime. You notice right away whether you have spent enough time during the week focusing on cardiovascular conditioning.

First, take a few deep breaths! Then, consider that the trail is a mirror for your physical conditioning. While hiking, you might discover your ankles are prone to turning awkwardly, especially on the way down when you are tired. Or you wake up the next day with cramped quads or sore calves. Your aching shoulders holler.

A 10-mile walk is long; add in elevation gain, and the trail offers ruthless physical feedback. Repetitive movement taxes the affected muscles. It is essential, and some experts argue critical to your health, to push your body's physical limits. Head out for a 10-mile hike and you will test your body. Building your endurance for long hikes through lower body and overall trunk strengthening will make your hike more enjoyable and lessen the effects you feel the next day. Supporting your body is essential, no matter if you hike daily or only escape to the wilderness occasionally.

This chapter covers major areas of the body a hike affects, from the soles of the feet to the spine. Each section highlights yoga poses that can support a specific area, especially if you are prone to injury, for example, in one of your knees. Please note that this is meant to be a glimpse into the poses and that they are most beneficial when included in a full practice with a warm-up and cool down. All poses in this chapter are included in the strength and recovery practices in

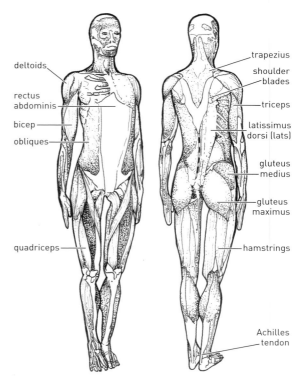

Figure 1. Full body musculature, front and back

POSE BASICS

....

Bring your feet together: This is a cue for neutral alignment in your feet. Yoga poses start with feet pointed straight ahead. For most people, it is big toe knuckles touching, with a slight gap at the heels so the outer edges of your feet are roughly parallel to each other.

Four corners of your feet: This refers to your big toe knuckle, pinky toe knuckle, and the two sides of your heels. Balance and your foundation start here by distributing your weight evenly among these four corners of your feet in all poses. If your foot is off the floor, stretch out your toes and continue to activate the four corners.

Core lock: Pull your belly button up and in toward your mid-back to stabilize your spine and trunk.

Hip-width distance: Make fists with your hands, fold forward and place them between your feet to set your feet at hip-width distance. In some cases, like Downward-Facing Dog, you will have to visualize it.

Sit bones: The bones at the base of your pelvis, which you might feel after sitting for a long time on a hard bleacher, are a reference point for alignment (see figure 4 below).

Pelvic bowl: Your pelvis is shaped like a bowl. Out of habit, most of us stand with it tilting slightly forward or back. Engage your core lock and tilt your tailbone toward the floor to move it into a neutral position. You can bring your hands to your hips to check your pelvic bowl position.

chapter 4; photographs of each pose described below appear as part of those practice instructions in that chapter.

SUPPORT YOUR FEET

Your feet bear your weight throughout a hike and dig deep to support you for hours at a stretch, coping with constant changes underfoot from rocks to tree roots and squelching through puddles. Your feet have twenty-eight bones each, with four layers of musculature, a bottom layer called your plantar fascia (see figure 2), and the pads of your feet. When the bones and muscles work together, they create lift, balance, and

INDIVIDUAL POSES COVERED IN THIS CHAPTER

» Mountain Pose
» Tree
» Toes Pose
» Squat
» Chair
» Crescent Lunge

» Downward-Facing Dog
» Rag Doll
» Standing Leg Extension
» Half Moon
» Half Pigeon
» Plank

» Side Plank
» Rag Doll with a Bind
» Reverse Tabletop
» Seated Twist
» Locust

movement in your foot, according to Leslie Kaminoff in *Yoga Anatomy*. Feet adapt incredibly well to uneven terrain, critical on a hike where the ground underfoot does not resemble the smooth, artificially even surfaces common in our modern world. Over time, if they are not challenged, the deeper muscles that support your feet weaken and only the surface layer, the plantar fascia, prevent collapse.

The good news is the roots and rocks woven throughout a trail force your feet to use the deeper muscles that support the three arches of your feet. While fitted, supportive boots are helpful, particularly on longer hikes where the strain on your feet is intense, performing yoga poses in bare feet will also condition and strengthen them.

COMMON INJURY: PLANTAR FASCIITIS
Many hikers suffer from plantar fasciitis, pain and inflammation on the band of tissue on the bottom of the foot, which occurs when the arches of a person's foot are not strong enough to support their weight downhill. When your foot musculature is weak, explains Seattle physical therapist Mark Trombold, the surface layer of plantar fascia, which are like springy strings on the bottom of your foot, get smashed repeatedly, leading to plantar fasciitis.

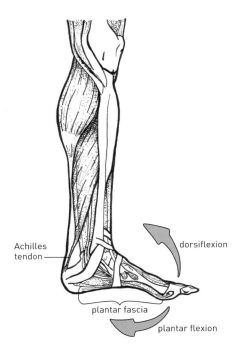

Achilles
tendon

dorsiflexion

plantar fascia

plantar flexion

Figure 2. Muscles of the feet and ankles

A foundational pose for your entire practice, Mountain Pose starts with awareness in your feet. It engages your whole foot and creates strength. The pose also illuminates weaknesses in your feet, allowing you to work that area.

» Stand with your feet directly underneath your hips with the outer edges of your feet parallel to your mat, arms relaxed by your sides.

» Lift and spread out your toes, creating gaps between every toe from your big toe to your pinky toe. Notice how this action lifts the arches of your feet.

» Soften your toes on the floor. Press the four corners of your feet into the floor.

» Keep your feet grounded and spin your inner ankles toward the back of your mat. Energetically draw your outer ankles down toward the floor.

» Fold forward toward your shins.

» Cross your wrists, palms facing away from each other, and bring your palms to your inner calves. Press opposite palms into opposite inner calves.

Mountain Pose

Tree

Notice the action in your feet, calves, and inner thighs.

» Stand up slowly. Keep your awareness in your feet. Close your eyes and notice how your feet flex and balance to keep your body upright.
» To strengthen, stand straight in the pose with your arms at your sides. Rise to the balls of your feet and balance for five breaths.

Tree

A simple balancing pose, Tree focuses attention on your feet and ankles to engage microstabilizing muscles, which develops stability and strength. Your inner thigh muscles lengthen and your rear muscles engage. You also will open your hip on your lifted leg.

» Stand with your feet together. Feel the four corners of your feet on the floor or mat.
» Lift one foot to either your inner calf, or above your knee joint to your inner thigh. If balancing is challenging, prop the foot of your bent leg against the ankle of your standing foot with the ball of your foot on the floor.
» Pull your belly in toward your spine to engage your core. Look at a spot on the wall.

» Bring your palms together at the center of your chest. Stay for five breaths.

STRENGTHEN YOUR ANKLES

Your ankles allow your feet move in four directions—you can wiggle your feet side to side, and flex up and point down because of your ankle joint. On the trail, your ankles constantly flex up and down while you hike. Every hiker also knows that when your body and mind tire out, you are more prone to turn an ankle, particularly if your ankles are weak. Good, supportive boots protect your feet and ankles when you are carrying an overnight pack, but it is also essential to strengthen and mobilize your ankles so they are strong and robust for long excursions in the woods.

Point your toes toward the floor away from your knee. This is plantar flexion. Your feet spend a lot of time in this position. Most people sleep with their feet in plantar flexion under the weight of sheets and a comforter, says Trombold, and shoes tend to lift your heels in the same direction during the day. Now flex your toes toward your knee for dorsiflexion to lengthen your calves in the opposite direction—notice the stretch into your calves.

Work your feet in both directions to develop strong, stable ankles.

Poses that are good for your feet also are good for your ankles, and vice versa. Tree pose, detailed above, supports stabilizing your ankle. The following poses will help you work more specifically on ankle flexibility.

COMMON INJURY: ACHILLES TENDINITIS

The Achilles tendon (see figure 2) connects your calf muscle at the back of your lower leg to your heel bone. Achilles tendinitis is caused by an extreme range of motion of your foot in dorsiflexion (foot flexed toward your shin) and plantar flexion (toes pointed away from your knee). With tendinitis, the connecting tissue becomes inflamed and tender, and can be exacerbated by carrying heavy loads while hiking. You can support your connective tissue by working on mobility and strengthening your ankle before your next hike.

Toes Pose

Many people find this pose quite intense. Toes Pose opens your toes, and stretches both your

Toes Pose

Achilles tendon and the fascia in the soles of your feet. You may not have stretched your ankles and feet in this direction before. Work up toward holding this pose. You can modify Toes Pose by tucking a rolled-up blanket behind your knees. Do not stay in the pose if it is painful for you.

» Come to your knees on a mat. Tuck your toes underneath you until you are on the balls of your feet—tuck your pinky toes in if they escape.

» Sit up slowly and lift your chest over your hips until you feel the sensation in your feet.

» Breathe deeply for thirty seconds, or stay up to one minute.

» Counter pose: Shift forward onto your hands and knees. Release your toe tuck and point your toes on the floor. Bring your hands to the ground behind you and lean back on your feet to stretch into your shins, the front of your foot and your ankles in the opposite direction to counter the intensity.

Squat

A squat is a natural position for the body, but most adults lose their ability to stay in this pose

Squat

comfortably if they don't squat regularly. In addition to working ankle mobility and flexibility on the front side of your ankle, it strengthens the arches of your feet. A squat also opens your spine, lower back, and hips. You can modify this pose by placing a folded blanket under your heels to accommodate tight ankles. Move away from this modification as soon as you can in order to work toward more ankle flexibility.

» Stand with your legs as wide as a mat.
» Bend your knees to lower your hips toward the floor. If your heels lift off the floor, widen your stance until you can flatten your feet. Your toes can turn out wider than your heels.

» Lift the arches of your feet. Press your elbows into your knees and lift your chest up toward the ceiling. Don't forget to pull your belly button in!
» Play with sitting in a passive squat, then engage your pelvic floor and lift your hips an inch out of the bottom of the squat into an active one.

PROTECT YOUR KNEES AND THIGHS

The uphill can feel like the hardest part of a steep hike, especially when you are hiking with chatty buddies who keep asking probing life questions! Thank goodness for lookouts where you can take a breather. But the toughest portion physically on steep hikes is the downhill. If your quads ache above all after a big hike, this section is for you.

When you come down an incline, the four muscles of your quadriceps slow your descent by resisting gravity. Add in a heavy pack, and the physical load is even greater. If you slam each foot down on the ground on the way down, your thighs and knees work even more to mitigate the brunt of your body weight and pack. Move slowly, your feet landing soft and ninjalike as you go downhill, and the load spreads throughout your legs.

Trekking poles can significantly reduce the load on your legs while moving downhill, particularly when carrying a lot of weight. The more you strengthen your quads and work on balance, the more likely you are to sneak up on a bear, rather than vice versa.

COMMON INJURY: PATELLAR TENDINITIS

The four quadricep muscles connect via tendons to your patella, or kneecap, to stabilize it. The patellar tendon begins underneath the kneecap and attaches to the shinbone (see figure 3). Weak or tight quadriceps and weak hips, combined with the constant jarring impact of walking steeply downhill, can lead to inflammation of the tendon. You can support your legs by doing poses that strengthen your quads and the tendons and ligaments around your knees.

Chair

A leg strengthening pose, Chair also develops foot and ankle stability, and requires you to use your core and activate your spine, all while engaging your thigh muscles to strengthen and support

Chair

your knees. It may take time for Chair to win the entry for your favorite pose, but it surely is a useful pose to have on your side.

- » Stand with your feet together on your mat. Spread out your toes, and lift the arches of your feet off the ground.
- » Lower your hips toward the floor until you feel your legs engage. Keep your toes soft and in view just past your knees.
- » Soften your shoulders down away from your ears. Engage your back to pull your shoulder blades to your spine.
- » Pull your belly in to activate your core.
- » Reach your arms up to the ceiling, parallel to your ears with palms facing toward each other.

Crescent Lunge

Crescent Lunge

Holding Crescent Lunge tests your balance, stabilizes your knees and ankles, and teaches you to breathe through challenge! It also strengthens your thighs, hamstrings, and glutes.

- » Step into a long lunge with your right foot forward, left foot back. Stack your right knee over the ankle of your right foot. Lift your left heel so your toes are bent and the sole of your foot is perpendicular to the ground. Move your feet hip-width distance apart for stability.
- » Lift your chest over your hips and extend your arms up to the ceiling.
- » Squeeze your back hamstring straight.
- » Pull your belly up and in to support your core.
- » Square your pelvis toward the front of your mat.
- » Reach your arms up parallel to your ears, pinky fingers forward.
- » Stay for five breaths, then switch sides.
- » To intensify, lower your back knee so it hovers two inches from the ground. Hold for five breaths. Straighten your back leg. Switch sides.

OPEN YOUR HAMSTRINGS

Your hamstrings are workhorses (see figure 3). When you walk, run, or hike, your hamstrings contract to propel you forward. They extend your leg behind you, flex your knees, and straighten your legs. Your hamstrings also sync with your quads to keep your pelvis stable.

You need strong thigh muscles for hiking but many people's quads are a stronger muscle group than their hamstrings. Over time, if your quads dominate, your hamstrings can suffer and get overstretched. Tight hip flexors pull on your strong thighs to make your hamstrings overly long. Sitting all day with your hamstrings in one position doesn't help either.

It's healthy to give your hamstrings some love by building strength and engaging your thigh muscles to stretch deep into the belly of your hamstring muscle. But be mindful of how you stretch your hamstrings to avoid overdoing it; it's important to breathe and focus on where you are stretching. When your hamstrings are opened properly, your legs will be more balanced in strength and openness, supporting you when going up and downhill on a hike and in other activities.

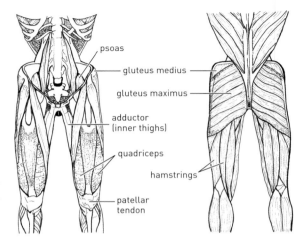

Figure 3. Muscles of the hips, glutes, and hamstrings

Downward-Facing Dog

Downward-Facing Dog is a widely used pose for good reason—it has benefits for the whole body. An inverted V-shape, it lengthens your hamstrings, your calves, and your spine, and in the pose, you practice grounding into your hands and

Downward-Facing Dog

learning to open and strengthen your shoulders. This pose is a good place to pay attention to your sit bones, the bones at the base of your pelvis (see figure 4). If you bike, you are very familiar with this part of your anatomy! In Downward-Facing Dog, practice spinning your sit bones up to the ceiling to lengthen your spine and engage your core.

» Come to your hands and knees, with your hands positioned underneath your shoulders, index finger pointing straight forward.
» Tuck your toes underneath you, and lift your hips up to the ceiling. Walk your feet back about six inches.

» Bend your knees and lift your tailbone until your spine lengthens. Spin your sit bones to the wall behind you.
» Roll your shoulders up to your ears, then use your back muscles to pull your shoulders down your back and in toward your spine. Squeeze your upper arms toward each other.
» Drive your heels toward the floor (they don't need to touch the floor).
» Pull your belly in toward your spine.
» Lift the muscles just above your knees to engage your thighs and open into your hamstrings. Stay for fifteen full breaths.

Rag Doll

Rag Doll is a soft forward fold that works from your feet to open tenderly into your hamstrings. Gravity also gives your spine traction to release tension in your lower back, shoulders, and neck.
» Stand with your feet hip-width distance apart.
» Lift and spread out your toes, creating gaps between every toe from your big toe to your pinky toe. Notice how this lifts the arches of your feet.

Rag Doll

» Soften your toes to the floor. Press the four corners of your feet into the floor.
» Spin your inner ankles toward the back of your mat and energetically draw your outer ankles toward the floor.
» Fold your chest toward the floor. Bend your knees until your belly touches the tops of your thighs to take pressure off your lower back and hamstrings. Squeeze your inner thighs up toward your pelvis.
» Hold your elbows and hang your upper body, letting go of your head. You will feel the release from your neck all along your upper back as well as in your hamstrings. Stay for five full breaths.

RELEASE YOUR HIPS AND GLUTES

Your pelvis grounds and stabilizes your body. You use the muscles attached to your pelvis daily, relying on the psoas muscle deep in your hip to get out of bed. Your gluteus maximus and gluteus medius, the big butt muscles, and hamstrings kick in when you walk (see figure 3). And yet most people don't know how to engage their glutes. Weak glutes, a result of sitting and general underuse, can lead to an overreliance on your lower back (rather than using your meaty rear muscles and your core) when walking or twisting. Your hip flexors also get shorter from sitting at a 90-degree angle all day.

Your pelvis has big flat bones with lots of muscles attached. It's easy for tension to get locked up in your hips, buried among all those muscles and connectors, and it takes time to release. Tension in your hips often works its way into your low back. Be mindful of the burden your hips and glutes take on every day, especially when asking more of your body during long treks with a lot of weight. Hip-release poses help your muscles relax and let go, while strengthening your glutes will provide more durability when you need the endurance.

Standing Leg Extension

Balancing poses challenge many elements of your lower body, from your feet up to your core. This variation on Hand-to-Knee Pose (presented in Strength Practice II) also strengthens your psoas and your butt muscles.

» Stand with your feet together, toes pointed toward the front of your mat. Press the four corners of your feet into the floor.
» Squeeze your thigh muscles and pull your belly in toward your spine to support your lower back.
» Lift your right knee into your chest. Hold your knee with your right hand.
» Extend your right leg forward, flexing your toes. Reach your arms to the ceiling, parallel to your ears. Keep your shoulders stacked over your hips, your core engaged.
» Stay for five breaths. Switch legs.

Standing Leg Extension

Half Moon

A balancing and strengthening pose, Half Moon works deeply into your butt muscles for both legs. Your glutes contract to balance your lower leg and lift your upper leg into the pose.

» Stand with your feet together.
» Line up a block (at its tallest height) underneath your right shoulder, just to the right of your standing pinky toe. Bring your right hand to the block.
» Shift your weight into your right foot. Lift your left leg and roll your left hip on top of your right hip. Lift your left arm to the ceiling.
» Press firmly into your standing foot with your toes pointing straight forward. Squeeze your thighs.
» Flex the toes of your lifted leg. Bring your lifted leg in line with your hip.
» Keep the weight on your lower hand light; rely on your standing leg for strength.
» Stay for ten breaths.
» Release: Fold forward.
» Do the other side.

Half Moon

Half Pigeon

After a long day on the trail, it is important to relax the muscles that support your pelvis. Half Pigeon works in your hip to release your piriformis, a hip stabilizer (not shown in figure 3), and also releases in your butt muscles. If you backpack frequently, it becomes particularly important to soften your hip area from the intensity of additional weight it bears over many miles.

» From a seated position, bend your right leg in front of you. Move your right thigh parallel to the outer edge of your mat with your right foot

Half Pigeon

tucked in toward your pelvis. Flex your right foot to protect your knee.

» Extend your left leg straight behind you so that the top of your thigh is on the ground.
» Flex your toes on your back foot and come up to the ball of your foot.
» Roll up to center so your pelvis is squared toward the front of your mat. Place a block under your right hip if you have trouble staying centered.
» Lengthen your chest and lower your torso toward the floor. Stay here for twenty breaths. Switch sides.

TIGHTEN YOUR CORE

Your trunk holds you up—and together! During a hike, it carries you and your pack, whether you are going up and down a mountain or meandering through rolling meadows. Your trunk muscles keep your spine stable. Your back and shoulder muscles, including your latissimus dorsi (lats), connect into your glutes, so the stronger you keep your back muscles overall, the stronger you will feel during a hike.

Your core lock engages multiple levels of muscles that support your spine, including your rectus abdominis, the central washboard muscles seen on some and used by all, that play a role in forward folds and protects the lower spine (lumbar) in backbends. Your obliques along the side of your trunk contribute to twisting, while the transverse addominus, the deepest abdominal muscle, supports uddhiyana bandha.

Endurance is an important element to core stability. Hikes last far longer than the time most people spend working on strength, so focus on timed holds. Your body will be grateful for the extra support.

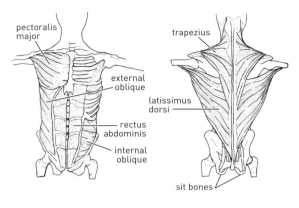

Figure 4. Muscles of the core

Plank

Plank pose is commonly used as a core strengthener. In yoga, the emphasis on doing a Plank on your hands rather than your elbows brings awareness to your palms as your foundation, and also strengthens your oblique muscles along the lateral sides of your torso. And you build shoulder and thigh strength.

» Come to your hands and knees on your mat. Stack your hands underneath your shoulders, index finger pointed straight ahead.
» Step your feet to the back of your mat. Tuck your toes and lift your knees off the floor, and squeeze your legs straight.
» Keep your hips just below level with your shoulders.
» Lift your head so your neck is level with your shoulders.
» Spiral your inner thighs up to the ceiling. Lengthen the backs of your knees and squeeze your thighs.

- » Press your palms firmly into the floor. Squeeze your upper arm bones toward each other.
- » Spin the inner eye of your elbows forward, and pull your shoulder blades together.
- » Lift your belly in toward your spine and wrap your front ribs together. Tilt your tailbone toward your heels.
- » Breathe and hold for one minute. If you can't hold for one minute, build up to it. Repeat three times.
- » To modify the pose, bring your knees to the floor. Keep your hips in one even plane between your shoulders and your knees, belly muscles fully engaged.

Side Plank

Side Plank challenges your external oblique muscles in your torso as well as other parts of your core. It works deep into your glutes and the lower arm and shoulder holding you up, firing up the muscles on half of your body. It also strengthens your hands and wrists. The goal is for your body to stabilize using neutral alignment of your spine and legs.

Side Plank

- » From Plank pose (see above), bring your feet to touch. Roll onto the outer edge of your right foot with your left foot stacked on top.
- » All your weight will be on your right hand. Your right hand faces the front of the mat and is stacked just a couple of inches forward of your shoulder.
- » Lift your left hand up to the ceiling, palm facing the same direction as your chest.
- » Flex your toes toward your knees and squeeze the muscles of your legs to the bone.
- » Keep your body at one angled plane from shoulders to feet.

» Set your gaze and look up to the ceiling.
» Stay for five breaths. Switch to your left hand.

RELEASE YOUR SHOULDERS

When you walk, your arms swing easily, naturally—you don't have to think about it. When your left foot steps forward, your right arm swings forward, and vice versa, keeping the two halves of your body balanced as you walk. The same rhythm applies while hiking. Your arms move in sync with the motion of your body. If you hike with poles, move them the same way, with opposite pole swinging forward from the leg that is moving forward.

Add endurance into the equation, and your natural rhythm gets disrupted. When you tire, your shoulders roll forward, your arms go limp, and you lose the natural cadence of your arm motion while walking. It makes walking heavier and harder. Spend time releasing your trapezius muscles, which get trapped up by your ears when you hunch on the trail or at a desk. Your deltoids in your shoulders (see figure 5) and your pectoral muscles in your chest (see figure 4) will also be giddy if you choose poses to counter and release a long day on the trail.

Rag Doll with a Bind

A bind adds shoulder opening to the grounding Rag Doll pose that already releases your legs and spine. If lifting your bound hands off your lower back is

Rag Doll with a Bind

challenging, hold a strap or towel with your hands behind your back and fold forward from there.

» Stand with your feet hip-width distance apart (or wider). Stretch out your toes and activate your feet. Fold your chest toward the floor.
» Bring your hands to your lower back. Lift your chest and interlace your fingers, with your palms facing in.
» Bend your elbows and squeeze your shoulder blades together. Straighten your arms and fold forward over your legs.
» Turn your head side to side to release your neck.
» Stay for five breaths.

Reverse Tabletop

Reverse Tabletop deeply stretches your pectoral muscles, deltoids, and biceps, opening your chest, shoulders, and upper arms. It reverses the feeling of gravity pulling forward on your shoulders. Your triceps straighten your arms.

» From a seated position, place your hands behind you on the mat with your fingertips facing your body.

Reverse Tabletop

» Walk your feet so they are flat on the floor at hip-width distance.
» Ground into the four corners of your feet, and lift your hips toward the ceiling.
» Press your palms into the ground.
» Lengthen the crown of your head behind you and look up. Gently release your head onto your shoulders.
» Stay for five breaths.

ALIGN YOUR SPINE

Your spine is the central pillar of your body, and you want to keep it supple and strong. But during a hike, your spine has little chance to twist or move in any direction other than holding your upper torso and head relatively vertical (see figure 5).

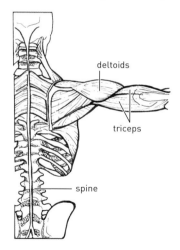

Figure 5. Muscles of the spine and shoulders

Twists will rotate your spine, keeping it flexible by encouraging the muscles between vertebrae and around your spine to open up. Backbends strengthen the muscles that arch your back and keep your spine aligned and healthy.

Seated Twist

A simple twist you can do anywhere, Seated Twist will offer release from long periods of sitting or from a big day outside.

Seated Twist

» From a seated position, extend your right leg straight toward the front of your mat, toes flexed. Bend your left knee and walk your left foot in close to your hip.
» Place your left hand on the floor behind you. Reach your right arm up to the ceiling. Wrap your right arm around your bent leg.
» Stay for ten breaths. Switch sides.

Locust

Backbends build strength in your spine and also work deeply into the big back muscles in your torso that support your spine. Locust pose focuses on the muscles that arch the back and is helpful for strengthening your low back.
» Lie on your belly. Bring your feet to hip-width distance, toes pointed.
» Reach your hands alongside your body, hands down by your hips, palms facing down.
» Bring your feet to hip-width distance, toes pointed. Pull your belly in toward your spine.

Locust

» Press the tops of your feet into the floor, and lift your knees off the ground. Keep your upper legs engaged, and lift both legs off the floor.
» Lift your upper arm bones toward the ceiling, and float your hands above your hips.
» Set your gaze on a point on the ground below your nose. Stay for ten breaths.

CHAPTER 4
YOGA PRACTICES FOR HIKERS

I OFTEN REMIND STUDENTS when they approach poses as if they can perfect them to remember it is called a yoga *practice*. The power comes from doing it over and over. When you put your body into different shapes that challenge your strength and flexibility, pay attention to alignment, and meld poses with your breath, it is a formidable combination. The more you practice and pay attention to your body in poses, the more you rewire your body and your mind. And that repeated effort gives you access to the subterranean levels of change and growth available in a yoga practice.

In this chapter, you will learn about a power yoga practice. Physical power in your body can be interpreted as bursts of speed to hurl yourself in various directions in space. In yoga, power stems from holding poses to build stability, building heat in your body from those holds, and experiencing freedom physically through alignment.

You will encounter challenge—that is a major component of your yoga practice. Rather than muscling through or forcing your body, consider breathing more deeply, listening and seeing if you can shift your alignment or your perspective in a pose you initially find tough. Take Child's Pose to return to your intentional ujjayi breath.

The sequences in this chapter are designed for two different approaches—strength and recovery. The Strength Practices will support you on the trail, creating stability and endurance in your lower body, spine, and core while softening your hips and shoulders. The later sequences include poses to practice mid-hike or at the end of a long day backpacking to support your body to stay at its most optimal.

In the Strength Practices, the poses connect you to your body so that you can let go mentally. Strength Practice I builds your strength in a short time. Your heart rate will elevate and you will sweat! Do it regularly to get stronger and practice noticing your body sensations. In Strength Practice II you build upon what you learned in the first, adding on more challenging poses and pushing your endurance for a longer stretch of time. Both practices start by activating your core, then move you into Sun Salutations, a traditional way to open a vinyasa practice. They build heat through repetition and help you practice connecting breath with movement. Once your body becomes accustomed to opening your practice this way, you will notice more ease and flow.

The standing poses for both practices build stability, challenge balance, and open your spine. They are strong poses designed to push you to your edge. The balancing poses strengthen your feet and test your body's limits to keep you upright, while arm balances test your skills and determination! Keep going.

Backbends open your chest and heart. Most of us habitually hunch forward, our posture sloppy from years of slouching. Backbends require us to reverse those years of habit. You may feel some resistance to backbends when first starting, partly because of your body's physical ways, and also the energetic opening experience that comes with a backbend. It can feel uncomfortable to release in your chest and around your heart if you are not used to it. Be patient and relax your chest. You never know what you may find.

Inversions turn your perspective upside down. Seeing your legs in the air may be all it takes. When your body is upside down, more blood moves to your heart, pumping more efficiently and slowing your heart rate and your blood pressure. Your heart gets a break and in turn, you relax.

You may be tempted to skip Final Rest. Savor it. It's the key to letting all the energy you've opened up in your body resettle. It trains you to

UNDERSTANDING THE POSES

Each pose description includes the following:

» **Name:** Common English name for the pose.
» **Introduction:** Context for the pose, relationship to the body, and how the pose supports you on the trail.
» **Setup:** Getting into the pose.
» **Alignment:** Specific cues to pay attention to for proper body alignment.
» **Release:** Some poses have directions for a specific release.

» **Gaze & focus:** Where to set your drishti (gaze) during the pose and where to focus your attention within your body during a pose.
» **Deepen:** Ways to deepen a pose for the next level of challenge.
» **Common challenges:** Physical challenges you may experience during the pose.
» **Modifications:** Alternatives to modify the full pose.

For poses that are already modifications of the full pose, challenges and modifications are not listed.

restore. It offers a space of stillness—all too rare in a busy day.

All the practices include recovery poses, particularly important for athletes who push their limits day in and day out. If you normally take a rest day after a long day on the trail, do the Recovery Practice. It is designed for a body that feels achy and tired. Your muscles and energy contract after a lot of intensity, and the recovery sequence will allow your body to both open and heal from a big day outdoors.

These practices are intended to support your time hiking, and a regular practice is key to seeing a shift. Commit to at least one Strength Practice twice a week, but know that it is designed to be practiced daily. Build from the 25-minute sequence to the 45-minute one. Do the Recovery Practice once a week, even if you haven't been in the mountains.

SEQUENCE FOR STRENGTH PRACTICE I

- » Supine Butterfly
- » Happy Baby
- » Boat
- » Plank
- » Low Cobra
- » Downward-Facing Dog
- » Child's Pose

- » Squat
- » Rag Doll
- » Halfway Lift
- » Mountain Pose
- » Sun Salutation A
- » Sun Salutation B
- » Warrior 2
- » Triangle

- » Side Angle
- » Wide-Legged Forward Fold
- » Twisted Crescent Lunge
- » One-Legged Chair
- » Tree
- » Low Lunge

- » Half Splits
- » Bridge
- » Reclined Half Pigeon
- » Seated Forward Fold
- » Seated Twist
- » Legs Up the Wall
- » Corpse Pose

GET READY

The Strength Practices are based on a power vinyasa practice, which weaves held poses for stability and challenge with a flow connecting breath and poses to build heat. They are designed to be challenging. You'll find as you grow in strength and mobility, you will build endurance and cultivate ease in the flow. If you start to lose track of your breath or need a rest at any time, remember you can take Child's Pose. Return to your ujjayi breath and then resume the sequence when you are ready.

KEY

Many of the cues are based in Mountain Pose. It is the foundation for your entire practice! The cues for poses also presume you are practicing in a room with walls and a ceiling, but feel free to interpret the cues if you are practicing outdoors. Please note that you have seen some of these poses

"Practice, practice, practice. That's it."

—Sri K Pattabhi Jois, in an interview

in chapter 3. For those poses, you will see some additional alignment cues to support a deeper understanding and experience of the pose.

Each pose should be held for five full breaths (each breath is made up of both an inhale and an exhale), unless otherwise noted. If there is a necessary transition between poses, you'll see a notation for a sequence transition.

STRENGTH PRACTICE I
TIME: 25 MINUTES
EQUIPMENT: YOGA MAT, BLOCK, AND STRAP

RELEASE AND ACTIVATE
This first phase of the sequence is a time to focus on your breath and your core, and in the process, release mental lists. Bring your attention to your physical body and notice your ability to listen to it and learn.

Supine Butterfly

Supine Butterfly

Starting your yoga practice lying on your back gives your body time to relax; the contact between your spine and the floor sends a signal to your brain that it's time to let go. Gravity draws your legs down toward the floor, naturally opening your hips. Your shoulders relax down into your mat; close your eyes if you like.

Give yourself time in this pose to feel the floor under you and to let your mind settle. Focus on your active ujjayi breath.

SETUP Lay down with your back on your mat.
• Bring the soles of your feet together so your legs form a diamond shape.

ALIGNMENT Let your arms relax on the floor, palms facing up. • Notice the connection of your spine to the floor and the natural curve of your lumbar spine at your lower back. • Hug your belly up and in toward your spine to activate your core. • Bring in your ujjayi breath.

GAZE & FOCUS Close your eyes. • Bring your attention to your spine on the floor and an active core.

COMMON CHALLENGES Tight hips or lower back pain prevents your knees from releasing toward the floor.

MODIFICATIONS Bring your feet as wide as your mat and rest your knees together to bring your lower back to the mat.

Happy Baby

Happy Baby opens your hips and brings your spine into neutral alignment. This is a wonderful pose to check in at the beginning of practice and again at the end to see what has changed in your spine

Happy Baby

and hips. If you can roll around on the floor and embody the name of this pose, you'll love the pose even more.

SETUP From Supine Butterfly, pull your knees into your chest. • Take your knees wide outside your chest. • Reach inside your legs for the inner arches of your feet, and lift your feet toward the ceiling.

ALIGNMENT Flex your feet toward your knees. Bend your knees at 90 degrees. Press your heels toward the ceiling. • Relax your shoulders. • Lengthen your lower back toward the floor while pulling on your feet with your hands. Press your feet into your hands.

GAZE & FOCUS Look at a spot on the ceiling.
• Lengthen your spine to the mat.

DEEPEN Switch your grip on your feet to the outside arch of your foot; pull your knees deeper down outside your ribs. • Stay in the pose for ten breaths for a deeper hip opening.

COMMON CHALLENGES Tight hips or lower back pain prevents you from reaching your feet.

MODIFICATIONS Hold the backs of your thighs instead of your feet. • Open your knees wider than your chest. • Place a block under your head.

SEQUENCE TRANSITION From Happy Baby, pull your knees into your chest and with momentum, rock up to a seated position.

Boat

You use your core intensely during a hike, especially if you are carrying heavy weight on your back. One of the most effective ways to strengthen your core, Boat pose challenges your trunk muscles in multiple ways. That said, people love to cheat in this pose! Be sure to lift your chest to get the full effect.

SETUP Hold the backs of your thighs, and balance between your sit bones at the base of your pelvis and your tailbone. • Lift your feet off the floor.

ALIGNMENT Pull your thighs toward your chest. Hold your shins parallel to the floor. • Squeeze your thighs toward each other. Spread out your toes so you see a gap between each one. • Pull your shoulder blades toward each other. Lift your chest toward the ceiling. • Reach your arms straight in front of you. • Stay for ten breaths. • Transition to Low Boat pose. Lower until your lower back is on the floor with your shoulders off the floor and your legs hovering above the mat. Squeeze your thighs

Boat, modified

MODIFICATIONS Hold the back of your thighs to keep your chest lifted.

SEQUENCE TRANSITION Bring your feet to the floor from Boat. • Hug your knees and lift your chest to the ceiling to release in your core. • From a seat, roll over your feet to hands and knees.

Plank

Your core is the key link for your entire body, and Plank is an effective way to build trunk strength and heat! Plank is also an excellent place to practice Mountain Pose, by keeping your legs fully engaged, pulling your shoulder blades into your spine, and lifting your head to be level with the rest of your spine.

SETUP Stack your hands underneath your shoulders, index finger pointed straight ahead. • Step your feet to the back of your mat. • Stay on the balls of your feet, lift your knees off the floor, and squeeze your legs straight.

together. Stay for five rounds of breath. • Lift back to Boat. Stay for ten breaths.

GAZE & FOCUS Set your gaze on your toes. • Concentrate on lifting your chest.

DEEPEN Once your hamstrings allow it, straighten your legs at a 45-degree angle away from the floor.

COMMON CHALLENGES Lower back weakness prevents you from lifting your chest.

ALIGNMENT Keep your hips just below level with your shoulders. Tilt your tailbone toward your heels. • Spiral your inner thighs up to the ceiling. Squeeze your thighs. • Lift your head so your neck is level with your shoulders. • Press your palms firmly into the floor. Squeeze your upper arm bones toward each other. • Spin the inner eye of your elbows forward, and pull your shoulder blades together. • Lift your belly in toward your spine and wrap your front ribs together. • Stay for ten breaths.

GAZE & FOCUS Set your gaze past the front of your mat. • Keep your legs and core firm. Breathe deeply to maintain the pose.

COMMON CHALLENGES Building strength to hold the full pose for ten breaths can take some practice.

MODIFICATIONS Bring your knees to the floor, toes curled under. • Keep your hips in one line with your shoulders.

SEQUENCE TRANSITION From Plank, shift to the tips of your toes and slowly lower to the floor, chest and pelvis touching down at the same time on the mat.

Plank

Plank, modified

Low Cobra

A gentle backbend, Low Cobra still has plenty of power. When practiced diligently with strong legs and a lift in your chest and spine, it builds strength in your back and opens your chest.

SETUP Press the tops of your toes into the floor. • Squeeze your thighs and lift your knees off the mat. • Place your hands next to your lower ribs so your elbows are at a 90-degree angle.

Low Cobra

ALIGNMENT Press your pelvis into the floor. • Engage your core and lift your chest off the floor. Hug your arm bones toward your spine. • Tilt your tailbone toward your heels slightly. • Lift your hands an inch off the floor to take weight off your hands.

GAZE & FOCUS Lift your gaze forward about a foot in front of you. • Maintain strong legs and lift from your core.

DEEPEN Press your palms down and lift to Upward-Facing Dog (see Strength Practice II).

SEQUENCE TRANSITION Lower your chest to the floor. • Press up to your hands and knees.

Downward-Facing Dog

New students are often skeptical that Downward-Facing Dog can become a resting pose. Just like a tough hike at the beginning of the season that feels moderate by the end, Downward-Facing Dog changes the more you do it. As your body awareness grows, you will experience length, strength, and softening all at once. In a flow sequence, it's a time to return to your ujjayi breath, to open your spine and hamstrings, and to open and strengthen tight ankles.

SETUP From hands and knees, tuck your toes and lift your hips to the sky. • Move your feet back about six inches toward the back edge of your mat.

ALIGNMENT Point your index fingers to the front of your mat. • Flatten your palms until the knuckles at the base of your index and middle fingers are grounded on your mat. • Move your feet to hip-width distance. Spin your inner ankles back so the outer edges of your feet are parallel with the edge of your mat. • Bend your knees and lift your tailbone toward the ceiling until your spine lengthens. Spin your sit bones to the wall behind you. • Roll your shoulders up to your ears, then use your back muscles to pull your shoulders down your back and in toward your spine. Squeeze your upper arms toward each other. • Press your chest toward your thighs; keep your shoulders engaged and do not hyperextend in your shoulders if you are extra flexible. • Drive your heels

Downward-Facing Dog

toward the floor (they don't need to touch the floor). • Pull your belly in toward your spine. • Lift the muscles just above your knees to engage your thighs and open into your hamstrings. • Create a long line from your wrists to your shoulders and hips; bend your knees as you need to.

GAZE & FOCUS Look backward at the floor between your big toes. • Lift your tailbone high toward the ceiling.

DEEPEN Once the pose feels more comfortable, press your heels deeply toward the mat until your toes can spread and soften.

COMMON CHALLENGES Tight hamstrings can lead to a rounded spine. • If you have a wrist injury, it may be painful to stay on your hands.

MODIFICATIONS For tight hamstrings, bend your knees and lift your tailbone toward the ceiling. Pull your shoulders toward your spine. Press your chest toward your legs. • For wrist pain, come down to your elbows for Dolphin pose: Bend your elbows so they are stacked directly under your shoulders. Walk your feet in toward your elbows as close as you can. Lift your tailbone to the sky.

Child's Pose

In a world of constant stimulation, Child's Pose offers a quiet, internal space. It brings your focus inward to your body and your breath, and it relaxes your spine and lower back, your hips and your shoulders.

Child's Pose

SETUP From Downward-Facing Dog, lower your knees to the floor. • Release your toes and bring your big toes together to touch. • Move your knees to the edges of your mat. Sink your hips back over your heels. • Walk your hands forward at shoulder-width distance, and bring your forehead to the ground.

ALIGNMENT Let go of tension in your shoulders. • Engage your core gently, pulling your belly up and in toward your spine. • Come into your ujjayi breath. • Stay for ten breaths.

GAZE & FOCUS Close your eyes. • Deepen your ujjayi breath. Pay attention to the feeling of the mat under your hands and forehead.

COMMON CHALLENGES A tight lower back or hips can prevent your forehead from touching the ground. • Knee injuries can prevent you from bending your knees comfortably.

MODIFICATIONS Bring a block under your forehead to relax your neck. • Roll over onto your back for Supine Butterfly or lay flat on your belly.

SEQUENCE TRANSITION Return to Downward-Facing Dog. • Step or jump to the front of your mat.

Squat

A squat releases your lower back and hips, and allows your body to move into the natural curves of your spine. It also opens your ankles. This is a great pose to do mid-hike to release your lower back and hips from the repetitive movement of walking on uneven terrain.

Squat

SETUP Walk your feet as wide as your mat. • Bend your knees to lower your hips toward the floor. If your heels lift off the floor, widen your stance until you can get your feet flat. Your toes can turn out wider than your heels. • Bring your hands together, palms touching, in front of your chest.

ALIGNMENT Shift your weight into the outer arches of your feet, and lift your inner arches. Squeeze your heels in toward each other like you are trying to wrinkle your mat. • Lift your belly button in toward your spine. • Press your elbows into your inner knees. • Lift your chest toward the ceiling. • Stay for ten breaths.

RELEASE Lift your hips and relax your upper body forward to your feet in a deep Forward Fold.

GAZE & FOCUS Set your gaze on a spot on the wall ahead. • Lengthen your spine and keep your knees aligned over your feet. • Play with sitting in a passive squat, then engage your pelvic floor and lift your hips an inch out of the bottom of the squat into an active one.

DEEPEN Bring your feet wider and sink your tailbone closer toward the floor. • Work your feet toward parallel.

COMMON CHALLENGES Tight hips prevent you from grounding your heels.

MODIFICATIONS If you have trouble lowering down below your knees, stay in a higher position or bring a folded blanket under your heels.

Rag Doll

Rag Doll releases compression in your spine through gravity. The pose also connects you to your feet and legs, grounding into the lower half of your body and releasing your hamstrings, all areas that can use some additional space after carrying a heavy pack.

SETUP Stand with your feet hip-width distance apart. • Stretch out your toes and activate your feet. Fold your chest toward the floor. • Hold your elbows and hang your upper body, letting go of your head.

ALIGNMENT Lift and spread out your toes, creating gaps between every toe from your big toe to your pinky toe. Notice how this lifts the arches of your feet. • Soften your toes to the floor. Press the four corners of your feet—your big toe and pinky toe knuckles, and the two sides of your heels—into the floor. • Spin your inner ankles toward the back of your mat and energetically draw your outer ankles toward the floor. • Bend your knees slightly until your belly comes down to the tops of your thighs. Squeeze your inner thighs up toward your pelvis.

Rag Doll

• Turn your head side to side to soften your neck. Stick out your tongue to release your jaw. • Sway gently side to side.

GAZE & FOCUS Close your eyes or set your gaze on a spot between your feet. • Release your spine and neck.

DEEPEN As you get more open in your hamstrings and lower back, your legs straighten more. Keep your knee joints soft still in the pose.

Halfway Lift

A transition pose, Halfway Lift builds strength in your lower back when you hold the pose. It also teaches you to activate your core while hinging at your hips, the biggest joint in your body. In turn, you activate your hamstrings and glutes.

SETUP From Rag Doll, release your hands to the floor. • Bring your big toes together. • Place your hands on your shins. Lift your chest parallel to the floor.

ALIGNMENT Root your feet firmly into the floor. Bend your knees as needed and squeeze your thighs.
• Stick your butt out toward the wall behind you. Lift your chest up to be even with your hips. • Lengthen the crown of your head away from your tailbone.
• Hug your shoulder blades to your spine to activate your centerline. Pull your belly up and in.

RELEASE Fold forward to your feet and exhale.

GAZE & FOCUS Look at a spot on the floor in front of your toes. • Create extension in your spine and wrap

Halfway Lift

your shoulder blades toward your spine. Engage your core.

DEEPEN Place your fingers or hands flat on the floor on the outsides of your feet.

COMMON CHALLENGES Your back rounds because of tight hamstrings.

MODIFICATIONS Bend your knees. Place your hands above your knees on your thighs or on a block in front of your feet.

Mountain Pose

If you were to set your sights on mastering any pose, make it Mountain Pose. This aptly titled pose holds the key to the universe of yoga poses, teaching proper alignment of the feet, legs, pelvis, core, shoulders, and spine. Like its namesake, it starts with a wide, strong foundation and rises through your core to lengthen through the top of your head. Once you have mastered the pose, it will bring extraordinary power to your practice.

SETUP Come to standing, with your feet directly underneath your hips, outer edges of your feet parallel to your mat, arms relaxed by your sides.

ALIGNMENT Point your toes straight ahead, and bring the outer edges of your feet parallel with the edges of your mat; this position may make you slightly pigeon-toed. Lift your toes and connect with the four corners of your feet to the mat. Soften your toes back to the floor. • Lift the arches of your feet, and with your feet grounded, press your outer shins out until you feel your legs engage. With your feet grounded, spiral your inner ankles toward the back of your mat. Energetically, drive your outer ankles down to the floor. • Squeeze your thigh muscles to the bone. If your knees have become stiff, soften the joints slightly. • Tilt your tailbone down toward the floor. Gently pull in your belly button to engage your core. Squeeze your front ribs toward each other. • Roll your shoulders up to your ears, then soften them down away from your ears. Pull your upper arm bones toward your shoulder blades to engage your shoulders. • Contract the muscles under your shoulder blades. • Gently pull your belly button in

Mountain Pose, arms extended

to engage your core. Hug your front ribs toward each other. Breathe into your back ribs. • Let your hands relax by your sides, and spin your palms to face forward. • **Alternative arms:** Reach your arms up to the ceiling in line with your shoulders. Spin your palms to face inward with your thumbs toward the back of your mat. Stretch your fingers out wide. • Lift the crown of your head up toward the sky to lengthen your neck. Soften your jaw. • Take ten deep ujjayi breaths.

GAZE & FOCUS Set your eyes on one point in front of you. • Ground your feet and legs, relax your shoulders, and breathe deeply.

VINYASA: BREATH AND MOVEMENT

A flow practice builds heat by connecting breath and poses in your practice. Challenge yourself to breathe according to the sequence of Sun Salutation A and B. Keep your breath steady and rhythmic, and slow your transitions to match your breath. As your body tunes in to the practice, notice what shifts in your experience of the practice.

Sun Salutation A

At this point in Strength Practice I, you have already learned all the poses for a Sun Salutation A. This sequence links poses together with cues and breaths for each pose. It builds heat in your body and is a powerful way to warm up your spine and to focus on the breath and foundational elements of the practice. Repeat the entire sequence three times.

Mountain Pose, inhale with your arms up. • Forward Fold, exhale. • Halfway Lift, inhale. • Plank lowered to floor, exhale. • Low Cobra, inhale. • Downward-Facing Dog, exhale, hold pose for five breaths. • Step or jump forward. • Halfway Lift, inhale. • Forward Fold, exhale. • Mountain Pose, inhale.

Sun Salutation B

Your body has now warmed up with Sun Salutation A. The Sun Salutation B sequence goes deeper into your hip flexors and builds even more internal fire for the next series of standing poses with two new poses: **Chair** and **Warrior 1**, described below. Do three full rounds of Sun Salutation B as follows:

Chair, inhale with your arms up. (First round: hold for five breaths.) • Forward Fold, exhale. • Halfway Lift, inhale. • Plank to floor, exhale. • Low Cobra, inhale. • Downward-Facing Dog, exhale. • Warrior 1, right side, inhale, (First round: hold for five breaths.) • Plank to floor, exhale. • Low Cobra, inhale. • Downward-Facing Dog, exhale. • Warrior 1, left side, inhale. (First round: hold for five breaths.) • Plank to floor, exhale. • Low Cobra, inhale. • Downward-Facing Dog, exhale, hold for five breaths. • Step or jump forward to the front of your mat. • Halfway Lift, inhale. • Forward Fold, exhale.

NEW POSES FOR SUN SALUTATION B

Chair

Contrary to its name, Chair is hardly restful. Without a chair underneath you, you build strength in your legs and your core, with particular strength in hamstrings, quads, glutes, core, and your shoulder girdle. Gravity is your main source of resistance, and this pose may feel challenging. Remember to breathe.

SETUP Stand with your feet together on your mat (ankles and heels may be slightly apart). • Lower your hips toward the floor until you feel your legs engage. • Reach your arms up to the ceiling, parallel to your ears with palms facing toward each other.

ALIGNMENT Keep your toes soft and in view just past your knees. • Spread out your toes. Lift the arches of your feet off the mat and spin your inner ankles toward the back of your mat. • Squeeze your inner thighs toward each other. • Tilt your tailbone toward the floor. Pull your belly in to activate your core. • Lift your chest over your hips and pull your front ribs together. • Soften your shoulders down away from your ears. Engage your back to pull your shoulder blades together. • Straighten your arms, stretch out your palms and spread your fingers wide toward the ceiling.

GAZE & FOCUS Lift your eyes off the floor and look at a spot on the wall in front of you. • Focus on

Chair

strength in your legs and a strong lift in your chest toward the ceiling.

DEEPEN Sink your hips deeper toward the floor. Keep your spine lifted toward the ceiling.

COMMON CHALLENGES Weak quadriceps may pull your knees away from each other. • Tight shoulders prevent you from bringing your arms directly overhead.

MODIFICATIONS Lift the arches of your feet to hug your knees toward each other. • Bend your elbows even with your shoulders at 90-degree angles like a cactus. • Hug your shoulder blades together to engage your shoulders. Squeeze your front ribs in toward each other.

Warrior 1

Warrior poses are intentionally challenging. Warrior 1 is the first you will encounter—it is a foundational pose in Sun Salutation B. The pose opens and strengthens your ankles and your hip flexors. It also builds your hamstring strength.

In addition, your core engagement and shoulder awareness will grow. It is a whole body posture that will challenge you in a new way. While the fundamentals may get easier as you get stronger, you can constantly adjust and refine alignment to challenge yourself.

SETUP From Downward-Facing Dog, step your right foot next to your right thumb. • Spin your left heel and ground it into the mat. • Lift your arms up to the ceiling.

ALIGNMENT Point your back foot out about 60 degrees on your mat, with your toes slightly in front of your back heel. • Press the outer edge of your back foot into the mat to connect all four corners of your foot to the floor. • Align your feet so your heels are in one line. Point your front foot toward the front of your mat. Bend your front knee over your ankle. • Spin the hip of your back leg toward the front of your mat while still grounding your back foot. You will feel an opening in your hip flexor. • Lift your belly button in toward your spine. Squeeze your front ribs toward each other. • Soften your shoulders away from your ears, and squeeze your shoulder blades

Warrior 1

HEALTHY, HAPPY KNEES

A common misalignment in Warrior 2 and Side Angle is to collapse in your front knee. Weak or tight hips and butt muscles more accustomed to softening while sitting rather than engaging while walking or moving can cause your front knee to collapse inward. The collapse puts unhealthy pressure on your knee joint, an area that already needs all the support it can get to stay strong and stable during hikes.

In Warrior 2, squeeze your thigh bones toward your centerline and stack your front knee over your ankle. In Side Angle, the action intensifies. Pull your front thigh bone into your hip socket and squeeze your front outer hip and butt cheek to keep your knee stacked. The alignment will build strength in your glutes, inner thighs, and thigh muscles, and your poses will become strong and stable.

toward your spine. Reach your arms to the ceiling, keeping your arm bones parallel with your ears.
• Stretch out your hands toward the ceiling; spread out your fingers.

GAZE & FOCUS Set your gaze on the wall in front of you. • Squeeze your back leg straight. Hug your core up and in toward your centerline.

DEEPEN Lengthen your stance and bend your front knee to a 90-degree angle.

COMMON CHALLENGES Tight hip flexors and psoas prevent you from bending your front knee to 90 degrees and pull at your lower back. • Tight ankles prevent you from grounding your back foot.
• Knee injury prevents you from keeping your heel grounded on your back foot.

MODIFICATIONS Shorten your stance slightly for both challenges until your ankle and hip flexors become more mobile. • Lift your back heel for a Crescent Lunge modification (see Strength Practice II).

SEQUENCE TRANSITION After you complete three rounds of Sun Salutation B, move through Chair, Forward Fold, Halfway Lift, Plank to the floor, Low Cobra, and Downward-Facing Dog. • Step your right foot to Warrior 1. • Continue into the strength poses below.

STRENGTH

The next series of standing poses build strength and power throughout your body. Twists open your spine and chest, while holding standing poses work the smaller muscles in your joints to create stability. Use drishti to stay focused, and soften your jaw to relax your face.

Warrior 2

Warrior poses rely on your leg strength, and are a good place to explore the balance of effort and ease. Warrior 2 offers great strength, building your quads and hamstrings for the hiking season. It also teaches you to set your gaze, soften your shoulders, and breathe deeply into the challenge.

Warrior 2

SETUP From Warrior 1 on the right side, exhale, turn your chest to face left, and reach your arms toward the front and back of your mat. • Walk your your back foot out toward a 90-degree angle.

ALIGNMENT Point your front foot toward the front of your mat. Stack your front knee over your ankle. (Widen your feet if your knee is bending past the top of your ankle.) • Line your back foot up with the back edge of your mat at roughly 90 degrees, but no wider than that, from your front foot. Lift the inner arch of your back foot off the floor. • Hug your feet toward each other to activate your inner thighs toward your pelvis. • Press your front heel firmly into the mat. • Stack your chest over your hips. Lengthen your tailbone down toward the floor. Lift your belly button in toward your spine. • Release your shoulders away from your ears. Hover your arms parallel to the floor. • From your spine, stretch your fingers to the front and back walls.

GAZE & FOCUS Turn your head toward your front hand and set your gaze on your fingertips.
• Squeeze your thigh bones in toward each other.
• Relax your jaw and eyes. Breathe into the challenge.

DEEPEN Widen your stance and bend your right knee to a 90-degree angle over your front ankle.

COMMON CHALLENGES Weak or tight outer hips and glutes can cause your front knee to collapse inward rather than staying stacked over your front ankle.

MODIFICATIONS Shorten your stance. Keep your knee aligned over your front ankle to build strength and prevent injury.

SEQUENCE TRANSITION From Warrior 2, straighten your front leg.

Triangle

A powerful grounding pose, Triangle relies on the bones of your body to open and strengthen. You'll get into your deeper psoas muscle in your hip; lengthen your hamstrings; and create a long, neutral spine. Triangle pose gives you greater stability against gravity and encourages you to listen to your body more deeply. Challenge yourself by moving your drishti to the ceiling.

SETUP With both legs straight, reach your front hand toward the front of your mat until your torso is parallel to the floor. • Shift your front hip toward the back of your mat. • Place your right hand on your front shin or on a block outside your right foot.
• Reach your upper hand toward the ceiling.

ALIGNMENT Ground the four corners of both feet into the floor. • Pull your front thigh bone up into your hip socket; your back hip will roll slightly forward toward the floor. • Lift the top of your right kneecap to lengthen into your hamstrings. Keep a slight bend in your front knee so you don't lock or hyperextend into the joint. • Hug your shoulders in toward your spine. • Stretch your chest toward the front of your mat; spin your upper ribs toward the ceiling. Stretch out your fingers on your upper hand.

GAZE & FOCUS Look up at the ceiling and set your gaze on one spot. • Press your big toe knuckle of your front foot into the floor. Focus on the stability of your legs and length in your spine.

DEEPEN Widen your stance. Reach your lower hand deeper toward your ankle or the floor.

COMMON CHALLENGES Tight hamstrings or a tight psoas prevent you from reaching your shin. • You overextend in your front knee joint.

MODIFICATIONS Use a block at the tallest height out-side your front foot. If necessary, stack two blocks to

Triangle

get enough height to lengthen your spine. • Soften your front knee joint and lift the muscles above your knee.

SEQUENCE TRANSITION From Triangle, come up to Warrior 2. • Bend your front leg for Side Angle.

Side Angle

If I were permitted to have a favorite pose, it would be this one. One of the most challenging standing poses when done with proper alignment, Side Angle strengthens your glutes and legs, and opens your spine. It will test your limits. Breathe through the challenge.

SETUP Lower your front forearm onto your front thigh. Reach your upper arm up to the ceiling, your palm facing the same direction as your chest.

ALIGNMENT Ground the four corners of both feet into the floor. Squeeze both feet toward the center of your mat. • Stack your front knee over your front ankle. • Pull your front thigh bone into your hip socket until you feel your outer glute engage.

Side Angle

Keep your right hip even with your bent front knee. • Lift the arch of your back foot and squeeze your back inner thigh. • Engage your belly to lighten the weight of your front arm on your thigh. • Pull your shoulder blades toward your spine. Spiral your upper ribs up toward the ceiling. • Spread out your fingers on both hands.

GAZE & FOCUS Set your gaze on your upper fingertips. • Squeeze your front hip and bend your front leg deeper.

DEEPEN Lower your front hand to a block or the floor just inside your front foot. Extend your upper arm in a diagonal line forward.

COMMON CHALLENGES Weak glutes cause your front knee to collapse inward.

MODIFICATIONS Shorten your stance slightly as long as you keep your front knee aligned over your ankle.

SEQUENCE TRANSITION Lift your torso to Warrior 2. • Straighten your front leg. • Spin your front foot parallel with your back foot.

Wide-Legged Forward Fold

Wide-Legged Forward Fold will open different regions of your hamstrings and inner thighs, perhaps in ways you never imagined. When your hamstrings are tight from a hike, you will come to appreciate the extra time you spend in this pose.

SETUP With your feet parallel to each other, widen your heels just outside your toes until the outer edges of your feet are parallel to the mat. Bring your hands to your hips. • On an inhale, lift your chest to the ceiling; on an exhale, fold forward.

ALIGNMENT Bring your hands to the floor under your shoulders. Point your fingers the same direction as your toes. • If your hamstrings and lower back allow, walk your hands back between your feet. • Lift the arches of your feet; squeeze your inner thighs up toward your pelvis. • Pull your chest deeper toward the floor with your hands. • Left side: Interlace your hands at your lower back. Hug your shoulder blades in toward your spine. Straighten your arms, press your hands away from your lower back, and fold forward.

Wide-Legged Forward Fold

COMMON CHALLENGES Tight hamstrings or a tight lower back prevent your hands from reaching the floor.

MODIFICATIONS Use a block under your hands. Bend your knees to give your spine more space.

SEQUENCE TRANSITION Bring your hands to your hips. • Come up to standing. • Turn your right foot to face the front of your mat. • Lower your left knee to the ground

Twisted Crescent Lunge

A deep twist that challenges balance, Twisted Crescent Lunge opens your hip flexors, builds strength in your legs, and supports an opening twist in your spine. The pose builds stability in your lower body and releases your spine, important tools for staying healthy and strong on the trail.

SETUP Stack your front knee over your ankle in a Low Lunge. Bring your palms together in front of your chest. Hook your left elbow over your right

RELEASE Walk your hands back underneath your shoulders.

GAZE & FOCUS Look at a spot on your mat or between your feet. • Squeeze your thigh muscles and shift your weight slightly forward toward your toes.

DEEPEN Straighten your legs. Pull your head toward your mat.

knee. If you need a block, set it near the inside edge of your front foot.

ALIGNMENT Shift your weight forward toward your right foot, keeping your knee pointing forward over your ankle; don't let it cave in or out. • Lift your upper elbow toward the sky; press down into your palms. • Lengthen your spine through the crown of your head to create more space for the twist. • Hug your shoulder blades toward your spine, and deepen your twist. • Pull your belly in toward your spine. • Bring your lower hand to the floor, or a block on the inside edge of your front foot. Stretch your upper fingers out wide and toward the ceiling.

GAZE & FOCUS Set your gaze at a spot on the ceiling. • Squeeze your shoulder blades toward each other. Engage the muscles underneath your shoulder blades to deepen your twist.

DEEPEN Tuck your back toes to the ball of your foot and lift your back leg off the floor for the full pose. Bring your lower hand to the floor or a block outside your front leg.

Twisted Crescent Lunge, modified

COMMON CHALLENGES You will need to develop strength and stability in your legs to hold the full pose. Squeeze your inner thighs for balance.

MODIFICATIONS Keep your back knee on the floor. Pad your knee if you feel pain in your kneecap.

SEQUENCE TRANSITION Bring your hands to the front of your mat and step your feet to the back of your mat for Plank. • Shift forward to your tiptoes and lower to the floor. • Lift your chest for Low Cobra. • Tuck your toes and lift your hips for Downward-Facing Dog. • Step into Warrior 1 on your left foot. Move through the strength poses from Warrior 2 through Twisted Crescent Lunge on your left side. • Step or hop to the front of your mat.

BALANCE
When you lift one foot off the floor, your body must maintain balance in a new way, from your feet to your core to your gaze. The balancing poses ask you to adapt, working functional strength and flexibility that benefits all kinds of movement in your life.

One-Legged Chair

This pose's combination of hip opening and balance will challenge you. Your hips work hard for you on the trail. One-Legged Chair allows the big muscles around your hip joint to gain mobility and also strengthens your standing leg and glute muscles.

SETUP Bring your big toe knuckles to touch, and lower your hips into Chair pose. • Lift your left ankle over your right knee. Flex your left foot toward your knee.

ALIGNMENT Ground your standing foot into your mat. Keep your upper foot flexed. • Lower your hips down toward the floor to strengthen your standing leg. • Hug your shoulder blades in toward your spine. • Reach your arms parallel to your ears. • Hug your belly in to support the pose.

GAZE & FOCUS Look at a spot on the wall in front of you. • Sink your hips lower toward the floor. Focus on balance.

One-Legged Chair

DEEPEN Stick your glutes out toward the back wall. Lower your chest to your upper shin, and extend your arms forward and parallel to the floor to stretch more deeply into your hip.

COMMON CHALLENGES Tight hips make it challenging to sit deeply into the pose.

MODIFICATIONS Sit as low as your body will allow.

SEQUENCE TRANSITION Do the left side for One-Legged Chair. • Lower your upper foot to the ground. • Switch to the right leg. • Lower your right foot to the ground into Mountain Pose.

Tree

Tree pose embodies the art of balancing. Your standing foot spreads wide and stretches into the earth. Your standing leg is straight and strong. When you hug into your core, you can extend your arms and energy up and out. Let go of the worry that you might step out of the pose. Instead, shift your gaze skyward and see what is possible.

Tree

SETUP Stand with your feet together in Mountain Pose. Lift your right foot to either your inner calf or above your knee joint to your inner thigh. Bring your palms together at the center of your chest.

ALIGNMENT Ground the four corners of your standing foot into your mat. • Press your lifted foot into your standing leg. • Hug your shoulder blades to your spine. Press your palms together. • Pull your belly in toward your spine; lift your lower ribs away from your pelvis. • Lift your hands to the ceiling, palms facing in.

GAZE & FOCUS Set your gaze on a spot in front of you. Once you are stable, move your gaze up the wall to the ceiling. • Ground your standing leg and stretch your spine skyward.

DEEPEN Walk your gaze up to the ceiling behind you.

COMMON CHALLENGES You are still building strength in your feet and have trouble staying upright with only one foot on the floor.

MODIFICATIONS Prop the foot of your bent leg against the ankle of your standing foot with the ball of your foot on the floor.

SEQUENCE TRANSITION Release into Mountain Pose. • Do Tree on your other leg. • From Mountain Pose, reach your arms to the ceiling. • Fold your chest to your feet. • Lift your torso to Halfway Lift. • Plant your hands for Plank. • Shift forward and lower to the floor. • Lift your chest to Low Cobra. • Tuck your toes and come to Downward-Facing Dog.

OPEN YOUR SPINE AND HIPS

Your spine and hips take the brunt of the work when climbing or descending on the trail. Your spine and core stabilize your upper body, and your hips transfer weight down to your lower body. Your hips in particular will appreciate the release after a long mileage day.

Low Lunge

A modified Crescent Lunge, Low Lunge minimizes the factors of balance and strength. Our hip flexors shorten from sitting all day, and are in constant use on hikes. Use this lunge to give your hip flexors some space.

SETUP From Downward-Facing Dog, step your right foot between your hands. Lower your back knee to the floor and keep your back toes tucked. • Bring your hands to your front thigh.

ALIGNMENT Square your hips toward the front of your mat. Pull your front foot and back knee toward each other to integrate. Your hips will lift slightly higher than before. • Once your centerline is established, slowly shift your weight forward toward your front foot. Stack your front knee over your ankle. • Squeeze your belly in toward your spine and hug your front ribs together. • Reach your arms up toward the ceiling, palms facing in. Breathe deeply into the stretch in your hip flexor.

GAZE & FOCUS Look at a spot on the wall in front of you. • Hug your inner thighs toward each other to keep your body strong while opening into your hip.

Low Lunge

DEEPEN Point your back toes and bring the top of your foot to the floor. Press into the top of your toes and foot. Lift your back knee off the floor. Squeeze your inner thighs toward your pelvis.

Half Splits

Your only choice in this pose may be mindfulness! Half Splits is a deep stretch into your hamstrings and good practice to release mindfully by engaging your thighs and breathing. This pose will support your awareness of the effects hiking has on your body and areas of tightness that you can slowly soften.

SETUP From Low Lunge, straighten your front leg and flex your front foot toward your knee. Stack your hips over your back knee. • Slide your front foot forward slightly.

ALIGNMENT Bring your hands down on either side of your front leg. • Lift the muscles above your front knee to engage your thighs to open your hamstrings; do not force the stretch. • Spiral your inner thighs

toward each other and down toward the floor.
• Lengthen your chest toward your front foot.
• Anchor your belly up and in toward your mid-back.

RELEASE Shift your weight forward to Low Lunge.

GAZE & FOCUS Look at your front toes. • Squeeze
your quads to open deep into your hamstrings.

DEEPEN Tuck your back toes and carefully move
into full splits, inching your back leg out and your
front leg forward. Hug your thigh bones in toward
your pelvis to stay stable in your centerline. • Keep
your hips square to the front of your mat. • Bring a
block under your pelvis to support the full pose.

COMMON CHALLENGES Tightness in your hamstrings
or lower back prevents you from bringing your
hands to the floor.

MODIFICATIONS Place a block on either side of your
legs to use for stability as you lengthen your spine
in the pose.

Half Splits

SEQUENCE TRANSITION Do Low Lunge to Half Splits
on your right leg. • Return to Downward-Facing
Dog. • Repeat on the left leg. • Plant your hands on
your mat and step backward to Plank. • Lift your
hips to Downward-Facing Dog. • Bring your knees
to the front of the mat. • Shift onto your sit bones.
• Roll down onto your back, with your arms at
your sides.

Bridge

Despite the temptation to rest on your back, it's not time yet! Bridge is a modification for Wheel, which you will learn in Strength Practice II, but more importantly, this backbend teaches you to use your legs and to open your chest by integrating and opening your spine and shoulders.

SETUP Walk your feet closer to your body until your fingertips brush your heels. Set your feet parallel and hip-width distance. • Press into the four corners of your feet to lift your hips to the ceiling. • Move your shoulders together and interlace your hands underneath your body.

ALIGNMENT Press your feet into your mat until your legs engage. • Stack your knees over your ankles. • Spin your inner thighs toward each other and down toward your mat. • Position your hands at your spine just above the tailbone. Feel the ridge of muscles around your spine engage. Lift your spine until you feel the engagement between your shoulder blades. • Lift your chest toward the back wall. • Squeeze your front ribs together.

Bridge

RELEASE Reach your arms up to the ceiling. Slowly release your spine toward the floor, one vertebrae at a time.

GAZE & FOCUS Look at a spot on the ceiling. • Press deeply into your feet for strong legs.

DEEPEN Lift your right knee into your chest. Press strongly into your rooted foot. • Extend your right leg, foot flexed, to the ceiling, keeping your hips level. Switch sides.

TAMI ASARS
Author, *Hiking the Wonderland Trail* and *Day Hiking: Mount Adams and Goat Rocks*
North Bend, Washington

Q: Why did you start doing yoga?
A: I was doing a lot of hiking and backpacking and doing long days, 20- to 30-mile days. Just the way my body, especially my knees and hips, was aligning, was causing a lot of pain. I thought if I did more stretching, it would help.

Q: What's changed in your body since you started?
A: One of the things I found was that when I climbed [a trail], my knee was tending to go inward. Doing Warrior pose, you pull your knee back out more. I realized on the trails, if I pushed my knee back out more than letting it naturally flop in, I was able to feel better. I didn't have as much exhaustion.

Q: Has yoga affected your hiking?
A: Carrying a heavy pack long distances, my back would bother me in the morning. Now I hop into the tent and do a couple of Downward Dogs. The other thing is focusing on breathing through the pain. Sometimes that gets you on the hills when you're bonking or not feeling well, you realize you're not listening to your body and just powering through it. Yoga does get you to be aware of your breath and aware of your body so much more.

Q: What poses speak to you the most?
A: The Warriors. When I hike uphill and downhill, my calf muscles are always tight. Stretching my calves, strengthening my quads, and focusing on alignment helps me stay focused during the day. I do them on my sleeping pad before I get going in the morning. Often by myself, I find a little spot and work it out. It's a nice peaceful thing to do, especially when I'm tired.

COMMON CHALLENGES Tight shoulders prevent you from interlacing your hands.

MODIFICATIONS Use a strap between your hands for a bind. Or press your palms into the floor.

SEQUENCE TRANSITION Do Bridge twice for five breaths each. • Lower your hips to the floor for Reclined Half Pigeon.

Reclined Half Pigeon

Reclined Half Pigeon is a supportive way to open your muscular hip region. Hip opening can be an intense experience—there is no need to force the opening, but rather surrender into it. Breathe deeply and move gently to deepen into the pose.

SETUP Bring your feet flat to the floor. Cross your right ankle over your left knee. Keep your right foot flexed toward your knee to protect your knee joint. • Reach your right hand between your legs and your left hand behind your left thigh to support it.

Reclined Half Pigeon

ALIGNMENT Pull your left leg toward you to get a deep stretch in your outer right hip. • Relax your shoulders toward the floor. Pull your left leg even closer toward you. • Breathe deeply for ten breaths.

GAZE & FOCUS Close your eyes or look at a spot on the ceiling. • Notice the sensations in your hip and breathe into it to release the muscles.

DEEPEN Straighten your free leg up to the ceiling and press through your heel.

COMMON CHALLENGES Tight hips prevent you from holding the back of your leg.

MODIFICATIONS Take a strap around the back of your left leg, and pull your leg toward your chest.

SEQUENCE TRANSITION Repeat Reclined Half Pigeon on your left side. • Pull your knees into your chest. • Rock yourself up to a seated position.

RECOVER AND RESTORE

The end of a practice gives your body time to soften and relax. Throughout these final poses, notice how your body sensations and your mental state have shifted through the practice.

Seated Forward Fold

Gravity comes into play in all forward folds as you pull your torso toward your legs. In a Seated Forward Fold, you also stretch your calves, hamstrings, glutes, and the muscles along your spine—a stretch that feels exceptionally good after many hours of hiking.

Seated Forward Fold

SETUP From your seated position, extend your legs straight to the front of your mat. Reach your hands toward the outer edges of your feet.

ALIGNMENT Flex your toes toward your knees. • Squeeze your quads. • Pull your chest toward your feet. • Relax your head.

GAZE & FOCUS Look at your toes as you fold. • Lower your gaze to your shins to lengthen your neck as you relax into the pose. • Lengthen your chest toward your feet. • Extend from your lower spine.

DEEPEN Press the backs of your knees toward the floor without overextending the joint, and squeeze your quads. • If your hands reach past your feet, use a block at the soles of your feet to give you more room to deepen.

COMMON CHALLENGES A tight lower back, hamstrings, or hip flexors can tend to contract and prevent your torso from folding forward.

MODIFICATIONS Place a block or blanket underneath your sit bones to relax your hips and core for the forward fold. • Alternatively, bend your knees to reach for your feet, or use a strap to lengthen your reach to your feet to allow your hip flexors and core to relax.

Seated Twist

Final twists, such as this Seated Twist, release the spine after the intensity of a practice, plus they support mobility in your lower back.

SETUP From Seated Forward Fold, extend your left leg straight to the front of your mat, toes flexed. • Place your right foot on the floor outside your left thigh. • Place your right hand on the floor behind you. • Reach your left arm up to the ceiling. Wrap your left arm around your bent leg.

ALIGNMENT Lengthen your spine on your inhale. • Twist toward your bent leg on your exhale.

GAZE & FOCUS Move your gaze past your right shoulder. • Inhale to lengthen your spine and exhale to deepen your twist.

DEEPEN Hook your left elbow outside your right leg. Cross your lower leg underneath you.

SEQUENCE TRANSITION Repeat the twist on the left side. • Bring your feet to the floor and lower down to your back.

Legs Up the Wall

Inversions allow gravity to lighten the load your heart usually takes on to pull blood up from your legs. Legs Up the Wall lets gravity do the work and is a restorative pose. Feel free to take the name of this pose literally by moving to a wall—or practice it on your mat.

SETUP Walk your feet in and lift your hips like you are going to Bridge pose. Position a block at its lowest height underneath your sacrum. • Set your hips down, adjusting the block to find a comfortable resting point. • Lift your legs to the ceiling.

ALIGNMENT Flex your toes toward your knees.
• Relax your shoulders, face, and hands.

GAZE & FOCUS Set your drishti on your feet.
• Breathe deeply and relax. Keep your legs still.

DEEPEN Choose a more active inversion with Shoulder Stand (see Strength Practice II).

COMMON CHALLENGES Tight hamstrings make it uncomfortable or difficult to keep your legs vertical.

MODIFICATIONS Loop a strap over the soles of your feet. Flex your feet. Hold onto the ends of the strap. Bring your elbows to the floor.

SEQUENCE TRANSITION Bring your feet back to the floor. • Lift your hips and move the block aside.

Legs Up the Wall

FINAL REST

Some people, especially active folks, can find stillness uncomfortable. Let go of your fidgety side. Take on Final Rest, and be soft and still.

Corpse Pose

Corpse Pose will either be the best pose you have ever tried, or the worst! Commit to closing your eyes and being quiet. If you are cold, cover yourself with a blanket.

Corpse Pose

SETUP From your back, straighten your legs on your mat. • With your arms at your sides, turn your palms to face the sky.

ALIGNMENT Slide your shoulders under you. • Relax the muscles in your legs, shoulders, and face. • Move into your natural breath. • Stay in this pose for three minutes.

GAZE & FOCUS Close your eyes. • Stay awake and still. Notice your natural breath.

DEEPEN Take a five-minute final rest.

STRENGTH PRACTICE II
TIME: 45 MINUTES
EQUIPMENT: YOGA MAT, BLOCK, AND STRAP

This 45-minute strength sequence builds off the first, adding on more challenge in the early Sun Salutation A and B plus new and added challenge during the standing poses. Once you are

SEQUENCE FOR STRENGTH PRACTICE II

- » Supine Butterfly
- » Reclined Half Pigeon
- » Happy Baby
- » Yogi Bicycle
- » Boat
- » Plank
- » Downward-Facing Dog
- » Halfway Lift
- » Sun Salutation A
- » Sun Salutation B
- » Warrior 2
- » Triangle
- » Side Angle with a Half Bind
- » Wide-Legged Forward Fold
- » Skandasana
- » Crescent Lunge
- » Twisted Crescent Lunge
- » Side Plank
- » Dolphin
- » Hand-to-Big-Toe Forward Fold
- » Gorilla
- » Eagle
- » Hand-to-Knee Balancing Pose
- » Airplane
- » Pyramid
- » Revolved Triangle
- » Half Moon
- » Crow
- » Flip Dog
- » Bow
- » Bridge
- » Wheel
- » Lizard
- » Half Pigeon
- » Seated Forward Fold
- » Head-to-Knee Seated Forward Fold
- » Reverse Tabletop
- » Shoulder Stand
- » Ear Pressure Pose
- » Fish
- » Supine Twist
- » Corpse Pose

comfortable with Strength Practice I, dive in. Or, if you are ready for a challenge, take on this practice now! All poses should be held for five breaths unless otherwise noted.

RELEASE AND ACTIVATE

Lying on your back sends a signal to your brain to relax. Let go of any tension in your body at the beginning of your practice. Bring in your ujjayi breath before you start.

Supine Butterfly

As you learned in Strength Practice I, Supine Butterfly activates your hips and sends a signal to your brain that all is well.

SETUP Lay down with your back on your mat.
• Bring the soles of your feet together so your legs form a diamond shape.

ALIGNMENT Let your arms relax on the floor, palms facing up. • Notice the connection of your spine to the floor and the natural curve of your lumbar spine at your lower back. • Hug your belly up and in toward your spine to activate your core. • Bring in your ujjayi breath.

GAZE & FOCUS Close your eyes. • Bring your attention to your spine on the floor and an active core.

COMMON CHALLENGES Tight hips or lower back pain prevents your knees from releasing toward the floor.

MODIFICATIONS Bring your feet as wide as your mat and rest your knees together to bring your lower back to the mat.

Supine Butterfly

Reclined Half Pigeon

Be gentle opening into your hips at the beginning of this practice. Use this time to notice any tension that has built up from hiking.

SETUP Bring your feet flat to the floor. • Cross your left ankle over your right knee. Keep your left foot flexed toward your knee to protect your knee joint.

Reclined Half Pigeon

DEEPEN Straighten your free leg up to the ceiling and press through your heel.

COMMON CHALLENGES Tight hips prevent you from holding the back of your leg.

MODIFICATIONS Take a strap around the back of your right leg, and pull your leg toward your chest.

SEQUENCE TRANSITION Repeat Reclined Pigeon on your right side. • Pull your knees into your chest.

Happy Baby

Open your hips and lengthen your spine and relax. Experiment too by switching your hands between the inner and outer arches of your feet.

SETUP Take your knees wide outside your chest. Reach inside your legs for the inner arches of your feet and lift your feet toward the ceiling.

ALIGNMENT Take your knees wide outside your chest. • Flex your feet toward your knees. Bend your knees at 90 degrees. Press your heels toward

• Reach your left hand between your legs and your right hand behind your right thigh to support it.

ALIGNMENT Pull your right leg toward you to get a deep stretch in your outer left hip. • Relax your shoulders toward the floor. Pull your right leg even closer toward you. • Breathe deeply for ten breaths.

GAZE & FOCUS Close your eyes or look at a spot on the ceiling. • Notice the sensations in your hip and breathe into it to release the muscles.

Happy Baby

the ceiling. • Relax your shoulders. • Lengthen your lower back toward the floor while pulling on your feet with your hands. Press your feet into your hands.

GAZE & FOCUS Look at a spot on the ceiling.
• Lengthen your spine to the mat.

DEEPEN Switch your grip on your feet to the outside arch of your foot. • Pull your knees deeper down outside your ribs.

COMMON CHALLENGES Tight hips or a tight lower back prevent you from reaching your feet.

MODIFICATIONS Hold the backs of your thighs instead of your feet. • Open your knees wider than your chest. • Place a block under your head.

Yogi Bicycle

It never hurts to wake up your core early in your practice. Yogi Bicycle works your obliques on either side of your trunk, and the lift in the middle strengthens your lower abdominals. It also builds heat to warm up your muscles for the work ahead.

SETUP From Happy Baby, stay on your back, stacking your knees over your hips. • Bring your shins parallel to the floor. Flex your toes toward your knees.

ALIGNMENT Interlace your fingers and cup your palms behind your head. Lift your chin away from your chest. • On an inhale, lift your shoulder blades off the floor. • Exhale and twist your right elbow to your left knee; extend your right leg straight.

Yogi Bicycle

• Come back to center. • Inhale and lift your shoulders and your hips to the ceiling. • Exhale and twist your left elbow to your right knee; extend your left leg straight. • Repeat for twenty full rounds per side, for a total of forty.

GAZE & FOCUS Look at your extended foot, switching sides with each movement. • Keep your knees stacked over your hips rather than pulling your knee toward your chest. You want to work your core, not your hip flexors. • Lift your elbow and shoulder toward your knee.

DEEPEN Lift your shoulders higher off the floor.

Boat

Boat accesses deep core muscles that stabilize you even when you don't know it. Challenge yourself in this sequence by taking on additional Low Boats, see variation below.

SETUP From Yogi Bicycle, pull your knees into your chest and with momentum, rock up to a seated position. • Hold the backs of your thighs, and balance between your sit bones at the base of your pelvis and your tailbone. • Lift your feet off the floor.

ALIGNMENT Pull your thighs toward your chest. Hold your shins parallel to the floor. • Squeeze your thighs toward each other. Spread out your toes so you see a gap between each one. • Pull your shoulder blades toward each other. Lift your chest toward the ceiling. • Reach your arms straight in front of you. • Stay for ten breaths.

LOW BOAT VARIATION Every other time, lower your torso until your lower back connects to the floor,

Boat

Once your hamstrings allow it, straighten your legs at a 45-degree angle away from the floor.

COMMON CHALLENGES Lower back weakness prevents you from lifting your chest.

MODIFICATIONS Hold the back of your thighs.

SEQUENCE TRANSITION Bring your feet to the floor from Boat. • Squeeze your knees and lift your chest to stretch your abdominal muscles • Roll over your feet and come to your hands and knees for Plank.

Plank

Add some heat to your Plank pose with variations to fire up your abdominal and back muscles.

SETUP Stack your hands underneath your shoulders, index finger pointed straight ahead. Step your feet to the back of your mat. Stay on the balls of your feet, lift your knees off the floor and squeeze your legs straight.

your shoulders stay off the floor, and your legs hover off the mat straight ahead. • Squeeze your thighs together. • Look at your toes. • Use your core and lift back to Boat. • Repeat this cycle five times, holding each variation for five breaths.

GAZE & FOCUS Set your gaze on your toes.
• Concentrate on lifting your chest and lengthening your spine.

ALIGNMENT Keep your hips just below level with your shoulders. Tilt your tailbone toward your heels. • Spiral your inner thighs up to the ceiling. Squeeze your thighs. • Lift your head so your neck is level with your shoulders. • Press your palms firmly into the floor. Squeeze your upper arm bones toward each other. • Spin the inner eye of your elbows forward, and pull your shoulder blades together. • Lift your belly in toward your spine and wrap your front ribs together. • Stay for ten breaths.

Plank

GAZE & FOCUS Set your gaze past the front of your mat. • Keep your legs and core firm. Breathe deeply to maintain the pose.

DEEPEN **Plank Variation I:** Lift your right foot off the floor three inches, toes flexed. Squeeze your leg muscles, especially in your left leg. Hold for five breaths. Switch legs. • **Plank Variation II:** Bring your right knee to your chest. Keep your hips level with your shoulders and lift your gaze forward. Step your right foot back. Bring your left knee to your chest. Keep your head lifted. Hug your knee to your chest. Do both sides three times.

COMMON CHALLENGES Building strength to hold the full pose for ten breaths can take some practice.

MODIFICATIONS Bring your knees to the floor, toes curled under. Keep your hips in one line with your shoulders.

SEQUENCE TRANSITION From Plank, lift your hips to the ceiling for Downward-Facing Dog.

Downward-Facing Dog

Add hip opening to your Downward-Facing Dog by mixing in a Three-Legged Dog pose. Adding a leg lift and rotation stretches dynamically into your hip.

Downward-Facing Dog

SETUP Keep your hands at shoulder-width distance. Lift your hips up to the ceiling.

ALIGNMENT Point your index fingers to the front of your mat. • Flatten your palms until the knuckles at the base of your index and middle fingers are grounded on your mat. • Move your feet to hip-width distance. Spin your inner ankles back so the outer edges of your feet are parallel with the edge of your mat. • Bend your knees and lift your tail-bone toward the ceiling until your spine lengthens. Spin your sit bones to the wall behind you. • Roll your shoulders up to your ears, then use your back muscles to pull your shoulders down your back and in toward your spine. Squeeze your upper arms toward each other. • Press your chest toward your thighs; keep your shoulders engaged and do not hyperextend in your shoulders if you are extra flexible. • Drive your heels toward the floor (they don't need to touch the floor). • Pull your belly in toward your spine. • Lift the muscles just above your knees to engage your thighs and open into your hamstrings. • Create a long line from your wrists to your shoulders and hips; bend your knees as you need to.

GAZE & FOCUS Look backward at the floor between your big toes. • Lift your tailbone high toward the ceiling.

DEEPEN Once the pose feels more comfortable, press your heels deeply toward the mat until your toes can spread and soften.

COMMON CHALLENGES Tight hamstrings can lead to a rounded spine. • If you have a wrist injury, it may be painful to stay on your hands.

MODIFICATIONS For tight hamstrings, bend your knees and lift your tailbone toward the ceiling. Pull your shoulders toward your spine. Press your chest toward your legs. • For wrist pain, come down to your elbows for Dolphin pose: Bend your elbows so they are stacked directly under your shoulders. Walk your feet in toward your elbows as close as you can. Lift your tailbone to the sky.

THREE-LEGGED DOG VARIATION From Downward-Facing Dog, bring your feet together. Lift up your right leg and stretch it toward the wall behind you. • Bend your knee and roll your right hip on top of your left. • Lift your right knee up to the ceiling. • Keep your left shoulder level with your right. • Set your gaze on your back foot. • Stay for five breaths. Switch legs.

GAZE & FOCUS Set your gaze on the back of your mat. • Lift your upper knee another three inches toward the ceiling. Keep your shoulders squared to the floor.

SEQUENCE TRANSITION Do Three-Legged Dog on the right side. • Repeat on the left side. • Lower your upper leg to the floor. • Step or hop to the front of your mat. • Bring your feet together.

Halfway Lift

An inhale moves you into an extension of your spine in Halfway Lift pose. Lead with your breath to create more space between your vertebrae.

SETUP Bring your hands to your shins. Lift your chest parallel to the floor. Squeeze your shoulder blades to your spine. Hug your belly muscles in toward your back, and lift your chest parallel to the floor.

ALIGNMENT Root your feet firmly into the floor. Bend your knees as needed and squeeze your thighs.

Halfway Lift

• Stick your butt out toward the wall behind you. Lift your chest even with your hips. • Lengthen the crown of your head away from your tailbone. • Hug your shoulder blades to your spine to activate your centerline. Pull your belly up and in.

RELEASE Fold forward to your feet and exhale.

GAZE & FOCUS Look at a spot on the floor in front of your toes. • Create extension in your spine and wrap your shoulder blades toward your spine. Engage your core.

DEEPEN Place your fingers or hands flat on the floor outside your feet.

COMMON CHALLENGES Your back rounds because of tight hamstrings.

MODIFICATIONS Bend your knees. Place your hands above your knees on your thighs or on a block in front of your feet.

VINYASA: BREATH AND MOVEMENT

The following flow practice intensifies with the addition of Chaturanga and Upward-Facing Dog. Challenge yourself to continue breathing according to the sequences to build strength, heat, and lung capacity.

Sun Salutation A

You will follow roughly the same sequence for Sun Salutation A as you did in Strength Practice I, with the addition of two new poses: **Chaturanga** and **Upward-Facing Dog**, described below. Do the following sequence three times.

Mountain Pose, inhale with your arms up. • Forward Fold, exhale. • Halfway Lift, inhale. • Chaturanga, exhale. • Upward-Facing Dog, inhale. • Downward-Facing Dog, stay for five breaths. • Step or jump to the front of your mat. • Halfway Lift, inhale. • Forward Fold, exhale. • Mountain Pose, inhale with your arms up.

NEW POSES FOR SUN SALUTATION A

Chaturanga (Low Plank)

A low plank, as Chaturanga is sometimes called, is a step up from the strength needed to lower with control to the floor in Strength Practice I. Chaturanga strengthens your legs, torso, arms, and wrists, and yet it's one pose where many people overrely on shoulder ligaments rather than their big trunk muscles for strength. Learn to integrate your shoulders into your spine through Mountain Pose to develop a strong, powerful Chaturanga.

SETUP From Plank, the fourth pose in Sun Salutation A, shift your weight forward until you're on the tops of your toes. • Lower your body in a strong plank, your core strong and active, until your shoulders are even with your elbows.

ALIGNMENT Squeeze your thigh muscles to the bone. • Pull your shoulder blades toward your spine to keep your chest open. • Engage your core as you lower. • Tilt your tailbone toward your heels to

Chaturanga (Low Plank)

engage your front ribs and core muscles. • Point your elbows to the back of your mat, keeping them about two inches or so away from your ribs and stacked directly over your wrists. • Ensure your shoulders are even with your elbows at a 90-degree angle or higher than your elbows. • Practice lowering from Plank into Chaturanga with a one-breath exhale.

GAZE & FOCUS Look past the front edge of your mat to keep your head in line with your spine. • Squeeze your shoulder blades toward your spine, and focus on using your back and belly muscles to hold.

DEEPEN Hold Chaturanga for five breaths.

COMMON CHALLENGES Weakness in core and shoulders leads to shoulders rolling forward toward your mat or dropping below a 90-degree angle.

MODIFICATIONS Bring your knees to the floor. Keep your hips in one diagonal line with your shoulders and lower to a 90-degree bend in your elbows. If you need further modification, lower to the floor.

Upward-Facing Dog

A backbend that develops strength in your back and shoulders, energizes your spine, and opens your chest, Upward-Facing Dog is a strong, fiery pose. Low Cobra, practiced in Strength Practice I, builds your strength for Upward-Facing Dog.

SETUP From Chaturanga, roll onto the tops of your feet. Pull your chest forward and up to the ceiling and straighten your arms. Stack your shoulders over your wrists.

ALIGNMENT Press the tops of your toes into your mat. • Lift your knees off the floor and press the pinky toe edge of your feet into the floor; squeeze your thighs. • Press all the knuckles of your hands firmly into the floor to lift your chest higher to the ceiling. • Roll your shoulder blades toward each other. • Lift your belly in toward your spine.
• Lengthen the top of your head toward the ceiling.

GAZE & FOCUS Keep your gaze level with your head and look at a spot on the wall in front of you. • The only contact points with the floor are your hands and feet. Press firmly into your foundation and lift your chest so your shoulder blades squeeze in toward your spine.

DEEPEN Lift your gaze toward the ceiling.

COMMON CHALLENGES Lower back pain can prevent you from executing the pose.

Upward-Facing Dog

MODIFICATIONS Substitute with Low Cobra (see Strength Practice I).

Sun Salutation B

In this round, you continue with the new poses you learned in Sun Salutation A—Chaturanga and Upward-Facing Dog—plus you will build ankle stability by adding an ankle balance in Chair pose. Do three full rounds of Sun Salutation B.

Chair, inhale with your arms up. (First round: hold for five breaths. Second round: Add Ankle Balance Variation.) • Forward Fold, exhale. • Halfway Lift, inhale. • Chaturanga, exhale. • Upward-Facing Dog, inhale. • Downward-Facing Dog, exhale. • Warrior 1, right side, inhale. (First round: hold for five breaths. • Chaturanga, exhale • Upward-Facing Dog, inhale. • Downward-Facing Dog, exhale. • Warrior 1, Left side, inhale. (First round: hold for five breaths.) • Chaturanga, exhale. • Upward-Facing Dog, inhale. • Downward-Facing Dog, exhale, stay for five breaths. • Step or jump forward. • Halfway Lift, inhale. • Forward Fold, exhale.

NEW POSES FOR SUN SALUTATION B

Chair

Adding on a foot and ankle balance challenge builds stability in your ankles, essential even when you wear supportive boots on the trail.

SETUP Stand with your feet together on your mat. Lower your hips toward the floor until you feel your legs engage. • Reach your arms to the ceiling, parallel to your ears with palms facing toward each other.

ALIGNMENT Keep your toes soft and in view just past your knees. • Spread out your toes. Lift the arches of your feet off the mat and spin your inner ankles toward the back of your mat. • Squeeze your inner thighs toward each other. • Tilt your tailbone toward the floor. Pull your belly in to activate your core. • Lift your chest over your hips and pull your front ribs together. • Soften your shoulders down away from your ears. Engage your back to pull your shoulder blades together. • Straighten your arms, stretch out your palms, and spread your fingers wide toward the ceiling.

GAZE & FOCUS Lift your eyes off the floor and look at a spot on the wall in front of you. • Focus on strength in your legs and a strong lift in your chest toward the ceiling.

DEEPEN Sink your hips deeper toward the floor. Keep your spine lifted toward the ceiling.

ANKLE BALANCE VARIATION Interlace your hands overhead, palms pressing away from your head. • Come up on the balls of your feet, lifting your heels as high as you can. • Hug your inner ankles together. • Stay soft in your face and your shoulders. • Look at a spot on the wall in front of you. • Balance for five breaths.

COMMON CHALLENGES Weak quadriceps may pull your knees away from each other. • Tight shoulders prevent you from bringing your arms directly overhead.

MODIFICATIONS Lift the arches of your feet to hug your knees toward each other. • Bend your elbows even with your shoulders at 90-degree angles like a cactus. Hug your shoulder blades together to engage your shoulders. Squeeze your front ribs in toward each other.

Chair

Warrior 1

A foundational pose in Sun Salutation B, Warrior 1 opens and strengthens your ankles and hip flexors and builds your hamstring strength.

SETUP From Downward-Facing Dog, step your right foot next to your right thumb. • Spin your left heel and ground it into the mat. • Lift your arms up to the ceiling.

ALIGNMENT Point your back foot out about 60 degrees on your mat, with your toes slightly in front of your back heel. • Press the outer edge of your back foot into the mat to connect all four corners of your foot to the floor. • Align your feet so your heels are in one line. Point your front foot toward the front of your mat. Bend your front knee over your ankle. • Spin the hip of your back leg toward the front of your mat while still grounding your back foot. You will feel an opening in your hip flexor. • Lift your belly button in toward your spine. Squeeze your front ribs toward each other. • Soften your shoulders away from your ears, and squeeze your shoulder blades toward your spine. Reach your

Warrior 1

arms to the ceiling, keeping your arm bones parallel with your ears. • Stretch out your hands toward the ceiling; spread out your fingers.

GAZE & FOCUS Set your gaze on the wall in front of you. • Squeeze your back leg straight. Hug your core up and in toward your centerline.

DEEPEN Lengthen your stance and bend your front knee to a 90-degree angle.

COMMON CHALLENGES Tight hip flexors and psoas prevent you from bending your front knee to 90 degrees and pull at your lower back. • Tight ankles prevent you from grounding your back foot.
• Knee injury prevents you from keeping your heel grounded on your back foot.

MODIFICATIONS Shorten your stance slightly for both challenges until your ankle and hip flexors become more mobile. • Lift your back heel for a Crescent Lunge modification (see Strength Practice II).

SEQUENCE TRANSITION After you complete three rounds of Sun Salutation B, move through Chair,

Forward Fold, Halfway Lift, Chaturanga, Upward-Facing Dog, to Downward-Facing Dog. • Step your right foot to Warrior 1. • Continue into the Strength poses below.

STRENGTH

Create more stability in your lower body by adding on new, challenging standing poses in this section of the practice.

Warrior 2

Widen your stance and bend your front knee deeper to challenge yourself in your evolving Warrior 2. Practice bringing ease into your face and your experience of the pose, and imagine a relaxed mental state in all situations, even when confronted with a downpour or the toughest stretch of the trail.

SETUP From Warrior 1 on your right side, exhale, turn your chest to face left, and reach your arms toward the front and back of your mat. • Walk your back foot out toward a 90-degree angle.

Warrior 2

feet toward each other to activate your inner thighs toward your pelvis. • Press your front heel firmly into the mat. • Stack your chest over your hips. Lengthen your tailbone down toward the floor. Lift your belly button in toward your spine. • Release your shoulders away from your ears. Hover your arms parallel to the floor. • From your spine, stretch your fingers to the front and back walls.

GAZE & FOCUS Turn your head toward your front hand and set your gaze on your fingertips.
• Squeeze your thigh bones in toward each other. Relax your jaw and eyes. Breathe into the challenge.

DEEPEN Widen your stance and bend your right knee to a 90-degree angle over your front ankle.

COMMON CHALLENGES Weak or tight outer hips and glutes can cause your front knee to collapse inward rather than staying stacked over your front ankle.

MODIFICATIONS Shorten your stance. Keep your knee aligned over your front ankle to build strength and prevent injury.

ALIGNMENT Point your front foot toward the front of your mat. Stack your front knee over your ankle. (Widen your feet if your knee is bending past the top of your ankle.) • Line your back foot up with the back edge of your mat at roughly 90 degrees, but no wider than that, from your front foot. Lift the inner arch of your back foot off the floor. • Hug your

SEQUENCE TRANSITION From Warrior 2, straighten your front leg.

Triangle

A pose to ground you, Triangle relies on your bone structure rather than muscle strength to bring attention to your hamstrings, hips, and spine. Challenge your stability and see what is possible in the pose with a longer stance.

SETUP With both legs straight, reach your front hand toward the front of your mat until your torso is parallel to the floor. Shift your front hip toward the back of your mat. Place your right hand on your front shin or on a block outside your right foot.
• Reach your upper hand toward the ceiling.

ALIGNMENT Ground the four corners of both feet into the floor. • Pull your front thigh bone up into your hip socket; your back hip will roll slightly forward toward the floor. • Lift the top of your right kneecap to lengthen into your hamstrings. Keep a slight bend in your front knee so you don't lock or

Triangle

hyperextend into the joint. • Hug your shoulders in toward your spine. • Stretch your chest toward the front of your mat; spin your upper ribs toward the ceiling. Stretch out your fingers on your upper hand.

GAZE & FOCUS Look up at the ceiling and set your gaze on one spot. • Press your big toe knuckle of your front foot into the floor. Focus on the stability of your legs and length in your spine.

DEEPEN Widen your stance. Reach your lower hand deeper toward your ankle or the floor.

COMMON CHALLENGES Tight hamstrings or a tight psoas prevent you from reaching your shin. • You overextend in your front knee joint.

MODIFICATIONS Use a block at the tallest heightoutside your front foot. If necessary, stack two blocks to get enough height to lengthen your spine.
• Soften your front knee joint and lift the muscles above your knee.

Side Angle with a Half Bind

To counter your shoulders locking up from carrying a pack—while giving you something to focus on other than your legs—add some shoulder opening to your Side Angle. Challenge yourself with a half bind, and release tightness in your neck.

SETUP From Triangle, come up to Warrior 2. Lower your front forearm onto your front thigh. Reach your upper arm up to the ceiling, your palm facing the same direction as your chest.

ALIGNMENT Ground the four corners of both feet into the floor. Squeeze both feet toward the center of your mat. • Stack your front knee over your front ankle. • Pull your front thigh bone into your hip socket until you feel your outer glute engage. Keep your right hip even with your bent front knee. • Lift the arch of your back foot and squeeze your back inner thigh. • Engage your belly to lighten the weight of your front arm on your thigh. • Pull your shoulder blades toward your spine. Spiral your upper ribs up toward the ceiling. • Spread out your fingers on both hands.

ADD-ON BIND Wind the top of your upper hand toward your lower back, rolling your upper shoulder in toward your chest. • Walk your fingers down behind your back toward your front inner thigh. If you can't reach your thigh, grab the waistband of your clothing. • Lengthen the crown of your head and turn your face to the ceiling to release in your neck.

GAZE & FOCUS Set your gaze on the ceiling. • Breathe into your upper shoulder as it releases through the bind.

DEEPEN Reach your lower hand under your front thigh and clasp your bound hand to create a full bind.

COMMON CHALLENGES Weak glutes cause your front knee to collapse inward.

MODIFICATIONS Shorten your stance slightly as long as you keep your front knee aligned over your ankle.

SEQUENCE TRANSITION Stretch your upper arm to the ceiling to release. • Come up to Warrior 2.

Side Angle with a Half Bind

• Straighten your front leg. • Turn your right toes to face the left edge of your mat so your feet are parallel.

Wide-Legged Forward Fold

Now that you have practiced squeezing your thigh muscles to open your hamstrings, focus on hugging your shoulder blades to your spine to deepen the Wide-Legged Forward Fold.

Wide-Legged Forward Fold

SETUP With your feet parallel to each other, widen your heels just outside your toes until the outer edges of your feet are parallel to the mat. Bring your hands to your hips. On an inhale, lift your chest to the ceiling; on an exhale, fold forward.

ALIGNMENT Bring your hands to the floor under your shoulders. Point your fingers the same direction as your toes. • If your hamstrings and lower back allow, walk your hands back between your feet. • Lift the arches of your feet; squeeze your inner thighs up toward your pelvis. • Pull your chest deeper toward the floor with your hands. • Interlace your hands at your lower back. Hug your shoulder blades in toward your spine. • Straighten your arms, press your hands away from your lower back, and fold forward.

RELEASE Walk your hands back underneath your shoulders.

GAZE & FOCUS Look at a spot on your mat between your feet. • Squeeze your thigh muscles and shift your weight slightly forward toward your toes.

DEEPEN Straighten your legs. Pull your head toward your mat.

TRIPOD HEADSTAND VARIATION Bring the crown of your head—the spot between your forehead and the top of your head—to the floor. • Walk your wrists back so you have a triangular base between your hands and your head. Stack your elbows over your wrists. Hug your elbows in toward each other. • When your arms feel stable, engage your core. Slowly lift your feet off the floor, working in a controlled lift, until your legs are stacked over your head. Hug in toward your centerline, squeezing your core throughout the headstand.

COMMON CHALLENGES Tightness in your hamstrings or a tight lower back prevents your hands from reaching the floor.

MODIFICATIONS Use a block under your hands. Bend your knees to give your spine more space.

SEQUENCE TRANSITION Stay in a Wide-Legged Forward Fold and walk your hands under your shoulders.

Skandasana

This pose adds a side-to-side movement to your practice, moving you laterally and working deeply into your hips. A deep side lunge, Skandasana is particularly effective for hikers, stretching into your hips, groin, and hamstrings.

SETUP In a Wide-Legged Forward Fold, turn your left toes out at a slight angle. Bend your left knee over your back toes.

ALIGNMENT Deepen into the lunge toward your left foot. Keep your right foot parallel. Ground into the four corners of both feet and lift the arches of your feet off the floor. • Stack your hands underneath your shoulders. Lengthen your chest parallel with your hips. Widen your sit bones out behind you.

Skandasana

• Lift your front ribs into your body. • Engage your inner thighs toward your pelvis. • Hug your shoulders into your back, and engage your core.

SKANDASANA VARIATION Turn your left toes out to a 45-degree angle, and bend your knee even deeper with your left heel *still grounded.* • Flex your right toes up to the sky, your heel on the ground. • Bring both hands together in front of your chest, pressing your left elbow into your inner knee.

GAZE & FOCUS Look at one spot on the floor directly at a natural point between your hands. • Play with the bend in your knee and keep your core engaged.

COMMON CHALLENGES Tightness in your hips and lower back prevents your hands from reaching the floor.

MODIFICATIONS Stay in the pose with feet flat on your mat. Stack your hands under your shoulders on a block.

SEQUENCE TRANSITION Ground both feet. • Straighten your left leg. • Bring your hands back to the front of your mat. • Lift your left heel for a lunge facing the front of your mat.

Crescent Lunge

A great stabilizing pose, Crescent Lunge develops the muscles around your front knee, and strengthens your thighs, hamstrings, and glutes. Here, you learn to stabilize into the centerline by hugging your inner thighs to your pelvis and engaging your core.

SETUP From a lunge position in your legs, stack your front knee over your ankle. • Lift your back heel so your toes are bent and the sole of your foot is perpendicular to the ground. Squeeze your back hamstring straight. • Lift your chest over your hips and extend your arms straight up to the ceiling.

ALIGNMENT Move your feet hip-width distance apart for stability. • Lift your back hamstring up to the ceiling. If your heel is pressing back toward the floor rather than lifted vertically over the ball of your foot, lengthen the distance between your front and back foot. • Square your pelvis toward the front of your mat. Squeeze your front heel and back foot toward each other. • Pull in your core lock. • Release your shoulders away from your ears. Reach your arms up to the ceiling parallel to your ears, pinky fingers forward.

GAZE & FOCUS Look at a spot on the wall in front of you. • Ground your front foot and straighten your back leg.

DEEPEN Lengthen your stance and bend your front knee to a 90-degree angle.

COMMON CHALLENGES Your front foot moves around.

MODIFICATIONS Ground into the big toe knuckle at the base of your front foot, and your heel. Lower your back knee to the floor for a Low Lunge if you need to.

Twisted Crescent Lunge

Adding a twist to an already challenging standing pose requires your body to stabilize in order to hold the pose. Twists create a healthy opening

Crescent Lunge

for your spine and release tightness that has accumulated in your lower back and shoulders from a hike. Your glutes also will activate.

SETUP From Crescent Lunge, bring your palms together in front of your chest. • On your exhale, hook your right elbow outside your left knee.

ALIGNMENT Squeeze your feet in toward each other to activate your inner thighs and stabilize your legs. Keep your front knee stacked over your ankle. • Squeeze your thigh muscles, straighten your back leg and lift your leg toward the ceiling. • Lift your upper elbow toward the ceiling. Press down into both palms equally. • Hug your belly in toward your spine, elevating your front ribs off your front thigh. • Pull your shoulders in toward your chest, and lengthen your chest forward to keep your spine long and straight and to deepen your twist. • Keep your shoulders higher than your hips. • Open your arms, with your lower hand on the floor or on a block outside your front leg. Lift your upper hand to the ceiling, palm facing the same direction as your chest. • Stretch your fingers away from your body.

Twisted Crescent Lunge

GAZE & FOCUS Set your gaze on a spot on the ceiling. • Squeeze your shoulder blades toward each other. Engage the muscles underneath your shoulder blades to deepen your twist.

DEEPEN Inch your back foot farther back and bend your front knee to a 90-degree angle.

COMMON CHALLENGES You will need to develop strength and stability in your legs to hold the full pose. Squeeze your inner thighs for balance.

MODIFICATIONS Keep your back knee on the floor. Pad your knee if you feel pain in your kneecap.

SEQUENCE TRANSITION Release your hands to the floor and step your feet to the back of your mat for Plank.

Side Plank

Side Plank brings the art of a static hold to one side of your body. It works the lower side of your body closest to the floor, from your legs to your obliques to your back muscles and shoulders. A strong Side Plank will develop your body's endurance and overall strength for long mountain treks.

SETUP From Plank, bring your feet together. Roll to the outer edge of your right foot, with your left foot stacked on top. • Stack your right shoulder over your right wrist; all your weight will be on one hand. • Lift your left hand up to the ceiling, palm facing the same direction as your chest.

ALIGNMENT Your right hand faces the front of the mat and is stacked just a couple of inches forward of your shoulder. • Stack your left foot on top of your right. Flex your toes toward your knees and squeeze the muscles of your legs to the bone. • Keep your body in one angled plane from shoulders to feet. • Hug your lower shoulder blade up and in toward your spine to take the weight out of your wrist. • Spread out the fingers on your upper hand. • Lengthen the crown of your head toward the front of your mat.

GAZE & FOCUS Look at the ceiling. • Create stability through your legs and core.

DEEPEN Lift your upper leg as high as you can toward the ceiling.

COMMON CHALLENGES You are still building strength and struggle to hold the pose.

MODIFICATIONS Bring your lower knee to the floor underneath your hip for support, keeping your foundation hand, lower knee, and feet in one line.

SEQUENCE TRANSITION Lower your hands to your mat for Plank. • Lower to Chaturanga. • Straighten

Side Plank

your arms for Upward-Facing Dog. • Lift your hips for Downward-Facing Dog. • Complete the left side of the strength poses from Warrior 2 to Side Plank. • Come to Downward-Facing Dog.

Dolphin

Dolphin can be a modification for Downward-Facing Dog if you are coping with wrist injuries, but Dolphin is usually not much of a break. With your elbows on the floor to alleviate pressure on your wrists, Dolphin builds shoulder and trunk strength.

SETUP From Downward-Facing Dog, lower to your elbows and knees on the floor. • Bring your hands to your triceps above your elbows to ensure your shoulders are stacked over your elbows. • Bring your thumbs to touch on the mat or interlace your hands in front of you. Tuck your toes and lift your hips up to the ceiling.

ALIGNMENT Lift your shoulders up to your ears and then draw your shoulder blades toward each other. Squeeze the muscles under your shoulder blades down your back. • Lift your hips in an inverted V. Walk your feet in closer toward your elbows and press your chest toward your feet, shoulders still integrated toward your spine. • Ground your hands and the edges of your wrists into the mat. • Bend your knees to lengthen your spine. Lower your heels toward the floor—they do not need to touch. • Release into Child's Pose.

GAZE & FOCUS Look back at the floor between your toes. • Lift your tailbone toward the ceiling and elongate your spine.

DEEPEN Bring your hands and forearms to parallel on the mat. Press into your palms and forearms.

Dolphin

SEQUENCE TRANSITION From Child's Pose, tuck your toes and lift to Downward-Facing Dog. • Step or hop to the front of your mat. • Stretch your chest to Halfway Lift. • Fold your chest to your feet.

Hand-to-Big-Toe Forward Fold

Active forward folds open your spine and create more space in your lower back. Harness your core to deepen your forward bend. In Hand-to-Big-Toe Forward Fold, your big toes serve as an anchor for your hands to pull your chest deeper into the fold, opening your lower back and your hamstrings. Keep your knees bent, particularly if your hamstrings are tight in general or from a day in the wilderness.

SETUP Stack your feet directly under your hips— place your fists between your feet to measure. • Loop your peace fingers (index and middle finger) around your big toes. Pull up on your big toes and press the four corners of your feet down toward the floor.

Hand-to-Big-Toe Forward Fold

ALIGNMENT Bend your elbows to the outer edges of your mat to pull your chest toward your shins.
• Relax your shoulders away from your ears.
• Hug your shoulder blades toward your spine. Engage your shoulders to go deeper into the pose.
• Bend your knees as needed—don't lock them!—and bring your belly down to your thighs. • Squeeze your thighs. • Release your head toward the floor.

GAZE & FOCUS Look at the floor between your feet.
• Engage your shoulders to pull your chest closer toward your feet.

DEEPEN Work your legs as straight as your hamstrings allow while hugging your thigh muscles; do not force your legs to straighten, and keep your knee joints soft.

SEQUENCE TRANSITION Release your big toes.

Gorilla

A big wrist and hand release, Gorilla is a counter pose to Downward-Facing Dog and Plank. It releases some of the effects of weight bearing in your wrists, and in this modern day of constant typing and texting, it's a great release for cramped hands.

SETUP From Hand-to-Big-Toe Forward Fold, keep your feet stacked under your hips. • Slide the palms of your hands underneath your feet so that the top of your hands touch your mat.

ALIGNMENT Wiggle your hands deeper under your feet until your toes reach your wrists. • Bend your elbows to the outer edges of your mat. • Hug your shoulder blades together to pull your chest deeper toward your spine. • Soften your knees and bring your belly down to your thighs. Engage your thigh muscles. • Release your neck and hang your head toward the floor.

GAZE & FOCUS Look at the floor behind your feet.
• Engage your shoulders to pull your chest closer to your shins.

DEEPEN Work your legs as straight as your hamstrings allow while still squeezing your thighs. Keep your knee joints soft.

Gorilla

COMMON CHALLENGES Tight hamstrings prevent you from sliding your hands under your feet.

MODIFICATIONS Make fists and place the tops of your hands on a block, curled fingers facing in toward your body. Bend your knees.

SEQUENCE TRANSITION Release your hands from under your feet. • Bring your feet together. • Stand in Mountain Pose.

BALANCE

Strong feet and ankles will not alleviate the constant pounding of hiking, but the stronger your feet and ankles, the more stable you will be on uneven terrain—and the quicker you will recover. Balancing poses build strength in the arches of your feet, which in turn strengthen your ankles. The more you practice engaging your core lock and focusing your drishti, the more ease you will feel while balancing. As your balance improves, you'll also notice a difference on longer hikes, particularly navigating the descent on a trail with a heavy pack.

Eagle

A balancing pose that generates from your centerline, Eagle builds balance and requires concentration and focus. Squeeze your inner thighs for strength and observe how the arm bind opens your shoulders and stretches your outer hips.

SETUP From Mountain Pose, extend your arms out wide and parallel to the floor, palms facing forward. Cross your right upper arm underneath your left upper arm. • Wind your forearms around each other. Bring your palms to touch for the full bind. • Lower into Chair in your legs. Cross your right thigh on top of your left thigh.

ALIGNMENT Ground into your standing foot. Squeeze your inner thighs all the way together. • Stack your shoulders over your hips; engage your core lock. • Lift your elbows level with your shoulders. Press your hands away from your face to stack your wrists over your elbows. • Soften your shoulders away from your ears; pull your arm bones in toward your shoulder sockets. • Stretch out your toes on your upper foot. • Release into Mountain Pose.

Eagle

GAZE & FOCUS Look past your arms to a spot on the wall. • Engage your belly firmly and set your gaze.

DEEPEN Bend your standing leg deeper and wrap your right foot around your calf. Challenge your balance by folding forward toward your knees, then come back up.

COMMON CHALLENGES Tight shoulders can prevent you from taking a full bind.

MODIFICATIONS Reach for opposite shoulders and lift your elbows even with your shoulders or hold your thumb.

SEQUENCE TRANSITION Release into Mountain Pose. • Do Eagle on the left side; wrap your left arm under your right and lift your left leg over your right leg.

Hand-to-Knee Balancing Pose

Your body relies on several systems for balance, including feet, core, and gaze. Hand-to-Knee Balancing Pose challenges your balance by using your standing leg as the foundation while your other leg switches positions and directions. You also move your gaze, testing your inner ear balance and eyes. It's a poetic little series of poses.

SETUP Stand in Mountain Pose. Ground into the four corners of your left foot. • Lift your right knee even with your hip, and hold your knee with your right hand.

ALIGNMENT Hug your belly in toward your spine. • Extend your free arm up to the ceiling, palm facing your body. • Lower your shoulders away from your ears and pull your shoulder blades toward each other. • Hold for five breaths.

GAZE Look at a spot on the wall in front of you.

DEEPEN Loop your peace fingers around your big toe. • Extend your leg forward for a balance challenge and hamstring opening. Squeeze your right thigh muscles to lengthen your hamstring. Maintaining a long, neutral spine is more important than the extension. Focus on standing up straight. • Pull the shoulder of your extended arm in toward your spine. Lengthen your leg last.

Hand-to-Knee Forward

HAND-TO-KNEE SIDE On an inhale, move your knee to the right. Extend your left hand toward the opposite side of the room, palm facing up. • Pull your right thigh bone into your hip socket to keep your pelvis level and your leg integrated into your body. • Lower your shoulders down your back and squeeze your shoulder blades toward each other. • Stay for five breaths. • Move your gaze over your left palm. • If you want to deepen, while holding your big toe, open your leg to the right. Hug your right thighbone into your hip socket to keep your pelvis level and spin your inner right thigh up to the ceiling. The tendency is to lose the centerline, which makes the balance harder! • Squeeze your thigh muscles on your standing leg. • Press through your lifted heel and hug your thigh muscles to the bone.

HAND-TO-KNEE FORWARD On an inhale, bring your back knee in front of you. Extend your right leg forward and parallel with the floor. • Press through your extended heel. Lift your arms straight up to the ceiling. • Stack your shoulders over your hips. Engage your core. If you feel it in your lower back, you are leaning back too far. • Engage your

Hand-to-Knee Side

shoulders toward each other. • Stay for five breaths.
• Set your eyes on your extended foot.

SEQUENCE TRANSITION Stand in Mountain Pose.
• Repeat Hand-to-Knee Pose and variations on the
left side. • **Challenge option:** Move from Hand-to-
Knee Variation 2 directly into Airplane by sweeping
your right leg back into the pose.

Airplane

As the name implies, this pose benefits from a lift
in your chest like the nose of an airplane. Your
standing leg becomes a lever, and the lean of your
chest counterbalances the lift of your leg behind
you, developing great functional strength and
flexibility for uneven terrain. Activate your core to
support your lower back.

SETUP Stand tall in Mountain Pose. Shift your weight
to your left foot. Extend your right foot toward the
back of your mat. Reach your hands back toward
your legs and float them above your hips.

Airplane

ALIGNMENT Lift your shoulders just above your hips.
• Hug your shoulder blades onto your spine.
• Rotate your thumbs away from your body, with
your palms facing down. • Rotate your right hip
down and level with your left hip; pull your right
thigh bone into your hip socket. • Engage your core
lock. • Elevate your right foot even with your head.
• Flex the toes on your back leg toward your kneecap.

GAZE & FOCUS Look at the floor in front of your standing foot. • Lift your back leg until you feel your hamstrings engage. Keep your belly lifted up and in.

DEEPEN Extend your arms forward and parallel with your head to transition into Warrior 3.

COMMON CHALLENGES A lack of strength and balance challenges you to stay steady in the pose.

MODIFICATIONS Bring your hands to a block placed directly under each of your shoulders to balance. Lift your chest and engage your back muscles and core. • Extend your back leg parallel with the floor.

SEQUENCE TRANSITION Step your upper foot down and behind you.

Pyramid

A pose of stability, Pyramid also opens your shoulders and spine with a hand bind behind your back. The balance in the pose comes from your adductors, your inner thigh muscles, which work tirelessly on a hike. Apply what you know about forward folds to deepen your hamstring stretch and to emphasize shoulder opening.

SETUP Set your feet up in a stance slightly shorter than Warrior 1, or the length of one leg. Position your feet about hip-width distance. • Point your back foot out at a 45-degree angle. • Reach behind your lower back for opposite elbows.

Pyramid

ALIGNMENT Ground the four corners of your feet into the floor, especially your back heel. • Lift your chest, inhale, and fold forward toward your front leg on your exhale. • Squeeze your thighs up and in toward your pelvis. Balance your weight between your front and back foot. • Soften your front knee joint. • Reach your chest toward your front shin.

GAZE & FOCUS Look at your front foot. • Hug your inner thighs toward each other. Squeeze your shoulders toward your spine to open your chest.

DEEPEN Interlace your hands at your lower back for a bind. Lift them away from your lower back.

COMMON CHALLENGES Tight hamstrings intensify the forward fold.

MODIFICATIONS Bend your front knee, squeeze your thigh muscles, and breathe deeply to release your hamstring.

SEQUENCE TRANSITION Come up to stand with your feet still in the Pyramid stance.

Revolved Triangle

A twist and a balance rolled up into one pose, Revolved Triangle can sometimes feel like trying to pat your head and rub your belly at the same time. You need stability in your legs to twist your spine. The pose will test your body awareness, determination, and focus, but over time, you can break through into a sensation of true freedom.

SETUP From your upright Pyramid stance, take your left hand to your left hip. • Extend your right arm up to the ceiling. • Lower your chest parallel to the floor, your core lock engaged. • Bring your right hand to a block at the tallest or middle height along the inside edge of your front foot.

ALIGNMENT Press your back foot into the floor and tilt your tailbone to press your sit bones to the wall behind you. • Squeeze your thigh muscles, including your inner thighs, toward your pelvis. • Pull your belly in toward your spine. • Stretch your chest parallel to the floor to lengthen your spine. • With your left hand still on your hip, squeeze your shoulder blades in toward your spine and spin your chest left and up toward the ceiling. • Reach your left arm up to the ceiling.

GAZE & FOCUS Look at your upper hand. • Press your back foot deeply into the mat, and distribute your weight evenly between front and back foot. • Rotate from your oblique muscles.

DEEPEN Bring your lower hand to the floor inside your foot, or place your block outside your front foot to challenge your balance and twist.

COMMON CHALLENGES Weak glutes or legs prevent you from grounding your back foot and keeping your hips even as you twist.

MODIFICATIONS Use the block at the tallest height or even your shin, avoiding your knee. • Focus on grounding your feet before you twist.

SEQUENCE TRANSITION Fold forward over your front leg to release.

Revolved Triangle

Half Moon

Another balancing pose, Half Moon requires engagement in your standing leg and strength in your glutes. You will be surprised at how much strength it takes to lift your upper leg higher and ground deeply into your standing foot.

SETUP Line up a block (at its tallest height) underneath your right shoulder, just to the right of your standing pinky toe. Bring your right hand to the block. • Shift your weight into your right foot. Lift your left leg and roll your left hip on top of your left. • Lift your upper arm to the ceiling.

ALIGNMENT Press firmly into your standing foot with your toes pointing straight forward. Squeeze your thighs. • Flex the toes of your lifted leg. Bring your lifted leg in line with your hip. You should be able to see your back toes. • Pull your upper thigh bone in toward your hip. Notice your upper glute engaging; lift your upper leg higher. • Extend your chest long, pulling your belly in toward your spine. • Keep the weight on your lower hand light; rely on your standing

Half Moon

leg for strength. • Pull your shoulder blades into your back. Extend your upper fingers to the ceiling.

GAZE & FOCUS Look at the floor. • Press deeply into your standing foot and radiate out from your core in every direction.

DEEPEN Move your gaze to the ceiling. Lighten the touch of your lower hand on the block or floor.

COMMON CHALLENGES You have trouble balancing in the middle of the room.

MODIFICATIONS Do this pose against a wall for support.

SEQUENCE TRANSITION Complete the poses from Airplane through Half Moon on your left side, standing on your right foot.

CHALLENGE OPTION Work all the poses on your right side from Hand-to-Knee Pose through Half Moon. Repeat all the poses on your left side. • Return to Mountain Pose.

Crow

Crow is yoga wrapped up into one tiny arm balance. It presents mental and physical challenges all at once. I have heard every reason possible why people can't do this pose—my arms aren't strong enough, I'm scared to fall over, what's the point of this pose? The point is to trust yourself and learn to do something that scares you—a whole new world of possibilities awaits.

SETUP From Mountain Pose, move your feet wide into a Squat. Set your hands on the floor a foot in front of you so they are underneath your shoulders. • Lift your hips until your shoulders come over your wrists and your hips are shoulder height or higher. Lift your hips above your shoulders, and walk your

Crow

feet in closer toward each other. • Bend your elbows slightly toward your feet. • Place your knees on your upper arms above your elbows. • Shift your weight forward to take all the weight into your arms.

ALIGNMENT Keep your gaze forward in front of your hands for balance. • Put all your weight into your hands. Lift one foot off the floor. Try the other foot. • If you can balance with one foot off the floor, slowly lift the other one. • Safety note: Do not hop into the pose. Move mindfully, leaning your weight into your arms with your gaze lifted so your head can counterbalance the weight of your body. Lift your feet slowly.

RELEASE Lower your feet to the floor for a squat.

GAZE & FOCUS Keep your gaze forward of your fingers. • Play with transferring your weight into your hands, with your head and gaze still lifted forward.

DEEPEN Bring your big toes together while hovering off the floor in the pose. Straighten your arms.

TRIPOD HEADSTAND VARIATION Lower the crown of your head—the spot between the top of your head and hairline—to the floor in front of your hands. • Make sure your hands and head are in a stable triangle shape. Wrap your elbows toward each other and pull your shoulders into your back. • Your knees still should be on your upper arms. Tilt your hips forward until they are stacked above your shoulders and slowly pull one knee in toward your chest. If you are stable, pull your other knee in toward your chest. • Hold with your knees in at your chest, and squeeze into your centerline. • If you are stable, extend one leg at a time toward the ceiling. If you feel unstable, bring your feet down or practice somersaulting out. Only take this pose if you feel comfortable rolling out. • **Note:** When you are new to inversions, practice against a wall until you are comfortable trying them in the middle of the room.

COMMON CHALLENGES If you have a wrist injury, be mindful in Crow.

MODIFICATIONS Squat with your heels on the floor.

A HEALTHY SPINE

Reversing your hunch from sitting at a computer all day takes practice—in case you missed that memo. Backbends are an effective way to signal to your brain that you want to open your chest, loosen your tight shoulders, and strengthen your lower back, which are all affected from rolling your shoulders forward all day.

The belly backbend Locust, for example, strengthens the muscles that arch your back, including the muscles along your spine, your lower back muscles, and your butt muscles. Upward-Facing Dog strengthens your arms in addition to opening your chest. Wheel, the deepest extension of the backbends, also stretches into your shoulders.

When first practicing backbends, most people tend to bend at the weakest point in their spine, particularly if their body is already open. Focus on keeping your core engaged, lengthening your lower back, and using your back strength to create a long, beautiful arc in your backbend.

Deep backbends foster healthy alignment, teach you to use your legs to access your core, strengthen and support your spine, and open your chest. Energetically, backbends also open your heart, and give you a path to connect to your body and energy. Instead of skipping them, learn to love them!

SEQUENCE TRANSITION Ground your feet at the front of your mat. • Fold your chest forward over your legs. • Stretch your chest to Halfway Lift. • Plant your hands for Plank. • Lower to Chaturanga.
• Straighten your arms for Upward-Facing Dog.
• Lift your hips into Downward-Facing Dog.

BACKBENDS

A backbend practice ramps up intensity, moving you even deeper into your spine. Build upon what you have learned about opening your chest, engaging your big back muscles, and learn to activate the smaller muscles around your spine to move safely into backbends.

Flip Dog

A fun backbend, Flip Dog opens your chest and strengthens your shoulder girdle. It looks intimidating, but is surprisingly easy. Let your neck relax once you're there and press into your legs for full strength in the pose.

SETUP From Downward-Facing Dog, lift your left leg to the ceiling. Bend your left knee and roll your hip open for Three-Legged Dog. • Look under your right arm for your upper foot and lower it to the floor behind you. • Turn your other foot around 180 degrees until both toes are flat and parallel on the ground. • Keep your right hand where it started on the ground and lift your left arm to the ceiling.

ALIGNMENT Set your feet hip-width distance. Reach your free arm overhead toward the floor. • Press into the four corners of your feet and lift your hips to the ceiling. • Bend your left elbow even with your shoulder for a cactus arm. Hug your shoulder blades toward each other to open your chest.

• Engage your core lock. • Soften your neck to let your head hang toward the floor.

RELEASE Lift your left arm to the ceiling. Hop back over to Three-Legged Dog.

GAZE & FOCUS Set your gaze on the front wall or the floor under you. • Press down into your feet to lift your hips higher. Hug your shoulder blades in toward your spine.

Flip Dog

DEEPEN Reach your hand overhead toward the floor.

COMMON CHALLENGES If you have shoulder pain, skip this pose if it exacerbates the injury.

MODIFICATIONS Stay in Three-Legged Dog.

SEQUENCE TRANSITION Hop back over into Three-Legged Dog. • Shift your weight forward into Plank. • Lower to Chaturanga. • Press your hands down to lift into Upward-Facing Dog. • Tuck your toes and lift to Downward-Facing Dog. • Do Flip Dog on the left side. • Move forward to Plank and lower to the floor.

Bow

Bow

Strong legs are instrumental to backbends, and Bow pose teaches your body how to engage your legs for backbends, in addition to opening up your quadriceps and strengthening your back.

SETUP From your belly on the floor, bend both knees. Reach for the outer edges of your feet with your hands.

ALIGNMENT Bring your knees to hip-width distance to support your lower back and tap into your leg strength. • Pull your belly in toward your spine. • Press your pelvis down toward the floor. Lift your feet up toward the ceiling. Use your leg strength to lift as high as you can.

RELEASE Let go of your feet gently. Roll your hips side to side on the floor.

GAZE & FOCUS Lift your eyes to the floor or the front of the room. • Engage your core and use your legs in the pose.

DEEPEN Reach for your ankles. Flex your toes and rock back to the tops of your thighs.

COMMON CHALLENGES Tight hamstrings or knee injuries prevent you from grabbing both of your feet at the same time.

MODIFICATIONS Bring your left forearm parallel to the front edge of your mat. Stack your left elbow under your left shoulder, palm facing down on the floor. Reach your right hand to your right foot. Press into your left elbow and lift your right foot up to the ceiling. Switch sides.

ALTERNATIVE Substitute with the Locust pose (see the Recovery Practice later in this chapter).

SEQUENCE TRANSITION Do a second Bow. • Plant your hands next to your ribs. • Straighten your arms and lift your legs for Upward-Facing Dog. • Lift up and back to Downward-Facing Dog. • Walk your feet forward between your hands. • Sit down and lower down to your back.

Bridge

Apply what you learned about leg strength in Bow for Bridge. The more you engage your legs, the stronger your backbends will be, and the more endurance you will have for a day on the trail.

Bridge

SETUP Walk your feet closer to your body until your fingertips brush your heels. Set your feet parallel and hip-width distance. Press into the four corners of your feet to lift your hips to the ceiling. • Move your shoulders together and interlace your hands underneath your body.

ALIGNMENT Press your feet into your mat until your legs engage. • Stack your knees over your ankles. • Spin your inner thighs toward each other and down toward your mat. • Position your hands at your spine just above your tailbone. Feel the ridge of muscles around your spine engage. Lift your spine until you feel the engagement between your shoulder blades. • Lift your chest toward the back wall. • Squeeze your front ribs together.

RELEASE Reach your arms up to the ceiling. Slowly release your spine toward the floor, one vertebrae at a time.

GAZE & FOCUS Look at a spot on the ceiling. • Press deeply into your feet for strong legs.

DEEPEN Lift your right knee into your chest. Press strongly into your rooted foot. Extend your right leg, foot flexed, to the ceiling, keeping your hips level. Switch sides.

COMMON CHALLENGES Tight shoulders prevent you from interlacing your hands.

MODIFICATIONS Use a strap between your hands for a bind. • Or press your palms into the floor.

SEQUENCE TRANSITION Keep your feet in Bridge to set up for Wheel.

Wheel

Wheel is where all the alignment you have learned comes together. A fully extended backbend, this peak pose requires powerful legs, integrated shoulders, and deep breathing. You will experience strength, heart opening, and an energy burst. If the last time you did this pose was around the age of six, today is the best day to start.

Wheel

ALIGNMENT Ground your feet deeply into the floor. • Spiral your inner thighs toward each other and down toward your mat. • Wrap your shoulder blades in toward your spine; press your hands deeply into the earth. • Pull your front ribs in toward each other. • Tilt your tailbone and pull your pubic bone toward your ribs to lengthen your lower back. • Let your head hang toward the floor.

RELEASE Tuck your chin, lower to the back of your head, and lower down the length of your spine.

GAZE & FOCUS Look at the floor behind you. • Push into your feet to get strong in your legs. Spin your inner thighs toward each other and down toward the floor.

DEEPEN Place a block between your inner thighs at the narrowest height as high up your thighs as it will go. Come up to Wheel while squeezing the block.

COMMON CHALLENGES Shoulder or wrist injuries may prevent you from accessing the full pose. • The pose puts pressure on your lower back.

SETUP From your Bridge with your feet at hip-width distance, plant your hands on either side of your head as wide as your mat, fingers turned in toward your shoulders. Point your elbows directly to the back of your mat. • Lift your hips like you are going into Bridge. Push down into the floor with your hands. • Set the crown of your head on the floor and wrap your elbows in toward each other so your upper arms are parallel. Press your hands down into the floor to straighten your arms.

MODIFICATIONS Stay in Bridge pose. • Or, for Wheel, place your hands as wide as your mat. Bring your feet wider and spin your inner thighs toward the floor. • Hug your belly in before you come up. If you are still feeling lower back pain, build strength in Bridge.

SEQUENCE TRANSITION Do Wheel three times total. • Lower down and bring the bottoms of your feet together for Supine Butterfly. Stay for five breaths. • Rock up to a seated position. • Move to Downward-Facing Dog.

RECOVERY

The lower half of your body takes much of the effects of a hike, and a backpacking expedition exacts an even greater toll. Treat your hips and lower back with care, taking the time to recover from this Strength Practice by spending time on hip opening poses and gentle forward folds.

Lizard

A deep, dynamic hip opener, your hips may be more inclined to shout at you than sigh with delight here. Either way, Lizard is a release valve for your glutes and hips. Catch your back foot for a stretch deep into your hard-working hiker thigh muscles.

SETUP From Downward-Facing Dog, step your right foot outside your right hand. Lower your back knee to the mat.

ALIGNMENT Flex your front foot and roll to the outer edge of your foot. The sole of your foot is off the

Lizard

floor and your right knee will roll open. • Angle your toes on your front foot to the outer edge of your mat. • Lower your elbows down beside your foot with elbows roughly in line with your heel. • Release your head toward your hands. • Stay for ten breaths.

GAZE & FOCUS Look at the inside of your front foot. • Notice the sensations in your hip and send your breath there.

DEEPEN Tuck your back toes, squeeze your quads, and lift your back leg to the ceiling.

BOUND LIZARD VARIATION Come up to your hands. Reach your right hand for your back foot. Stay on your left hand or lower your left elbow to a block or the floor. Slowly shift your weight toward your front foot. Stay another ten breaths. Look to a spot on the wall to the right or close your eyes.

RELEASE Let go of your back foot gently.

COMMON CHALLENGES Tight hips prevent you from coming down to your elbows.

MODIFICATIONS Place a block underneath your elbows. • If you have trouble grabbing your foot for the variation because of tightness in your hamstrings or hips, loop a strap around your foot and hold the strap for the stretch.

SEQUENCE TRANSITION Bring your hands to the floor and lift your chest to set up for Half Pigeon.

Half Pigeon

Our muscular hips deserve particular attention after a long trek on a trail. Your body may resist this stretch initially as you work into your piriformis, a deep hip stabilizer. Breathe deeply into the sensation in your body, and give the muscles around your hip time to soften as you work into the pose.

SETUP From Lizard, move your right foot across your mat and in toward your pelvis, keeping your right foot flexed to protect your knee. • Extend your left leg straight behind you so that the top of your thigh is on the ground.

ALIGNMENT Flex the toes on your back foot and come up to the ball of your foot. • Roll up to center so your pelvis is squared toward the front of your mat. Place a block under your right hip if you have trouble staying centered. • Pull your thigh bones in toward your pelvis. • Lengthen your chest and slowly lower your torso toward the floor. • Walk your arms in front of you. Soften your shoulders and face. • Place a block under your forehead if it doesn't touch your mat. • Stay for one minute.

GAZE & FOCUS Close your eyes. • Breathe deeply into your hips.

DEEPEN Shift your front shin closer to parallel with the front of your mat to get a deeper opening.

COMMON CHALLENGES Knee injuries prevent you from staying in this pose without sharp pain.

MODIFICATIONS Take Reclined Half Pigeon (see Strength Practice I).

SEQUENCE TRANSITION Plant your hands and step your front leg to the back edge of your mat for

Half Pigeon

Downward-Facing Dog. • Step your left foot forward for Lizard through Half Pigeon on the left side. • From Downward-Facing Dog, step forward and move to your sit bones for a seat.

Seated Forward Fold

Practice moving slowly into the Seated Forward Fold to deepen the stretch. Pay attention to your back muscles and lengthening through your chest to extend your spine.

SETUP From your seated position, extend your legs straight to the front of your mat. Reach your hands toward the outer edges of your feet.

ALIGNMENT Flex your toes toward your knees.
• Squeeze your quads. • Pull your chest toward your feet. • Relax your head.

GAZE & FOCUS Look at your feet. • Lengthen your chest toward your feet. Extend from your lower spine.

Seated Forward Fold

DEEPEN Press the backs of your knees toward the floor without overextending the joint, and squeeze your quads. If your hands reach past your feet, use a block at the soles of your feet to give you more room to deepen.

COMMON CHALLENGES A tight lower back, hamstrings, or hip flexors can tend to contract and prevent your torso from folding forward.

MODIFICATIONS Place a block or blanket underneath your sit bones to relax your hips and core for the forward fold. Alternatively, bend your knees to reach for your feet, or use a strap to lengthen your reach to your feet to allow your hips flexors and core to relax.

Head-to-Knee Seated Forward Fold

With this asymmetric forward fold, you can focus on stretching into each leg and one side of your trunk at a time. You'll most likely find one side easier than the other, revealing any unevenness between the two sides of your body.

Head-to-Knee Seated Forward Fold

SETUP From Seated Forward Fold, keep one leg extended straight. • Tuck your other foot in toward your pelvis, bringing the sole of the foot in against your inner thigh.

ALIGNMENT Flex the toes on your extended leg toward your knee. • Reach your hands for your extended foot. • Squeeze your thigh muscles to extend into your hamstring. • Lengthen your chest toward your foot. Release your head toward your

shin. • Keep your sit bones grounded. • Hold for ten breaths.

GAZE & FOCUS Close your eyes. • Ground your sit bones into the mat.

DEEPEN On your inhale lengthen your chest toward your foot; exhale and fold deeper.

COMMON CHALLENGES Knee injuries prevent you from bringing your foot in toward your pelvis.

MODIFICATIONS Slide your bent foot into your knee or lower leg instead of to your inner thigh.

SEQUENCE TRANSITION Do both sides for Head-to-Knee Seated Forward Fold.

Reverse Tabletop

A shoulder opener, Reverse Tabletop is also a back-bend that moves deeply into your chest, biceps, and your deltoids in your shoulders. Always an interesting challenge, it's a powerful, modified backbend.

Reverse Tabletop

GAZE & FOCUS Set your gaze on the ceiling or wall behind you. • Ground your feet deeper into the floor to activate your leg muscles.

DEEPEN Extend your legs straight on the floor. Press into your heels to lift your hips. Press the soles of your feet into the earth; spin your inner thighs down toward the floor.

COMMON CHALLENGES Weak hamstrings make it difficult to keep your legs internally rotated. Also, tight chest muscles can make breathing feel challenging.

MODIFICATIONS Play with moving your breath around to stay in the pose.

SEQUENCE TRANSITION Lower your hips to the floor. • Roll down to your back.

SETUP From a seated position, place your hands behind you on the mat with your fingertips facing your body. • Walk your feet in so they are flat on the floor at hip-width distance.

ALIGNMENT Ground into the four corners of your feet and lift your hips toward the ceiling. • Press your palms into the ground. • Lengthen the crown of your head behind you. Gently release your head onto your shoulders. • Rotate your inner thighs toward each other and down toward your mat.

Shoulder Stand

Going upside down is a hallmark of a yoga practice, inverting both your body and your perspective on the world. Shoulder Stand, the queen of all inversions, creates harmony in your nervous and endocrine systems. It is a restorative inversion, stimulating the heart and flushing your spine.

SETUP From a lying position, lift your feet up and over behind your head, reaching them toward the floor behind you so your pelvis stacks over your shoulders. • Wiggle your shoulders underneath you to create a solid base. Place your palms on your back.

ALIGNMENT Inch your shoulders in closer toward your spine to create a solid foundation. Bring your hands higher up your back. • Lift your hips higher by walking your elbows in toward each other. • Extend your legs up toward the ceiling. • Keep a gap between your chin and chest to keep your neck off the floor.

GAZE & FOCUS Set your drishti on the ceiling and keep it focused there; avoid turning your head from side to side—this will protect your neck. • Keep your legs still.

DEEPEN Lift your hips higher over your shoulders.

Shoulder Stand

COMMON CHALLENGES A tight lower back or hamstrings makes it difficult to get into the pose.

MODIFICATIONS Place a folded blanket under your shoulders for padding before moving into the pose. Or substitute with Legs Up the Wall pose (see Strength Practice I).

Ear Pressure Pose

Allow yourself to relax into Ear Pressure Pose and feel the benefits of this deep stretch into the mid-back and of turning your body upside down.

SETUP From Shoulder Stand, lower your knees toward your forehead. Keep your hips stacked over your shoulders.

ALIGNMENT Keep your hands on your back; relax your mid-back. • Rest your knees on your forehead. • If your body allows, bring your knees outside your ears. • If your knees come down by your ears, wrap your arms around the backs of your thighs. Otherwise, keep your hands on your back.

Ear Pressure Pose

RELEASE Roll slowly out of Ear Pressure Pose.

GAZE & FOCUS Close your eyes. • Soften your spine and mid-back.

COMMON CHALLENGES Your back doesn't allow your knees to reach your ears.

MODIFICATIONS Keep your knees on your forehead.

SEQUENCE TRANSITION Come up to a seated position.

Fish

A backbend counter pose to Shoulder Stand, Fish opens your chest and throat wide to the sky. Now is a perfect time to take a Lion's Breath, a big, open-mouthed *loud* exhale. Stick your tongue out to release your jaw!

SETUP From a seated position with your legs straight on the mat, slide your fingertips underneath your sit bones. Lower to your elbows, keeping your shoulders off the floor. • Press into your hands and puff your chest up to the ceiling. Lower the top of your head to the mat.

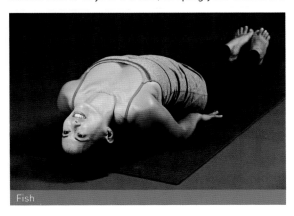

Fish

ALIGNMENT Lengthen the top of your head up and back toward the floor. • Press deeply into your hands and slide them underneath you to bring your head closer to the floor. • Stretch your feet toward the front of your mat. • Open your chest to the sky. • Take a Lion's Breath: Inhale deeply. On your exhale, stick out your tongue and roar loudly.

RELEASE Tuck your chin to release to the floor.

GAZE & FOCUS Close your eyes or look at a spot on the floor behind you. • Connect the top of your head to the floor to relax your neck. Breathe into your chest.

COMMON CHALLENGES You can't get your head to the floor.

MODIFICATIONS Place a block (in its widest direction) underneath your shoulder blades. Relax over your block for a more restorative Fish.

Supine Twist

A Supine Twist relaxes your spine and allows your body to wind down from the intensity of practice and/or many miles on the trail.

SETUP From a resting position on your back, pull your knees into your chest. Extend your arms open into a T. Lengthen your left leg to the floor.

Supine Twist

ALIGNMENT Lower your knees to your left, knees still hugging in toward your chest. • Shift your hips under you toward the right. • Keep both shoulders anchored on the floor. • Look away to your right hand so your neck also benefits from the twist. • Stay for ten breaths.

GAZE & FOCUS Look away from your knees toward your opposite hand. • Relax your body and allow gravity to take the weight of your legs toward the floor.

DEEPEN Pull your right knee into your chest, and straighten your left leg on the ground to deepen the twist. Roll your right knee toward your left side.

SEQUENCE TRANSITION Do the twist for both sides of your body.

FINAL REST

You've got this one! Lay down, relax all the muscles in your body, let go of your ujjayi breath, and all is well.

Corpse Pose

Corpse Pose

Practice making Corpse Pose the best pose you have ever tried. Commit to closing your eyes and being quiet. If you are cold, cover yourself with a blanket.

SETUP From Supine Twist, come to Corpse Pose with your arms at your sides, palms facing up.

ALIGNMENT Slide your shoulders under you. • Relax the muscles in your legs, shoulders, and face. • Move into your natural breath. • Stay in this pose for three minutes.

GAZE & FOCUS Close your eyes. • Stay awake and still. Notice your natural breath.

DEEPEN Take a five-minute final rest.

GET READY

Many hikers love to push, a lot of the time. It is good for your body. Pressing ahead on a long, hard day on a bright, gusty trail elevates your heart rate, and builds your body's endurance and capacity.

Your body also is meant to rest and recover. You may be excellent at the school of recovering prone on the couch. I love a good day of doing nothing, despite the advice of my trainers to do something every day, even on a rest day. Others of you may itch to move.

A middle ground does exist between relentless action and zero. When tired, and especially when sore, you may be tempted to take the couch approach. You already spent hours outdoors, and your glutes, calves and hamstrings throb, your feet are tender and your shoulders tight from hauling your pack. The idea of movement sounds like torture.

It is still wise to move your body. The temptation to stay still is strong, but you move through soreness faster by moving again. A restorative yoga practice offers a soft approach to your body, giving it the space it needs to heal from the previous day's intensity to support a faster recovery. You may be surprised by what you experience.

The following practice is intended for a day you can tell you need to take it down a notch. Addressing the major parts of the body that need a gentler touch after a long hike, it includes long stretches into your hips and shoulders, and mellow twists to open your spine. A focus on breathing and noticing the sensations of your body also will relieve stress any day of the week.

With a thirty-minute restorative yoga practice, you can hone in on what might hurt or feel like it needs some attention. More time in longer stretches lets you release more deeply and recover with ease.

RECOVERY PRACTICE

TIME: 30 MINUTES
EQUIPMENT: BLOCK, YOGA MAT, STRAP, AND
BOLSTER (OPTIONAL)

INTEGRATE AND ACTIVATE

Even in a recovery sequence, it's still important to warm the body before moving into deep stretches. Build heat with a combination of Sun Salutation A and a few more challenging standing poses before you move into more restorative poses. Use this time to settle your mind, get connected with your body, and prepare to release mentally and physically.

SEQUENCE FOR RECOVERY PRACTICE

» Child's Pose
» Cat–Cow
» Downward-Facing Dog
» Plank
» Low Cobra
» Rag Doll
» Halfway Lift

» Mountain Pose
» Sun Salutation A
» Low Lunge
» Twisted Crescent Lunge
» Airplane, Modified
» Revolved Triangle
» Tree

» Lizard
» Half Splits
» Half Pigeon
» One-Armed Shoulder Opener
» Locust
» Heart Throat Nose Pose

» Toes Pose
» Frog
» Reverse Tabletop
» Head-to-Knee Seated Fold with a Twist
» Seated Twist
» Legs Up the Wall
» Corpse Pose

Child's Pose

Start your recovery practice with Child's Pose to notice your physical body and your ujjayi breath, and to bring your mind to the present. Observe the feeling of your mat underneath your hands and forehead. Feel your breath move into your ribs. Listen to what your body is telling you.

Child's Pose

SETUP From a seat, move your knees to the edges of your mat, and bring your big toes together to touch. Sink your hips back over your heels. • Walk your hands forward at shoulder-width distance and bring your forehead to the ground.

ALIGNMENT Let go of tension in your shoulders. • Engage your core gently, pulling your belly up and in toward your spine. • Come into your ujjayi breath. • Stay for ten breaths.

GAZE & FOCUS Close your eyes. • Deepen your ujjayi breath. Pay attention to the feeling of the mat under your hands and forehead.

COMMON CHALLENGES A tight lower back or hips can prevent your forehead from touching the ground. • Knee injuries can prevent you from bending your knees comfortably.

MODIFICATIONS Bring a block under your forehead to relax your neck. • Roll over onto your back for Supine Butterfly or lay flat on your belly.

SEQUENCE TRANSITION Move forward to your hands and your knees.

Cat–Cow

Cat–Cow is a gentle way to warm up your spine, releasing tension there, including your neck. The pose also creates fluidity in your pelvis and lower back, particularly if you are feeling stiff after a long day of walking up and down steep terrain. It syncs your breath with your body's movement, preparing you for a vinyasa flow.

SETUP On your hands and knees, stack your hands underneath your shoulders, palms flat. Stack your knees under your hips.

ALIGNMENT Pull your navel up and in toward your spine. Keep your spine neutral to start. • **Cat:** On an exhale, arch your spine and roll your shoulders forward. Keep your belly engaged as you round your spine. Move your gaze down toward your legs. • **Cow:** On an inhale, lift your tailbone and chest

Cat

Cow

toward the ceiling. Soften your belly toward the floor while keeping your core engaged. Stretch the crown of your head toward the ceiling. • Repeat Cat–Cow cycle five times.

GAZE & FOCUS Let your drishti move naturally with the pose, or work with your eyes closed. • Move your spine slowly, and let the pace of your breath determine how long it takes to do each Cat and Cow. Take your time and breathe fully.

DEEPEN Shift your hips and neck into broad circular movements. Start clockwise, moving your right hip out past your mat, swing it back down over your heels, move to the left edge of your mat, and move your weight forward into your hands to complete a circle. • Do it three times, then repeat counterclockwise three times.

SEQUENCE TRANSITION Tuck your toes and lift your hips to the ceiling for Downward-Facing Dog.

Downward-Facing Dog

As you become familiar with it, Downward-Facing Dog may feel like the resting pose it is meant to be. Use the time in this pose to listen to your body, open into your shoulders, spine and hamstrings, and focus your gaze.

SETUP Lift your hips to the sky. Move your feet back about six inches toward the back edge of your mat.

ALIGNMENT Point your index fingers to the front of your mat. • Flatten your palms until the knuckles at the base of your index and middle fingers are grounded on your mat. • Move your feet to hip-width distance. Spin your inner ankles back so the outer edges of your feet are parallel with the edge of your mat. • Bend your knees and lift your tailbone toward the ceiling until your spine lengthens. Spin your sit bones to the wall behind you. • Roll your shoulders up to your ears, then use your back muscles to pull your shoulders down your back and in toward your spine. Squeeze your upper arms toward each

Downward-Facing Dog

other. • Press your chest toward your thighs; keep your shoulders engaged and do not hyperextend in your shoulders if you are extra flexible. • Drive your heels toward the floor (they don't need to touch the floor). • Pull your belly in toward your spine. • Lift the muscles just above your knees to engage your thighs and open into your hamstrings. • Create a long line from your wrists to your shoulders and hips; bend your knees as you need to.

GAZE & FOCUS Look backward at the floor between your big toes. • Lift your tailbone high toward the ceiling.

DEEPEN Once the pose feels more comfortable, press your heels deeply toward the mat until your toes can spread and soften.

COMMON CHALLENGES Tight hamstrings can lead to a rounded spine. • If you have a wrist injury, it may be painful to stay on your hands.

MODIFICATIONS For tight hamstrings, bend your knees and lift your tailbone toward the ceiling. Pull your shoulders toward your spine. Press your chest toward your legs. • For wrist pain, come down to your elbows for Dolphin pose: Bend your elbows so they are stacked directly under your shoulders. Walk your feet in toward your elbows as close as you can comfortably. Lift your tailbone to the sky.

SEQUENCE TRANSITION Shift your weight forward to stack your shoulders over your hands for Plank.

Plank

Feel free to bring your knees to the floor and modify your Plank rather than doing the intense version you learned in the Strength Practice. But don't forget to engage uddhiyana bandha!

SETUP Stack your hands underneath your shoulders, index finger pointed straight ahead. Step your feet to the back of your mat. • Stay on the balls of your feet, lift your knees off the floor, and squeeze your legs straight.

Plank

ALIGNMENT Keep your hips just below level with your shoulders. Tilt your tailbone toward your heels. • Spiral your inner thighs up to the ceiling. Squeeze your thighs. • Lift your head so your neck is level with your shoulders. • Press your palms firmly into the floor. Squeeze your upper arm bones toward each other. • Spin the inner eye of your elbows forward, and pull your shoulder blades together. • Lift your belly in toward your spine and wrap your front ribs together. • Stay for ten breaths.

GAZE & FOCUS Set your gaze past the front of your mat. • Keep your legs and core firm. Breathe deeply to maintain the pose.

COMMON CHALLENGES Building strength to hold the full pose for ten breaths can take some practice.

MODIFICATIONS Bring your knees to the floor, toes curled under. Keep your hips in one line with your shoulders.

SEQUENCE TRANSITION Roll forward onto your tiptoes. • Lower in one solid plank to the floor.

Low Cobra

Spend some time in this gentle backbend to open your chest.

SETUP Press the tops of your toes into the floor. • Squeeze your thighs and lift your knees off the mat. Place your hands next to your lower ribs so your elbows are at a 90-degree angle.

ALIGNMENT Engage your core and lift your chest off the floor. Hug your arm bones toward your spine.

Low Cobra

• Tilt your tailbone toward your heels slightly. • Lift your hands an inch off the floor to take weight off your hands.

GAZE & FOCUS Lift your gaze forward about a foot in front of you. • Maintain strong legs and lift from your core.

DEEPEN Press your palms down and lift to Upward-Facing Dog (see Strength Practice II).

SEQUENCE TRANSITION Tuck your toes and lift your hips for Downward-Facing Dog • Walk your feet to the front of your mat.

Rag Doll

Connect to your feet, relax your spine, and let go in your neck.

SETUP Stand with your feet hip-width distance apart. Stretch out your toes and activate your feet. Fold your chest toward the floor. Hold your elbows and allow your upper body to hang, letting go of your head.

Rag Doll

ALIGNMENT Lift and spread out your toes, creating gaps between every toe from your big toe to your pinky toe. Notice how this lifts the arches of your feet. • Soften your toes to the floor. Press the four corners of your feet—your big toe and pinky toe knuckles, and the two sides of your heels—into the floor. • Spin your inner ankles toward the back of your mat and energetically draw your outer ankles toward the floor. • Bend your knees slightly until your belly comes down to the tops of your thighs. Squeeze your inner thighs up toward your pelvis.

• Turn your head side to side to soften your neck. Stick out your tongue to release your jaw. • Sway gently side to side.

GAZE & FOCUS Close your eyes or set your gaze on a spot between your feet. • Stay in the release in your spine and neck.

DEEPEN As you get more open in your hamstrings and lower back, your legs straighten more. Keep your knee joints soft still in the pose.

SEQUENCE TRANSITION Release your elbows and bring your feet together.

Halfway Lift

Open your hamstrings, extend your spine, and practice hinging your hips in this pose.

SETUP Place your hands on your shins. Lift your chest parallel to the floor.

Halfway Lift

ALIGNMENT Root your feet firmly into the floor. Bend your knees as needed and squeeze your thighs. • Stick your butt out toward the wall behind you. Lift your chest even with your hips. • Lengthen the crown of your head away from your tailbone. • Hug your shoulder blades together and to your spine to activate your centerline. Pull your belly up and in.

RELEASE Fold forward to your feet and exhale.

GAZE & FOCUS Look at a spot on the floor in front of your toes. • Create extension in your spine and wrap your shoulder blades toward your spine. • Engage your core.

DEEPEN Place your fingers or hands flat on the floor on the outsides of your feet.

COMMON CHALLENGES Your back rounds because of tight hamstrings.

MODIFICATIONS Bend your knees. Place your hands above your knees on your thighs or on a block in front of your feet.

SEQUENCE TRANSITION Inhale and reach your arms up to the ceiling. • Relax your hands by your sides for Mountain Pose.

Mountain Pose

Practice a combination of effort and ease in your Mountain Pose by engaging your legs and core, while still staying relaxed in your jaw and eyes.

SETUP Stand with your feet directly underneath your hips, arms relaxed by your sides.

ALIGNMENT Point your toes straight ahead, and bring the outer edges of your feet parallel with the edges of your mat; this position may make you slightly pigeon-toed. Lift your toes and connect with the four corners of your feet to the mat. Soften your toes back to the floor. • Lift the arches of your feet, and with your feet grounded, press your outer shins out until you feel your legs engage and with your feet grounded, spiral your inner ankles toward the back of your mat. Energetically, drive your outer ankles down to the floor. • Squeeze your thigh

Mountain Pose, arms extended

muscles to the bone. If your knees become stiff, soften the joints slightly. • Tilt your tailbone down toward the floor. Gently pull in your belly button to engage your core. Squeeze your front ribs toward each other. • Roll your shoulders up to your ears, then soften them down away from your ears. Pull your upper arm bones toward your shoulder blades to engage your shoulders. • Contract the muscles under your shoulder blades. Send breath into your ribs in your mid-back. • Gently pull your belly button in to engage your core. Hug your front ribs toward each other. Breathe into your back ribs. • Let your hands relax by your sides, and spin your palms to face forward. • **Alternative arms:** Reach your arms up to the ceiling in line with your shoulders. Spin your palms to face inward with your thumbs toward the back of your mat. Stretch your fingers out wide. • Lift the crown of your head up toward the sky to lengthen your neck. Soften your jaw. • Set your gaze on one point. • Take ten deep ujjayi breaths.

GAZE & FOCUS Set your eyes at one point in front of you. • Ground your feet and legs, relax your shoulders, and breathe deeply.

Sun Salutation A

Follow the sequence for Sun Salutation A as outlined in Strength Practice I to warm up your body and to focus on your breath. Do three rounds.

Mountain Pose, inhale with your arms up. • Forward Fold, exhale. • Halfway Lift, inhale. • Plank to floor, exhale. • Low Cobra, inhale. • Downward-Facing Dog, exhale, hold pose for five breaths. • Step or jump forward to the front of your mat. • Halfway Lift, inhale. • Forward Fold, exhale. • Mountain Pose, inhale.

Low Lunge

Focus on the stretch in your hip flexors, which may be tense and tight after a long day on the trail.

SETUP Move through Sun Salutation A to Downward-Facing Dog. • From Downward-Facing Dog, step your right foot between your hands. • Lower your back knee to the floor and keep your back toes tucked or point your toes. • Bring your hands to your front thigh.

Low Lunge

ALIGNMENT Square your hips toward the front of your mat. Pull your front foot and back knee toward each other to integrate. Your hips will lift slightly higher than before. • Once your centerline is established, slowly shift your weight forward toward your front foot. Stack your front knee over your ankle. • Squeeze your belly in toward your spine and hug your front ribs together. • Reach your arms up toward the ceiling, palms facing in. Breathe deeply into the stretch in your hip flexor.

GAZE & FOCUS Look at a spot on the wall in front of you. • Hug your inner thighs toward each other to keep your body strong while opening into your hip.

DEEPEN Tuck your back toes and left your knee off the floor for Crescent Lunge (see Strength Practice II).

Twisted Crescent Lunge

Move gently into a twist to activate your core and back muscles and release your spine from a vigorous day outdoors. Keep your back knee on the floor to take the intensity down.

Twisted Crescent Lunge, modified

SETUP From Low Lunge, place your right hand to the inside of your front foot on a block or the floor. • Extend your left hand in line with your shoulder. On an inhale, stretch your chest longer to get more space in your spine. On an exhale, move deeper into the twist.

ALIGNMENT Shift your weight forward toward your left foot, keeping your knee pointing forward over your ankle; don't let it cave in or out. • Lift your left elbow toward the sky; press down into your palms. • Lengthen your spine through the crown of your head to create more space for the twist. • Hug your shoulder blades toward your spine, and deepen your twist. • Pull your belly in toward your spine. • Bring your lower hand to the floor, or a block along the inside edge of your front foot. Stretch your upper fingers out wide and toward the ceiling.

GAZE & FOCUS Set your gaze on a spot on the ceiling. • Squeeze your shoulder blades toward each other. Engage the muscles underneath your shoulder blades to deepen your twist.

DEEPEN Tuck your back toes to the ball of your foot and lift your back leg off the floor. Bring your lower hand to the floor or a block outside your front leg.

COMMON CHALLENGES You will need to develop strength and stability in your legs to hold the full pose. Squeeze your inner thighs for balance.

MODIFICATIONS Keep your back knee on the floor. Pad your knee if you feel pain in your kneecap.

SEQUENCE TRANSITION Bring your hands down to the floor on either side of your front foot, returning to Low Lunge.

Airplane, modified

If your feet are feeling the effects of the previous day, a modified Airplane creates a gentle challenge for tired feet.

SETUP From a Low Lunge, tuck your back toes. Walk your hands in front of you, and place two blocks at shoulder-width distance from each other

Airplane, modified

at about six inches in front of your foot. • Lift your back leg to be parallel with the floor.

ALIGNMENT Stretch your chest to be parallel with the floor. • Hug your shoulders in toward your back. • Squeeze your belly in toward your spine. • Press your standing foot and leg into the floor, and squeeze your thigh muscles. • Push through your back heel on your lifted leg, and spin your toes to point toward the floor. • Lift your back foot so it is even with your head. • Stay for five breaths.

GAZE & FOCUS Look at the floor just in front of the blocks. • Work on the inner spiral of your back leg, rotating your right hip even with your left hip. Squeeze your glute on your lifted leg.

SEQUENCE TRANSITION Step your back foot onto the floor for Revolved Triangle.

Revolved Triangle

Stay steady in your legs to challenge your balance. Engage your oblique muscles to create the twist.

SETUP Set your feet in a stance slightly shorter than Warrior 1, or the length of one leg. Position your feet about hip-width distance. Point your back foot out at a 45-degree angle. • Take your left hand to your left hip. Lower your chest parallel to the floor, your core lock engaged. Bring your right hand to a block at the tallest or middle height along the inside edge of your front shin.

ALIGNMENT Press your back foot into the floor and tilt your tailbone to press your sit bones to the wall behind you. • Squeeze your thigh muscles, including your inner thighs, toward your pelvis. • Pull your belly in toward your spine. • Stretch your chest parallel to the floor to lengthen your spine. • With your left hand still on your hip, squeeze your shoulder blades in toward your spine and spin your chest up toward the ceiling. • Reach your left arm up to the ceiling.

GAZE & FOCUS Look at your upper hand. • Press your back foot deeply into the mat, and distribute your weight evenly between front and back foot. Rotate from your oblique muscles.

DEEPEN Bring your lower hand to the floor inside your foot, or place your block outside your front foot to challenge your balance and twist.

COMMON CHALLENGES Weak glutes or legs prevent you from grounding your back foot and keeping your hips even as you twist.

MODIFICATIONS Use the block at the tallest height or even your shin, avoiding your knee. • Focus on grounding your feet before you twist.

Revolved Triangle

SEQUENCE TRANSITION Fold forward over your front leg to release. • Plant your hands on the floor and step your feet back to Plank. • Shift to your tiptoes and lower to the floor. • Lift your chest to Low Cobra. • Press back to Downward-Facing Dog. • Complete Low Lunge through Revolved Triangle on your right side. • Step or jump to the front of your mat.

Tree

Tree is a powerful grounding pose and focal point to bring your awareness to the present moment, helpful when you are tired.

SETUP Stand with your feet together in Mountain Pose. Lift your right foot to either your inner calf or above your knee joint to your inner thigh. • Bring your palms together at the center of your chest.

ALIGNMENT Ground the four corners of your standing foot into your mat. • Press your lifted foot into your standing leg. • Hug your shoulder blades to your spine. Press your palms together. • Pull your belly in toward your spine; lift your lower ribs away

Tree

from your pelvis. • Interlace your hands. Press them down toward the floor, then lift them up toward the ceiling, palms facing up to the sky.

GAZE & FOCUS Set your gaze on a spot in front of you. Once you are stable, move your gaze up the wall to the ceiling. • Ground your standing leg and stretch your spine skyward.

DEEPEN Walk your gaze up to the ceiling behind you.

COMMON CHALLENGES You are still building strength in your feet and have trouble staying upright with only one foot on the floor.

MODIFICATIONS Prop the foot of your bent leg against the ankle of your standing foot with the ball of your foot on the floor.

SEQUENCE TRANSITION Do Tree pose on both sides.
• Stand with your feet together in Mountain Pose.
• Inhale and reach your arms up to the ceiling, palms facing each other. • Bring your hands in front of your chest and fold your chest forward to your feet and exhale. • Lengthen your chest to Halfway Lift. • Plant your hands, and step back to Plank.
• Roll forward onto your tiptoes and lower to the floor.
• Lift your chest for Low Cobra. • Tuck your toes and lift your hips to Downward-Facing Dog. • Step your right foot to your right hand into Low Lunge.

RELEASE AND RESTORE
It's time to move into poses that both release and restore your body. Your trunk and lower body have shouldered much of the work. Focus on breathing and releasing in these deep stretches.

Lizard with Quad Stretch

Your body may resist the intensity of this pose at first. Use your breath to release deep into your hips.

SETUP From Low Lunge, bring both hands to the floor inside your front leg. • Angle your toes on your front foot to the outer edge of your mat.

ALIGNMENT Flex your front foot and roll to the outer edge of your foot. The sole of your foot is off the floor and your right knee will roll open. • Come up

ACTIVE & PASSIVE RELEASE

....

Your brain is in constant conversation with your muscles while you stretch so it's helpful to understand how you can release. If you're not making much progress in mobility, you may not be stretching the targeted muscles. Follow cues in the poses to stretch into the appropriate part of your body.

Passive release: When you are doing passive stretches, you use body weight, gravity, and muscles to stretch. A stretch held for a longer period of time will also stretch into fascia, the connective tissue holding your body together. You never want to force your body into a stretch, which causes the muscles to contract and blocks the deepening of the stretch. Work slowly, breathing to release into the muscle. Holding a passive stretch for thirty to sixty seconds gives the muscle time to relax.

Active release: Here, you focus on a combination of muscles for release by contracting one muscle to let another muscle relax and deepen in. For example, your thigh muscles extend or straighten your knee. Contracting your thighs also signal the hamstrings to relax. In a Seated Forward Fold, you reach for your feet and straighten your legs to stretch your hamstrings. But if you soften slightly at the knee, then contract your thigh muscle to straighten your knee again, you signal the muscle to soften even deeper into the stretch. You can use this active release in your practice.

In another method of stretching, sometimes called ballistic, your body remembers the length of muscles from the last time you practiced. Each time you do a Sun Salutation, your muscles reset to the length from the last time you did yoga. Essentially, you are opening muscles throughout your entire practice, not just when you stretch at the end.

Lizard

to your hands. Reach your right hand for your back foot. Stay on your left hand or lower your left elbow to a block or the floor in line with your front heel. Slowly shift your weight toward your front foot. Stay another ten breaths. Look to a spot on the wall to the right or close your eyes. • Let go of your back foot gently.

GAZE & FOCUS Look at the inside of your front foot. • Notice the sensations in your hip and send your breath there.

COMMON CHALLENGES Tight hips prevent you from coming down to your elbows.

MODIFICATIONS Place a block underneath your elbows. • If you have trouble grabbing your foot because of tightness in your hamstrings or hips, loop a strap around your foot and hold the strap for the stretch.

SEQUENCE TRANSITION Bring your front foot to point toward the front of your mat for a Low Lunge.

Half Splits

Combine engagement of your thigh muscles with softening to relax into this pose. Your hamstrings and you deserve the break.

SETUP From Low Lunge, straighten your front leg and flex your front foot toward your knee. Stack your hips over your back knee. Slide your front foot forward slightly.

ALIGNMENT Bring your hands down on either side of your front leg. • Lift the muscles above your front

Half Splits

knee to engage your thighs to open your hamstrings; do not force the stretch. • Spiral your inner thighs toward each other and down toward the floor. • Lengthen your chest toward your front foot. • Anchor your belly up and in toward your back.

RELEASE Shift your weight forward to Low Lunge.

GAZE & FOCUS Look at your front toes. • Squeeze your quads to open deep into the belly of your hamstrings.

COMMON CHALLENGES Tightness in your hamstrings or lower back prevent you from bringing your hands to the floor.

MODIFICATIONS Place a block on either side of your legs to use for stability as you lengthen your spine in the pose.

SEQUENCE TRANSITION Shift your weight onto your front foot for a Low Lunge.

Half Pigeon

By now, you may have a new appreciation for the release available in your hips after they are tense from a long hike. Challenge yourself to stay in Half Pigeon longer than you have before.

SETUP From Low Lunge, move your right foot across your mat and in toward your pelvis, keeping your right foot flexed to protect your knee. • Extend your left leg straight behind you so that the top of your thigh is on the ground.

Half Pigeon

ALIGNMENT Flex the toes on your back foot and come up to the ball of your foot. Roll up to center so your pelvis is squared toward the front of your mat. Place a block under your right hip if you have trouble staying centered. • Pull your thigh bones in toward your pelvis. • Lengthen your chest and slowly lower your torso toward the floor. • Walk your arms in front of you. Soften your shoulders and face. • Place a block under your forehead if it doesn't touch your mat. • Stay for one minute.

GAZE & FOCUS Close your eyes. • Breathe deeply into your hips.

DEEPEN Shift your front shin closer to parallel with the front of your mat to get a deeper opening.

COMMON CHALLENGES Knee injuries prevent you from staying in this pose without sharp pain.

MODIFICATIONS Take Reclined Half Pigeon (see Strength Practice I).

SEQUENCE TRANSITION Walk your hands back in toward your front leg. • Plant your hands on the floor and step your right foot back into Downward-Facing Dog. • Lift your right leg to the ceiling and roll your right hip open for Three-Legged Dog. • Lower your foot back to the floor. • Step your left foot into Low Lunge. • Complete Lizard through Half Pigeon on the left side. • Once you have completed both sides, walk your hands back in toward your front leg, and step your front leg back to Plank. • Lower from Plank to the floor.

One-Armed Shoulder Opener

Many poses you have learned strengthen your shoulders. This pose is a passive stretch deep into your shoulder girdle, reversing your body's inclination to hunch. It also supports the mobility of your shoulder joint and can provide release for your upper back, where many people hold stress.

SETUP From your belly on the floor, extend your right arm out so your wrist is level with your eyes, palm down. • Place your left hand next to your ribs on the floor, elbow bent at a 90-degree angle to the floor. • Roll over onto your right hip, bend your left leg and set your foot on the floor behind your right leg. • Rest your temple on the floor or on a block.

ALIGNMENT With your left hand, which has leverage, press gently into the floor until your body naturally stops you. • Relax your shoulder and your face. • Stay for ten full breaths.

GAZE & FOCUS Look at the floor or close your eyes. • Relax into the pose. Stay focused on your breath.

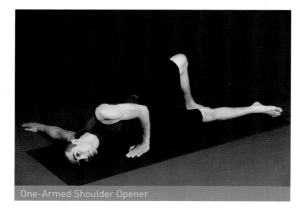

One-Armed Shoulder Opener

DEEPEN If your body allows, bend your lower leg and place your foot on the floor parallel with your left foot, like a bridge. • Reach your left hand up toward the ceiling, wind it behind your body, reaching for your extended lower hand to bind. Keep your lower arm in line with your shoulder.

COMMON CHALLENGES If you have a shoulder injury, particularly in your rotator cuff, your shoulder may not allow you to do this stretch.

MODIFICATIONS Substitute Locust pose with a bind at your lower back (see below).

SEQUENCE TRANSITION Roll back onto your belly.
• Set up for the left side of the One-Armed Shoulder Opener.

Locust

An active backbend, Locust builds strength in your lower back. Your body must lift to counter gravity, strengthening to extend your chest and legs. Think about lifting from the front side of your body. It is a heart opener after all.

SETUP On your belly, bring your feet to hip-width distance, toes pointed. Reach your arms alongside your body, hands down by your hips, palms facing down.

ALIGNMENT Press the tops of your feet into the floor, and lift your knees off the ground. Keep your upper legs engaged, and lift them off the floor. • Lengthen the crown of your head forward, and lengthen and lift your chest to the ceiling. Hug your shoulders

Locust

in toward your spine. • Lift your upper arm bones toward the ceiling and float your hands above your hips. • Pull your belly up and in to lift even higher into the pose. • Stay for five breaths.

GAZE & FOCUS Look past your nose at the front edge of your mat or the floor. • Squeeze your legs, engage your core, and lift from your chest forward and up to the sky.

DEEPEN Bring your inner thighs and ankles together and lift. • **Bound variation:** Interlace your hands at your lower back. If you have tight shoulders and want to work up to doing a bind, hold a strap with your hands to modify. Lift your hands off your lower back in the pose.

COMMON CHALLENGES You feel lower back strain.

MODIFICATIONS Keep the tops of your feet on the floor. Place your hands by your lower ribs. • Lift your chest into Low Cobra.

SEQUENCE TRANSITION Lower slowly to the floor from Locust. Wiggle your hips side to side to release your back. • Do a second Locust with the Bound variation. • Press up to your hands and knees.

Heart Throat Nose Pose

Another shoulder and heart opener, Heart Throat Nose Pose can feel comforting because we face the floor rather than the open air above. It creates a big opening into your chest and shoulders with a grounding quality with its connection to the earth.

Heart Throat Nose Pose

SETUP From hands and knees, walk your arms forward, keeping your hips stacked over your knees, until your forehead comes to the ground.

ALIGNMENT Activate your core to protect your lower back. • Melt the space between your shoulders toward the floor. • Stay for five breaths.

GAZE & FOCUS Set your gaze on the floor or close your eyes. • Soften into your upper back.

DEEPEN If your shoulders are open enough that your chest touches the floor, lift your chin and place it on the floor.

SEQUENCE TRANSITION Walk your hands in and come to a seated position on your knees.

Toes Pose

Your feet take a pounding on the trail, working hard to stabilize on whatever terrain you may encounter. In addition, most people spend at least some of their day up on the balls of their feet in shoes with a slightly lifted heel rather than flexing their feet and working into their Achilles tendon. Toes Pose can be an intense stretch into the soles of your feet. Breathe!

SETUP Tuck your toes underneath you until you are on the ball of your foot—tuck your pinky toe in if it escapes. • Sit up slowly and lift your chest over your hips until you feel the sensation in your feet.

Toes Pose

ALIGNMENT If the pose is immediately too intense, lean forward for a moment, then return to lift your chest upright. • Stay for ten full breaths.

RELEASE Shift forward onto hands and knees. Release your toe tuck and point your toes on the floor. Bring your hands by your hips and lean back to stretch into your shins, the front of your foot and your ankles in the opposite direction to counter the intensity. Stay for five breaths.

GAZE & FOCUS Set your gaze on a spot on the wall. • Notice if your mind wants to take you out of the pose. Stay with it.

DEEPEN Hold for twenty breaths.

COMMON CHALLENGES Knee pain prevents you from taking the pose.

MODIFICATIONS Roll up a blanket (or small towel) and place it behind your knees or on top of your ankles.

Frog

Frog

An intense pose that moves into your inner thighs and groin, Frog may take some time to love. But once you fall, you fall deeply. It takes practice to stay in the pose for more than a few breaths, but it's worth pursuing: you will open deeply into new regions of your hips, and learn more about how to stay in one place when confronted with challenge.

SETUP Fold up the short edges of your mat to pad your knees. Bring your inner knees wider than hip-width distance apart on the padded edges. • Come down to your elbows (you will be off your mat).

• Move your feet to 90-degree angles with your knees. Flex your feet and bring your inner ankles to the floor. • Stack a block under your forehead.

ALIGNMENT Ensure your hips are even with your knees. • If you don't feel sensation, move your knees wider. • Pull your thigh bones in toward your pelvis. • Stay for two minutes.

GAZE & FOCUS Close your eyes. • Stay with your breath and focus on the slow release in your groin.

DEEPEN Stay longer! Try staying in this pose for up to three or four minutes, and see what happens.

SEQUENCE TRANSITION Slowly slide forward onto your belly. • Come to a seated position at the front of your mat.

Reverse Tabletop

A modified backbend that releases into your chest and shoulders, Reverse Tabletop also helps your body release from the intensity of Frog.

Reverse Tabletop

SETUP From a seated position, place your hands behind you on the mat with your fingertips facing your body. Walk your feet in so they are flat on the floor at hip-width distance.

ALIGNMENT Ground into the four corners of your feet and lift your hips toward the ceiling. • Press your palms into the ground. • Lengthen the crown of your head behind you. Gently release your head onto your shoulders. • Rotate your inner thighs toward each other and down toward your mat.

GAZE & FOCUS Set your gaze on the ceiling or wall behind you. • Ground your feet deeper into the floor to activate your leg muscles.

COMMON CHALLENGES Weak hamstrings make it difficult to keep your legs internally rotated. • Tight chest muscles can make breathing feel challenging.

MODIFICATIONS Play with moving your breath around to stay in the pose.

SEQUENCE TRANSITION Lower your hips to the floor.

Head-to-Knee Seated Fold with a Twist

By adding a twist, this pose works the length of your spine and also moves into your side body.

SETUP From a seated position, extend your left leg toward the front left corner of your mat, toes flexed. • Tuck your other foot in toward your pelvis, bringing the sole of the foot in against your inner thigh.

ALIGNMENT Flex the toes on your extended leg toward your knee; squeeze your thigh muscles. • Twist: Place your left forearm on your left shin, or lower it to the floor just in front of your shin. • Extend your right arm up to the ceiling. Roll your shoulder blades in toward your spine. • Reach your upper hand toward your left foot, palm facing down. Rotate your chest to the ceiling. • If you can reach your foot, hold onto your big toe. Make sure to spin your chest toward the sky. • Stay for ten breaths.

GAZE & FOCUS Look up at the ceiling. • Ground your sit bones into the mat.

COMMON CHALLENGES Knee injuries prevent you from bringing your foot in toward your pelvis.

MODIFICATIONS Slide your bent foot into your knee or lower leg instead of to your inner thigh.

SEQUENCE TRANSITION Repeat the Head-to-Knee Seated Fold with a twist on the other side.

Seated Twist

Release your spine gently from practice and also from the effects of the trail through a Seated Twist pose.

SETUP Extend your right leg straight to the front of your mat, toes flexed. Place your left foot on the floor outside your right thigh. • Place your left hand on the floor behind you. Reach your right arm up to the ceiling. • Wrap your right arm around your bent leg.

ALIGNMENT Lengthen your spine on your inhale. Twist toward your bent leg on your exhale. • Stay for five breaths.

GAZE & FOCUS Move your gaze past your left shoulder. • Inhale to lengthen your spine and exhale to deepen your twist.

DEEPEN Hook your right elbow outside your left leg. • Cross your lower leg underneath you.

Seated Twist

SEQUENCE TRANSITION Repeat the Seated Twist on the other side. • Slowly roll down to the floor or move your mat to a wall.

Legs Up the Wall

If you haven't tried this pose at the wall, this is the moment. You'll truly appreciate this restorative inversion after all of the release in this sequence.

Legs Up the Wall

SETUP Move your mat to a wall. Bring your left hip to touch the base of the wall. • Lower yourself down to your back, and lift your legs up the wall. Scoot your sit bones to touch the wall.

ALIGNMENT Press your feet into the wall, lift your hips, and slide a block underneath your lower back. • Relax your legs. • Soften your shoulders, face, and hands.

GAZE & FOCUS Close your eyes. • Breathe deeply and relax. Keep your legs still.

SEQUENCE TRANSITION If you are coming out of Legs Up the Wall, pull your knees to your chest and roll to one side. • Move onto your back for Corpse Pose.

FINAL REST

You can stay in Legs Up the Wall pose for your Final Rest—it's a wonderful modification that restores your body. Or if you would like to rest in Corpse Pose, come back to the floor.

Corpse Pose

Corpse Pose is the embodiment of recovery. Commit to true stillness and relaxation. Take the time for a long rest.

Corpse Pose

SETUP From your back, straighten your legs on your mat. • With your arms at your sides, turn your palms to face the sky.

ALIGNMENT Slide your shoulders under you. • Relax the muscles in your legs, shoulders, and face. • Move into your natural breath. • Stay in this pose for three minutes.

GAZE & FOCUS Close your eyes. • Stay awake and still. Notice your natural breath.

DEEPEN Take a five-minute final rest.

SUPPORTED FINAL REST Sweeten your Final Rest with a bolster. Come up to a seated position. • Place a bolster at the base of your spine. Lay down along the bolster. • Release your hands to the floor. Close your eyes. Ahh!

CHAPTER 5
YOGA PRACTICES IN THE WOODS

SOMETIMES THE PEAK OF a hike is a snowcapped, craggy mountaintop that stuns you into awed silence. Sometimes the "peak" is an alpine lake so deeply blue you never imagined such a color existed, or it is the depths of a canyon down to a river or lake, even though you know that a climb awaits you on your return to the trailhead. The pinnacle of a hike could more aptly be titled the halfway point—the time when you sit down, contemplate a space and place bigger than your body, and eat the best lunch of your life.

Whether you hiked up or down, you challenged your body. If it wasn't the elevation, at the very least you worked on endurance and the balance required on uneven terrain. It is time to rest, refuel, and move your body in new directions to ease the muscles that have tightened up from the first half of your day. It also is an opportunity to reflect on where your legs have carried you, to contemplate the beauty of where you have arrived, and to take it all in. A yoga practice offers mindfulness in the moment and a connection to the source of why you travel to the wilderness—and can keep you limber for the return trip.

Doing some yoga poses at the end of your day will also help your body rejuvenate, particularly if you are out on a multiday backpacking trip. If you're anything like me, you'd rather make dinner immediately upon reaching your campsite—or just set up your tent and collapse. Instead, try doing a few poses while your body is still warm from your hike—when you're waiting for a friend to take off her boots, or when the water is heating up for your evening meal. Or sit by the campfire in a hip opening pose. It doesn't take much, and the rewards will be great.

PINNACLE PRACTICE

Take off your pack. Look around. Notice the color of the sky. Feel the temperature of the air on your skin. What do you smell? Gather in the view. Do you see mountaintops or trees or vast desert? Listen to what is around you. Do you hear birds, water, or other hikers? Breathe deeply for five breaths. Find a fairly even surface. Do a few yoga poses, in bare feet if possible. Or try the following sequence.

Mountain Pose

» Stand with your feet together.
» Reach your arms up to the sky. Feel the great stretch in your spine.
» Lift your face to the sun. Breathe deeply for five full rounds.

Squat

» Stand with your feet wider than your shoulders.
» Lower your hips down between your feet so your hips dip below your knees.
» Press your elbows into your inner knees.
» Lift your chest up to the sky. Stay for ten breaths.

Rag Doll

» Stand with your feet at hip-width distance.
» Bend your legs slightly at the knee.
» Fold your chest forward over your legs.
» Move your hands to your lower back, interlacing your fingers to bind your hands.
» Stretch your arms away from your back.

Horse Stance Twists

» Stand with your feet a leg's length distance apart from each other, turning both feet out at an angle.
» Bend your knees, tracking your knees over your ankles in the direction of your toes.

MICK PEARSON
Founder, Kaf Adventures
Seattle, Washington

Q: How did you get your start with yoga?
A: To me, yoga has been always outdoors. I was on a Boundary Waters trip in Minnesota with a friend and coworker. They were stretching. I asked, "What are you doing?" They said, "This is yoga." At some point, it morphed into a game, trying to pick up a bag while standing on one foot. That was the first time.

Q: Why do you do yoga outdoors?
A: Doing yoga outside is about the commonality of getting adults together to focus internally. It's a lot easier to focus internally when you're outdoors because you're in the womb of your existence. It's such a beautiful place to be, to sit. I think that's why we all go outside. We value it, we can feel the energy from the earth. Incorporate that with breath, movement, and overall intention around your own personal growth, and now you've got an entire group of individuals who are also trying to build community and that intentionality. That's the whole part of why I do outdoor education. It's about community and individual growth, and it's about learning a little bit of yourself and the people around you.

Q: What's different about taking people out on group hikes where they also do yoga?
A: Lots of people say they go outside for this one peak or activity or final destination. When you say I'm going outside to do yoga, already you can tell, it's not necessarily related to an outcome. Of course you want to get to the lake, etc., but maybe it's not as important how quickly you get to the lake or if you get to the lake at all. In our experience, it doesn't actually matter.

» Bring your hands to your inner thighs, and press until your arms are straight.
» Lower your right shoulder toward your left foot for a twist with your core engaged. Hold for five breaths.

» Come back to neutral.
» Lower your left shoulder toward your right foot. Hold for five breaths.

One-Legged Chair

» Stand with your feet together. Lower your hips toward the ground for Chair pose.
» Cross your right ankle over your left knee. Flex your upper foot.
» Insert your thumbs into your hip crease (the indentation where the top of your leg meets your hip socket), and press your hips back until you feel a stretch in your hip in your bent leg.
» Hold for five breaths. Repeat on the left side.
» Variation: Hold onto a tree or use a boulder or trekking pole for balance.

Low Lunge with Quad Stretch

» Stand with your feet together. Step your left foot far enough behind you so that you can lower your left knee to the ground. Bring your hands to the ground.
» Pull your left hip toward your right knee. Pull your belly in toward your spine.
» Reach your left hand for your back leg and pull your foot toward you.

» Rest your front hand on your front thigh. Stay for five breaths.
» Bring your hands back to the ground. Step your back foot forward to your right foot.
» Do the pose on the other side.

Upward-Facing Dog

» Lower down to your belly. Place your hands below your elbows next to your lower ribs.
» Press the tops of your feet down into the earth, and lift your knees off the ground.
» Plant your palms into the ground, and straighten your arms, with your shoulders stacked over your wrists.
» Lift your chest to the sky. Lift your gaze and feel the air on your face.
» Hug your shoulder blades in toward your spine.
» Stay for five breaths.

POST-HIKE PRACTICE

For a day out backpacking, add the following poses to the Pinnacle Practice (above) to help ease the intensity of the day. These additional poses help release your hips and lower back from the extra weight of your backpack. You can do this practice on the ground with boots on, if necessary, but barefoot on a tarp is nicer! Do all the poses in order on your right side, then switch to your left.

Twisted Crescent Lunge, Modified

» Come to a Low Lunge with your right foot in front, and your back knee on the ground behind you.
» Lower your left hand to the ground; squeeze your inner thighs in toward your pelvis.
» Stretch your right fingers up to the sky. Hug your shoulder blades toward your spine.
» Engage your core lock. Look up past your right hand to the clouds. Stay for five breaths.

Warrior 2

» Bring both hands to the ground in your Low Lunge. Tuck your back toes and spin your back heel to the ground. Come all the way up.
» Bend your right knee over your front ankle.
» Extend your arms out parallel to the earth away from your chest.

» Set your gaze on your front fingers. Stay for five breaths.

Triangle

» Keeping your front foot facing forward, straighten your front leg.
» Reach your front arm forward and lengthen your spine.
» Lower your right hand to your right shin. Stretch your left fingers to the sky and look up past your left hand.
» Stay for five breaths.

Skandasana

» Come up to stand from Triangle.
» Spin your right foot parallel with your left foot.
» Turn your left toes out slightly at an angle, and bend your left knee over your left ankle.
» Keep your right leg straight. Bring your hands to the ground under your shoulders.
» Lift your chest even with your hips.
» Pull your belly in toward your back.
» Stay for five breaths.

Half Splits

» From Skandasana, walk your hands to your right foot, and come back to a Low Lunge.
» Shift your weight back so your hips stack over your left leg.
» Come onto the heel of your right foot, sliding it forward if necessary.
» Squeeze your right thigh muscles and lower your chest gently over your right leg into a hamstring stretch.
» Stay for five breaths.

Lizard

» Shift your weight forward into a Low Lunge. Bring your hands to the ground inside your right foot.

» Turn your right toes out at an angle, and roll to the outer edge of your foot. Keep your foot flexed.
» Stay here with your hands on the ground or deepen by bringing your forearms to the ground.
» Stay for five breaths.

Half Pigeon

» Come up to your hands from Lizard.
» Walk your right foot in front of your body until your right knee comes to the ground. Keep your foot flexed.
» Square your hips toward the ground. Lift your chest up and lengthen your spine.
» Slowly lower your chest to the ground.
» Stay for ten breaths.

CHAPTER 6
FINDING A YOGA CLASS

I WAS MINDING MY own practice in class. My sister was with me; we were there to move, breathe, and get a break from the family vacation we were on in Taiwan. I was content to be in a challenging yoga class under the watchful eye of Patrick Creelman, an experienced teacher for the Pure Yoga franchise.

The class was up in Wheel pose. Patrick came over to me. "Move your feet closer together," he said. I was annoyed. I knew that would make the pose harder. He used his feet to inch mine closer together. I went up. Yep, harder. I also felt the backbend go deeper. My legs were shaking from the intensity.

We came down, and he called for another. Out of habit or rebelliousness, I can't say for sure, I inched my feet out wider. He came back to me and said, "Bring your feet closer together." I got the message. *You're strong enough. You can do this.*

You can learn many things about yourself in a home yoga practice. With breath, a focus on your feet and alignment, and a quiet space, you can move through a deeper understanding of your body, and shift your energy and mental space. It's the same energy you might feel if you love to hike solo. You focus, you breathe, and you are one with the trail.

But at some point, everyone needs to get *checked*, as Patrick told the class that day. A teacher is like your hardcore friend who encourages you to go on a more difficult hike than you feel up for, or the one who says it's time to plan a backpacking trip, even though you swore those days were behind you.

When I encounter a yoga teacher like Patrick, I remember why it's so important to be held accountable. If I practice alone, I can't always see the next step in my practice. Or, even if I do see it, I talk myself out of doing it. Without someone there to keep an eye on me, I might give up on myself. Practicing with a great teacher is a way of giving back to yourself. You will learn new poses, see new possibilities in your practice, and become immersed in a new community—all effective reasons to take a class.

I have practiced with hundreds of people at trainings. The words of my teachers landed in my body and chest, and opened me up in ways I had never felt before, physically and energetically. At times in final rest I remember feeling a deep sense of freedom; contentment; and true, uplifted joy akin to a hike on a cool, perfect day summiting a peak with the people I love most in the world.

A guided practice also offers a different kind of freedom: You don't have to think about the next pose or where to move your feet or hands. A teacher leads the way.

As you take on the practices in this book and get stronger, the next step will be finding a place to elevate your practice. While it is useful to understand the basics of the types of yoga available, it is more important to find a place that fits with your overall intention for your practice. With so many options available, the search can feel challenging. Start with the easiest options, such as a nearby community center, your office, or the classes at your gym. If none of those feel quite right, take advantage of a yoga studio's introductory offer, lasting from one week to one month, giving you a chance to take classes from multiple instructors and see if the studio community is a fit.

If one doesn't work out, try another. It's important to find one that suits you. Follow the four steps below to define what you want to get from a yoga class. *Stay open to the process!*

STEP 1: CHOOSE AN ENVIRONMENT

Identify what kind of environment you want to practice in. For some people, the convenience of a workplace class counterbalances the absurdity of practicing in a conference room! For others, the gym is perfectly acceptable. For those of you looking for a deeper quiet with like-minded people, a yoga studio may be the best fit. No matter where you go, try more than one teacher at a location, particularly if the place offers different styles.

WORKPLACE

Some workplaces now offer their employees yoga classes. These classes are frequently subsidized and so may be offered at a lower drop-in rate than they would be at a yoga studio. You will also get to know your coworkers in a different space. I taught a corporate class where the CEO showed up every week. You never know who will be practicing next to you!

GYM

Most classes are included in your gym membership, so it's a convenient, low-cost way to experience a guided class with a teacher who can check your form. Drawbacks may include a louder environment than you'd like, with people coming and going during the session.

YOGA STUDIOS

Yoga studios offer more daily classes and likely more variety in style than the gym or your workplace, although some specialize. The environment is designed to be clear and calming with an intention to create community. The best yoga studios foster powerful communities where teachers and students know one another, connect on a personal level, and are part of each other's daily lives. If you are looking to deepen your practice, a studio also generally offers workshops and trainings to give you more guidance.

STEP 2: IDENTIFY A STYLE THAT SPEAKS TO YOU

As yoga has exploded in popularity in the United States, the number of styles continues to expand. From a gentle yin practice to relax your body to flow practices where people pop upside down into handstands at every opportunity, the choices are vast. The following broad guidelines will get you started. The styles are listed roughly in order from more vigorous practices to gentler, though that varies depending on your idea of challenge!

HEATED VERSUS NOT HEATED

Heated yoga rooms are fairly common, particularly in yoga studios. There's a wide variety in approach. Bikram or Hot Hatha practices generally reach temperatures of at least 100 degrees. Most power or vinyasa flow practices, such as the ones in this book, are taught with some heat, generally in the mid-80s to mid-90s. Unheated classes are taught at room temperature.

The idea behind heat is that it opens your body and helps you sweat to detoxify. Some people love the intense rinse of a heated class. Others prefer to build heat internally through the practice. You may discover that you love a big, sweaty practice. Or you may find you need a balance between the two. Keep in mind that some people's bodies do not tolerate heat well.

FLOW

Ashtanga is the original flow practice. Sun Salutation A and B as you have learned in this book are rooted in this style, as is vinyasa flow, or connecting poses with breath. Many teachers credit Ashtanga for teaching them discipline and flow— it is considered an extremely rigorous practice.

Many descriptions of practices will use the word "flow," but they all are likely to rely on a connection of breath and poses moving together. Some work with one breath per movement throughout the entire practice, while other practices encourage students to hold poses longer, more common in "power yoga" classes. Some types of practices work with a set sequence, such as Ashtanga and Baptiste Power Yoga, while others will sequence to work different areas of the body and build up to different poses.

HATHA

All yoga is a hatha practice, but these days hatha usually indicates a nonflow practice; the best known of these, Bikram, founded by Bikram Choudhury, features classes held in intense heat. The studios use mirrors for you to focus your gaze, and the Bikram sequence is a set series of the same twenty-six poses.

Iyengar, created by yoga master B. K. S. Iyengar, is another nonflow practice that moves from pose to pose, working deeply and precisely into alignment with a focus on healing the body and mind through poses. An Iyengar practice uses many props and fine-tunes alignment with long holds.

ANNETTE MCGIVNEY
Southwest Field Editor, *Backpacker* magazine
Author, *Resurrection: Glen Canyon and a New Vision*
for the American West* and *Leave No Trace: A Guide
to Wilderness Etiquette
Flagstaff, Arizona

Q: Why did you start practicing yoga?
A: I had done enough trips with packs that were too heavy. I started having problems with my knees. My doctor said I might need to have surgery for torn cartilage. I went to the Flagstaff Athletic Club, which had some yoga classes, and started doing that.

Q: How did yoga help?
A: I didn't end up having knee surgery. It made me aware of my body in a way I had not been up to that point. Yoga made me use my body in a way that felt really good. I thought I had to run to get the emotional high that I needed or to hike to get my heart rate up. I was able to learn practicing yoga also would give me that sense of well-being.

Q: Has yoga helped your backpacking and other outdoor pursuits?
A: It has made me a better backpacker as far as sense of center of gravity and balance. If I'm carrying a 40-pound pack down a crazy steep drop-off in the Grand Canyon, I'm a better hiker and more stable.

Q: What else do you get from yoga?
A: Yoga also gives me that sense of grounded-ness, being connected to my body and being connected to the earth. You can do it anywhere. You can have that connection in your living room. When I'm hiking, I'm out there. I'm surrounded by trees, I'm part of the outside world. When I'm practicing yoga, I have that same connection, but it's this hyperawareness of my own body. It's an inner world instead of the outer world. It makes me tune into my hips and breathe into that space. That makes me feel whole, the way hiking to the top of a hill and breathing hard and getting there and looking at the view makes me feel whole also.

KUNDALINI

Kundalini means "serpent power" and is an energetic practice that might include waving your hands or closing and opening your hands over and over. It also includes meditation, poses, mantra, and breathing techniques.

GENTLE OR YIN

Also known as restorative yoga, this style is geared toward restoring your body from intense athletic days, or for people with injuries or other physical challenges who want to breathe and move at a slower, modified pace. A yin practice will take you through long deep holds, while a gentle class could show up as a modified flow practice or moving from pose to pose.

STEP 3: IDENTIFY TEACHERS WHO ELEVATE YOU

A great teacher inspires me to hold a pose longer or pop into an extra Wheel, especially when I don't want to. If a teacher is great *and* funny, she can make me laugh. I love those classes. When it comes to your yoga practice, a great teacher can be the difference between staying committed and giving up.

The first step to looking for a teacher is looking at her credentials. Make sure she comes from an established yoga training program. In addition to training, experience is a helpful indicator. The more time a teacher has spent understanding the body, how to read a class of different body types and experiences, and how to speak to the body in a way that makes sense to you, the more effective she will be for you and your practice. Most yoga teachers also assist in poses to support your alignment, and a great assist can make the difference between struggle and freedom in a pose.

Beyond that, a great teacher resonates with you personally. You may find you prefer the sequences taught by a particular teacher. You may find you need a funny teacher to get through a challenging class. You may be drawn to a gentle teacher who gives you space to grow, or you may find yourself going back to a teacher who has heart and passion to challenge you to explore new depths in your poses.

Lastly, find more than one teacher. Every teacher, whether at a community center near your home or at a yoga studio, has something to share. You may be surprised when a teacher you initially didn't like grows on you. Listen and learn along the way, and you will find new teachers to support you and learn something about yourself.

STEP 4: CREATE YOUR YOGA COMMUNITY

Like a hiking buddy who checks in on you regularly and gets you out on the trails more than you might venture out on your own, a community can help you stick with your yoga practice. As you search for a place to practice, observe the community. Do people chat before and after class? Does the person at the front desk know your name? Does the teacher ask people to introduce themselves to each other?

You may be tempted to isolate yourself in practice, particularly when you are new. But practicing with a teacher means practicing with other people, and community is a powerful element of yoga. Like the people you meet on the trail who become instant friends because they were in the same place at the same time with the same idea of fun, a class full of like-minded people may be just what you need to thrive.

CHAPTER 7
EATING MINDFULLY

WHAT YOU EAT FUELS your body. It's a simple concept, and yet it can feel very complicated when you dive into the world of nutrition. For someone who is active, it matters even more that you get enough calories to sustain yourself through a yoga class or on long days out in the woods.

There is no right way to eat mindfully. But the first step is to notice whether you pay attention to what you eat in the first place.

The world is rife with cleanses, diets, and other challenges. I have tried many of them, some for myself and some in the name of research. I have at times cut out sugar, alcohol, gluten, dairy, grains, legumes, red meat, processed food, caffeine, canola oil, sweetened drinks, and fruit. Thank goodness for vegetables. I've done an anti-inflammatory diet; I've eaten only fruit; I've gone Paleo; I've done a vegan cleanse; I've experimented with having five meals a day and with filling my plate two-thirds full of veggies and fruit.

But what's the point of all this cleansing? Every time I've experienced one, I've noticed something about my food habits. Eliminating a certain food or type of food for a short time has helped me recognize when I was eating out of habit and convenience versus choosing the best food for my body. Through my experience, I've found it is best to eat foods in which you recognize all the ingredients. It's even better if you know where it comes from, and it's helpful for the environment if it originates close to home.

But I've also learned that every person's body is different. What works for one person may not work for you.

Every year, I lead a three-day fruit cleanse with yoga students in my "40 Days to Personal Revolution" program. At the meeting leading up to the cleanse, I always hear diverse, creative excuses for why people can't do it. Some are traveling. Others already have dinner planned with friends on all three nights of the cleanse. Some question whether it's healthy to eat so much (natural) sugar for three days.

Ultimately for many students, doing the cleanse is simply a triumph of commitment. Some appreciate discovering how fixated they are on food. Others learn that they are addicted to their morning cup of coffee. One mom realized that she snacks constantly while fixing her kids' food for the day, a mindless habit.

The three-day fruit cleanse is one real-life step to bringing your yoga practice to your day-to-day life. You may already have noticed how your eating habits affect how you feel during yoga, for example. Having wine the night before an early morning class might make it feel rather challenging. Or you might be in a twist, and with a groan, realize that whatever you ate wasn't quite right.

These days, I know my body does best when I eat at home, cooking vegetables, whole grains and humanely raised meat, along with some fruit. I tend to eat seasonally, particularly with fruits and vegetables, and love to shop at my local farmers' market in the summer. If I'm eating out alone, I pick a salad or something healthy. If I'm out with friends or family, I enjoy myself. When I hike, my favorite thing to eat is a sandwich and a brownie from a local bakery. Of all the days to eat whatever I want, a day outside definitely wins.

Still, I like to take on a nutrition challenge every three months or so to direct some awareness to how I've been eating. Sometimes I do a cleanse because I want to lose a couple pounds. Sometimes I do a challenge to balance out energy slumps during the day. Other times, I've been eating out a lot, and I'm ready to bring some more mindfulness to my diet.

When focusing on food, it's helpful to add other mindfulness practices that bring health to your day, such as sleep habits. I prefer the rule to sleep at least seven hours a night, which is simple if not easy. However, when I pay attention to my sleep, I tend to sleep even more.

Below are a few practices to eating mindfully, two modified from some of my favorite resources on this topic: *Savor*, which delves into both nutrition and mindfulness practices; and *The Abascal Way*. Whatever way you choose to approach mindful eating, know that you can always make a shift simply by paying attention to what you eat!

Apple Meditation Practice

This practice is modified from *Savor: Mindful Eating, Mindful Life* by Thich Nhat Hanh and Dr. Lilian Cheung, which advises "Eating an apple consciously is to have a new awareness of the apple, of our world, and of our own life."

» Take an apple. Wash it. Before you take a bite, look at it. Take a few deep breaths in and out. Observe the color and the shape. Smell it. What kind of apple is it? Consider the tree where the apple grew, the orchard where the tree lives. Think about the person who plucked the apple, the people who drove or flew the apple to your city, the people who brought the apple to your grocery store.

» Slowly take a bite. Savor the texture as you bite into the apple. Notice the give of the skin and the crisp flesh underneath. Eat it slowly, taking twenty or so chews to finish your bite. Is it sweet, tart, juicy, or crisp? Notice how the texture changes as you chew. What does it feel like when you swallow?

» Savor the taste of the apple. Chew consciously, savoring the taste, and immersing yourself completely in the apple. Eat the entire apple this way.

Mindful Eating Practice

Bring mindfulness to your diet by eliminating one of the following. Or, if you are feeling bold, choose two or more! Note that both caffeine and sugar are stimulants (caffeine can affect sleep), while alcohol is a depressant. Sugar and alcohol are inflammatory for all people.

Choose to eliminate one or more of these items for one week:

» **Caffeine:** If you drink coffee regularly, replace your morning cup with two cups of green tea for two days before eliminating caffeine entirely.
» **Alcohol:** Abstain from all types of alcohol.
» **Processed foods:** Do not eat any packaged food that includes ingredients you can't identify.
» **Tobacco:** Cut out all tobacco.
» **Sugar:** Refrain from eating foods with added sugar, including all refined sugars and natural sweeteners like honey, agave, and maple syrup. This includes soft drinks. Note that many packaged foods use sugar identified by different names, like dextrose, maltose, sucrose, etc.

No Midnight Snacks! Practice

This practice is adapted from "The TQI Diet," described in *The Abascal Way* by Kathy Abascal.
» Stop eating two to three hours before bed.

As adults, we have one daily burst of hormone that occurs a few hours after we fall asleep, which helps maintain muscle mass as we age. But if you eat a bedtime snack, "the insulin released will shut down the important burst of growth hormone that night" writes Abascal.

Eating before bed over time also sends signals to your brain to change your normal hunger and satiety signals. Humans are supposed to be hungry in the morning, not at night. Leptin, the hormone that is tied to satiety also affects melatonin, which is released during the night. If you give up your bedtime snack, people typically notice "they are sleeping better and feel more clearheaded during the day," says Abascal.

LIKE YOGA, EATING MINDFULLY is a practice, and it takes time to shift patterns. Don't take it too seriously if you go off the path on occasion. Remember your intention. Observe what feels best in your body and choose from there.

RESOURCES

BOOKS

Abascal, Kathy. *The Abascal Way: To Quiet Inflammation*. Vashon: Tigana Press, 2011.

Baptiste, Baron. *40 Days to Personal Revolution: A Breakthrough Program to Radically Change Your Body and Awaken the Sacred within Your Soul*. New York: Simon and Schuster, 2004.

———. *Journey into Power: How to Sculpt Your Ideal Body, Free Your True Self, and Transform Your Life with Yoga*. New York: Simon and Schuster, 2002.

Desikachar, T. K. V. *The Heart of Yoga: Developing a Personal Practice*. Rochester, VT: Inner Traditions International, 1999.

Hartranft, Chip and Patañjali. *The Yoga-Sūtra of Patañjali: A New Translation with Commentary*. Boston: Shambhala Publications, 2003.

Iyengar, B. K. S. *Light on Life: The Yoga Journey to Wholeness, Inner Peace, and Ultimate Freedom*. Emmaus, PA: Rodale, 2005.

———. *Light on Yoga*. New York: Schocken Books, 1979.

Kaminoff, Leslie. *Yoga Anatomy*. Champaign, IL: Human Kinetics, 2007.

Long, Ray. *The Key Muscles of Yoga: Your Guide to Functional Anatomy in Yoga*. Bandha Yoga Publications, 2006.

———. *The Key Poses of Yoga: Your Guide to Functional Anatomy in Yoga*. Bandha Yoga Publications, 2008.

Nhat Hanh, Thich, and Lilian Cheung. *Savor: Mindful Eating, Mindful Life*. New York: HarperOne, 2010.

OTHER RESOURCES

Chopra Center for Wellbeing, www.chopra.com: Meditation resource

Yoga Alliance, www.yogaalliance.org: National yoga teacher directory

Yoga Journal, www.yogajournal.com: Leading national yoga magazine and website

INDEX

Nicole Tsong writes the popular "Fit for Life" column in the *Seattle Times*, published in *Pacific NW Magazine*. Tsong teaches yoga at Seattle's leading yoga studios, where she runs strong, essential, and fun classes, leads retreats, and trains and mentors new yoga teachers. She is a Certified Baptiste Teacher and a leader in the national yoga community. Tsong is a member of the board for Seattle-based nonprofit Yoga Behind Bars. She now lives in Seattle. Formerly an award-winning reporter for the *Seattle Times* and the *Anchorage Daily News*, she has traveled to Nome, Alaska, to cover the finish line of the world-renowned Iditarod dog-sled race and covered politics in Washington, DC.

Erika Schultz shares stories through documentary photography and video. A staff photographer for the *Seattle Times*, she was raised in central Wyoming and attended college at Northern Arizona University and Syracuse University in London. She is a cofounder of NW Photojournalism and an SPJ Western Washington board member.

Put your knowledge to practice with Nicole's companion video series, "Yoga for Hikers," available now at www.codyapp.com/yogaforhikers. Pair the book with instructional videos and a supportive online community to help further your hiking goals!

MOUNTAINEERS BOOKS

SKIPSTONE   BRAIDED RIVER

recreation · lifestyle · conservation

MOUNTAINEERS BOOKS is a leading publisher of mountaineering literature and guides—including our flagship title, *Mountaineering: The Freedom of the Hills*—as well as adventure narratives, natural history, and general outdoor recreation. Through our two imprints, Skipstone and Braided River, we also publish titles on sustainability and conservation. We are committed to supporting the environmental and educational goals of our organization by providing expert information on human-powered adventure, sustainable practices at home and on the trail, and preservation of wilderness. The Mountaineers, founded in 1906, is a 501(c)(3) nonprofit outdoor recreation and conservation organization whose mission is to enrich lives and communities by helping people "explore, conserve, learn about, and enjoy the lands and waters of the Pacific Northwest and beyond."

Our publications are made possible through the generosity of donors and through sales of more than 600 titles on outdoor recreation, sustainable lifestyle, and conservation. To donate, purchase books, or learn more, visit us online:

www.mountaineersbooks.org • mbooks@mountaineersbooks.org • 800-553-4453

Also available: